Aristotle's Gradations of Being in Metaphysics E–Z

Other Titles of Interest from St. Augustine's Press

Plato, *The Symposium of Plato: The Shelley Translation*. Translated by Percy Bysshe Shelley.

Aristotle, *Aristotle – On Poetics*. Translated by Seth Benardete and Michael Davis

Aristotle, *Physics, Or Natural Hearing*. Translated by Glen Coughlin.

St. Augustine, *On Order [De Ordine]*. Translated by Silvano Borruso.

St. Augustine, *The St. Augustine LifeGuide: Words to Live by from the Great Christian Saint*. Translated by Silvano Borruso,

Michael Davis, *The Poetry of Philosophy*

Thomas Aquinas, *Commentary on Aristotle's Nicomachean Ethics*

Thomas Aquinas, *Commentary on Aristotle's De Anima*

Thomas Aquinas, *Commentary on Aristotle's Metaphysics*

Thomas Aquinas, *Commentary on Aristotle's Posterior Analytics*

Thomas Aquinas, *Commentary on Aristotle's Physics*

Thomas Aquinas, *Disputed Questions on Virtue.* Translated by Ralph McInerny

Thomas Aquinas, *Commentary on the Epistle to the Hebrews*. Translated by Chrysostom Baer, O. Praem.

Thomas Aquinas, *Commentaries on St. Paul's Epistles to Timothy, Titus, and Philemon*. Translated by Chrysostom Baer, O. Praem.

John of St. Thomas, *Introduction to the Summa Theologiae of Thomas Aquinas*. Translated by Ralph McInerny.

John Poinsot [John of St. Thomas], *Tractatus de Signis Poinsot: The Semiotic of John Poinsot*.

Seth Benardete, *Sacred Transgressions: A Reading of Sophocles' Antigone*

Seth Benardete, *Herodoean Inquiries*

Josef Pieper, *Leisure, the Basis of Culture*

Josef Pieper, *Scholasticism: Personalities and Problems*

Josef Pieper, *The Silence of St. Thomas*

Francisco Suarez, *On Creation, Conservation, & Concurrence: Metaphysical Disputations 20–22*. Translated by A.J. Freddoso

Francisco Suarez, *Metaphysical Demonstration of the Existence of God.* Translated by John P. Doyle

Leo Strauss, *Xenophon's Socrates*

Leo Strauss, *Xenophon's Socratic Discourse: An Interpretation of the Oeconomicus*

Ronna Burger, *The Phaedo: A Platonic Labyrinth*

Stanley Rosen, *Plato's Sophist: The Drama of Original and Image*

Stanley Rosen, *Plato's Symposium*

Stanley Rosen, *Plato's Statesman*

Stanley Rosen, *The Ancients and the Moderns: Rethinking Modernity*

Aristotle's Gradations of Being in Metaphysics E–Z

Joseph Owens, C.Ss.R.

Edited with a Preface by
Lloyd P. Gerson

St. Augustine's Press
South Bend, Indiana
2007

Manufactured in the United States of America.

1 2 3 4 5 6 12 11 10 09 08 07

Library of Congress Cataloging in Publication Data
Owens, Joseph.
Aristotle's gradations of being in Metaphysics E-Z / Joseph Owens; edited with a preface by Lloyd P. Gerson. – 1st ed.
p. cm.
Includes bibliographical references and index.
ISBN 1-58731-028-7 (hardcover: alk. paper)
1. Owens, Joseph. Doctrine of being in the Aristotelian Metaphysics. 2. Aristotle. Metaphysics. 3. Philosophy, Medieval. 4. Metaphysics. 5. Ontology. I. Gerson, Lloyd P. II. Title.
B434.O84 2005
110 – dc22 2005005586

∞ The paper used in this publication meets the minimum requirements of the American National Standard for Information Sciences – Permanence of Paper for Printed Materials, ANSI Z39.48-1984.

St. Augustine's Press
www.staugustine.net

Table of Contents

Preface

In the mid-1990s Professor Joseph Owens of the Pontifical Institute of Mediaeval Studies and the University of Toronto began to experience some of the effects of advanced age and gradually ceased his daily office routine. When it became clear that he would not likely ever return to work, members of his religious community and colleagues in the Institute began sifting through his academic papers with a view to seeing what, if anything, could be brought forward to publication. Among the papers, they found a typescript of a book, *Aristotle's Gradations of Being in Metaphysics* E–Z. In the spring of 1999, that typescript was passed on to the editor-in-chief of the Pontifical Institute of Medieval Studies Press, Ron Thompson, who in turn asked me to have a look at it. Upon reading the work, it became clear to me that it was sufficiently close to completion to be capable of being massaged into publishable form. The present volume is the result. Its delay is owing to the ordinary vicissitudes of academic publishing as well as the sad fact that Owens has been in no way able to assist in the process of completion. I am reasonably confident that he would want this work to reach the scholarly world and that its form is, under the circumstances, close enough to what it would be if its author's own hand had guided it to publication. There is no doubt, however, that if Owens had himself submitted this book for publication, he would have incorporated the comments and criticisms of readers' reports into a final revision of the book. He would also have carried forward his survey and evaluation of the secondary literature on Aristotle's *Metaphysics* right up to the last minute. Owens liked to tell the story of the enterprising journalist who asked the Toronto fishmonger whether the Roman Catholic Church's relaxing of the ban on Friday meat-eating would be bad for business. "No," said the merchant, "fish can stand on their own two feet." So it is with this book, though I would urge the reader to bear in mind that it does not bear the author's *imprimatur*.

My colleagues and I have been aware of the gestation of *Aristotle's Gradations* for some time. The book constitutes Owens' final reflections on Aristotle's *Metaphysics* and on the scholarship on that work throughout the half century since the appearance of Owens' great work, *The Doctrine of Being in the Aristotelian Metaphysics* (1951). That work – essentially the published version of Owens' doctoral dissertation – has had a considerable influence on succeeding generations. From the time of that book's publication, Owens never ceased to be engaged with *Metaphysics*, with the scholarship on it, and with the critical response to his own interpretations. In decades of teaching and in a steady stream of publications, he came back again and again to the central problems posed by Aristotle's invention of a science of first philosophy. Many years ago, I recall a conversation with him during which we mused about whether he might call his book *Son of The Doctrine of Being* or *The Doctrine of Being Revisited.* The actual title of the book reflects Owens' reflective view of what he took the central interpretive crux to be.

As the reader will discover, this book displays Joseph Owens' distinctive philosophical voice, his extraordinary learning, and his constant engagement with the two foci of his academic career – ancient Greek and medieval philosophy. In my opinion, this book does not evince to any significant degree the diminution of intellectual powers that removed Owens from our midst almost immediately upon the book's completion. Having known him – first as a student and then as a colleague – for over thirty years, I am confident in saying on Owens' behalf that he would wish his book to be subjected to full critical scrutiny. Alas, it will have to be left to others to respond to whatever criticisms there may be.

I have thought it useful to include in this preface what is now certainly a complete bibliography of the writings of Joseph Owens along with reviews and critical studies of his works. I am extremely grateful to Professor Richard Ingardia for the substance of the bibliography, which comes mainly from his most valuable online Aristotle bibliography.

I am also pleased to acknowledge the generous financial and technical assistance of the Principal of St. Michael's College, University of Toronto, Professor Mark McGowan, and the President of the University of St. Michael's College, Richard Allway. Dr. Ian Bell was responsible for the painstaking work of producing an electronic version of the typescript of this book. I am also grateful to the Reverend Michael Brehl, C.SS.R., Joseph Owens' religious superior, without whose enthusiastic cooperation this work could not have appeared.

Joseph Owens died on October 31, 2005 while this book was in production.

LLOYD P. GERSON
University of Toronto

JOSEPH OWENS: A BIBLIOGRAPHY

1946

The Common Nature: A Study in St. Thomas Aquinas and Duns Scotus. Thesis for the M.S.L. degree, Pontifical Institute of Mediaeval Studies.

"An Aristotelian Text Related to the Distinction of Being and Essence," *Proceedings of the American Catholic Philosophical Association* 21: 165–172.

1948

The Doctrine of Being in the Aristotelian Metaphysics: A Study in the Greek Background of Medieval Thought, I–II. Thesis for the M.S.D. degree, Pontifical Institute of Mediaeval Studies, University of Saint Michael's College (Canada).

1949

"Up to What Point Is God Included in the Metaphysics of Duns Scotus?" *Mediaeval Studies* 10: 163–177.

"Report of a Recent Thesis Defended at the Pontifical Institute of Mediaeval Studies: The Doctrine of Being in the Aristotelian Metaphysics: A Study in the Greek Background of Mediaeval Thought," *Mediaeval Studies* 11: 239–245.

1950

"The Reality of the Aristotelian Separate Movers," *The Review of Metaphysics* 3, no. 3 (Mar.): 319–337.

1951

"Theodicy, Natural Theology and Metaphysics," *The Modern Schoolman* 28, no.1 (Jan.): 126–137.

The Doctrine of Being in the Aristotelian Metaphysics: A Study in the Greek Background of Mediaeval Thought, xxxi–539 pp. Toronto, Ontario: Pontifical Institute of Mediaeval Studies. [2nd edition, 1963]

1952

"The Conclusion of the Prima Via," *The Modern Schoolman* 30, no. 1 (Nov.): 33–53.

"Comments on Mr. Anderson's Theses," *The Review of Metaphysics* 5, no. 3 (Mar.): 467–469.

"The Doctrine of Being in the Aristotelian Metaphysics (Abstract)," *Sophia* 20: 375.

Reviews of Books by Owens

Borgmann, P. Review of *The Doctrine of Being in the Aristotelian Metaphysics: A Study in the Greek Background of Mediaeval Thought* (1951), by Joseph Owens. *Franciscan Studies* 34: 425–428.

Bourke, Vernon J. Review of *The Doctrine of Being in the Aristotelian Metaphysics: A Study in the Greek Background of Mediaeval Thought* (1951), by Joseph Owens. *Speculum* 27, no. 4 (Oct.): 576–578.

Bourke, Vernon J. Review of *The Doctrine of Being in the Aristotelian Metaphysics: A Study in the Greek Background of Mediaeval Thought* (1951), by Joseph Owens. *Theological Studies* 13: 165.

Fabro, Cornelio. Review of *The Doctrine of Being in the Aristotelian Metaphysics: A Study in the Greek Background of Mediaeval Thought* (1951), by Joseph Owens. *Giornale di Metafisica* 7: 661–668.

Heuston, J. M. Review of *The Doctrine of Being in the Aristotelian Metaphysics: A Study in the Greek Background of Mediaeval Thought* (1951), by Joseph Owens. *Philosophical Studies* (Maynooth) 2: 97–109.

Kutsch, Wilhelm. Review of *The Doctrine of Being in the Aristotelian Metaphysics: A Study in the Greek Background of Mediaeval Thought* (1951), by Joseph Owens. *Scholastik* 27: 409–410.

Taylor, Richard. Review of *The Doctrine of Being in the Aristotelian Metaphysics: A Study in the Greek Background of Mediaeval Thought* (1951), by Joseph Owens. *Philosophy and Phenomenological Research* 13, no. 2 (Dec.): 254–256.

Verbeke, Gérard. Review of *The Doctrine of Being in the Aristotelian Metaphysics: A Study in the Greek Background of Mediaeval Thought* (1951), by Joseph Owens. *Revue Philosophique de Louvain* 50: 471–478.

Critical Studies

Anderson, James F. "Some Basic Proposition Concerning Analogy," *The Review of Metaphysics* 5, no. 3 (Mar.): 465–472.

Anderson, James F. "Response III: On Fr. Owens' Comments," *The Review of Metaphysics* 5, no. 3 (Mar.): 470–472.

Anderson, James F. "A Notable Study of the Aristotelian Metaphysics," *The New Scholasticism* 26, no. 2 (Apr.): 229–239.

Fabro, Cornelio. "Il concetto dell'essere e la metafisica," *Giornale di Metafisica* 7: 661–668.

Verbeke, Gérard. "La doctrine de l'être dans la métaphysique d'Aristote," *Revue Philosophique de Louvain* 50: 471–478.

1953

"The Conclusion of the Prima Via I," *The Modern Schoolman* 30, no. 2 (Jan): 109–121.

"The Conclusion of the Prima Via II," *The Modern Schoolman* 30, no. 3 (Mar.): 203–215.

"Doctrine of Being in the Aristotelian Metaphysics: A Study in the Greek Background of Mediaeval Thought," *The Journal of Hellenic Studies* 73: 159.

Reviews of Books by Owens

Antonopoulos, J. Review of *The Doctrine of Being in the Aristotelian Metaphysics: A Study in the Greek Background of Mediaeval Thought* (1951), by Joseph Owens. *The Journal of Philosophy* 50: 161–168.

Bourke, Vernon J. Review of *The Doctrine of Being in the Aristotelian Metaphysics: A Study in the Greek Background of Mediaeval Thought* (1951), by Joseph Owens. *The Thomist* 16, no. 2 (Apr.): 300–301.

Gewirth, Alan. Review of *The Doctrine of Being in the Aristotelian Metaphysics: A Study in the Greek Background of Mediaeval Thought* (1951), by Joseph Owens. *The Philosophical Review* 62, no. 4 (Oct.): 577–589.

I. H. Review of *The Doctrine of Being in the Aristotelian Metaphysics: A Study in the Greek Background of Mediaeval Thought* (1951), by Joseph Owens. *Dominican Studies* 6: 234.

MinioPaluello, Lorenzo. Review of *The Doctrine of Being in the Aristotelian Metaphysics: A Study in the Greek Background of Mediaeval Thought* (1951), by Joseph Owens. *Journal of Hellenic Studies* 73: 159.

Moreau, Joseph. Review of *The Doctrine of Being in the Aristotelian Metaphysics: A Study in the Greek Background of Mediaeval Thought* (1951), by Joseph Owens. *Revue Philosophique de la France et de l'Étranger* 78: 473–477.

Rees, David A. Review of *The Doctrine of Being in the Aristotelian Metaphysics: A Study in the Greek Background of Mediaeval Thought* (1951), by Joseph Owens. *Classical Review* 3, no. 1 (Mar.): 22–24.

Staff. Review of *The Doctrine of Being in the Aristotelian Metaphysics: A Study in the Greek Background of Mediaeval Thought* (1951), by Joseph Owens. *The Thomist* 16, no. 2 (Apr.): 300–301.

Veatch, Henry B. Review of *The Doctrine of Being in the Aristotelian Metaphysics: A Study in the Greek Background of Mediaeval Thought*, by Joseph Owens. *The Modern Schoolman* 30, no. 2 (Jan): 146–151.

Critical Studies

Gewirth, Alan. "Aristotle's Doctrine of Being," *The Philosophical Review* 62, no. 4 (Oct.): 577–589.

Walton, William H. "Fr. Owens and the Metaphysics of Aristotle," *The Review of Metaphysics* 6, no. 2 (Dec.): 257–264.

1954

"A Note on the Approach to Thomistic Metaphysics," *The New Scholasticism* 28, no. 4 (Oct.): 454–476.

"The Special Characteristic of the Scotistic Proof that God Exists," *in Studi filosofici intorno all "esistenza" al mondo, al trascendente. Relazoni lette nella Sezione di Filosofia del Congresso internazionale per il IV Centenario della Pontificia Università Gregoriana*, 14–16 ottobre 1953. *Analecta Gregorian* Vol. 67, 311–27. Rome: Apud Aedes Universitatis Gregorianae.

Reviews of Books by Owens

Forest, Aimé. Review of *The Doctrine of Being in the Aristotelian Metaphysics: A Study in the Greek Background of Mediaeval Thought* (1951), by Joseph Owens. *Revue Thomiste* 54: 397–399.

Geiger, Louis-Bertrand. *Review of The Doctrine of Being in the Aristotelian Metaphysics: A Study in the Greek Background of Mediaeval Thought* (1951), by Joseph Owens. *Bulletin Thomiste* 9, no. 1: 150.

Hufnagel, A. Review of *The Doctrine of Being in the Aristotelian Metaphysics: A Study in the Greek Background of Mediaeval Thought* (1951), by Joseph Owens. *Freiburger Zeitschrift für Philosophie und Theologie 1*: 334–335.

Klenk, G. Fr. Review of *The Doctrine of Being in the Aristotelian Metaphysics: A Study in the Greek Background of Mediaeval Thought*, by Joseph Owens. *Gregorianum* 35: 176–180.

Muskens, Georgius L. Review of *The Doctrine of Being in the Aristotelian Metaphysics: A Study in the Greek Background of Mediaeval Thought* (1951), by Joseph Owens. *Museum: Maandblad voor Philologie en Geschiednis* 59: 42–44.

Vass, G. Review of *The Doctrine of Being in the Aristotelian Metaphysics: A Study in the Greek Background of Mediaeval Thought* (1951), by Joseph Owens. *Gregorianum* 35: 176–178.

1955

"The Causal Proposition – Principle or Conclusion? Part I," *The Modern Schoolman* 32, no. 2 (Jan): 159–171.

"The Causal Proposition – Principle or Conclusion? Part II," *The Modern Schoolman* 32, no. 3 (Mar.): 257–270.

"The Causal Proposition – Principle or Conclusion? Part III," *The Modern Schoolman* 32, no. 4 (May): 323–339.

"The Intelligibility of Being," *Gregorianum* 36: 169–193.

"Our Knowledge of Nature," *Proceedings of the American Catholic Philosophical Association* 29: 63–86.

Reviews of Books by Owens

Robinson, Daniel S. Review of *The Doctrine of Being in the Aristotelian Metaphysics: A Study in the Greek Background of Mediaeval Thought* (1951), by Joseph Owens. *The Personalist* 36: 179.

Critical Studies

Klubertanz, George P. "A Comment on 'The Intelligibility of Being'," *Gregorianum* 36: 194–195.

1956

Reviews of Books by Owens

Barth, Timotheus. Review of *The Doctrine of Being in the Aristotelian Metaphysics: A Study in the Greek Background of Mediaeval Thought* (1951), by Joseph Owens. *Wissenschaft und Weisheit* 19: 66–68.

Deku, Henry. Review of *The Doctrine of Being in the Aristotelian Metaphysics: A Study in the Greek Background of Mediaeval Thought* (1951), by Joseph Owens. *Philosophisches Jahrbuch* 64: 419.

H. D. Review of *The Doctrine of Being in the Aristotelian Metaphysics: A Study in the Greek Background of Mediaeval Thought* (1951), by Joseph Owens. *Philosophisches Jahrbuch* 64: 419.

1957

St. Thomas and the Future of Metaphysics, 97 pp. Milwaukee: Marquette University Press. [Reprinted 1973]

"Common Nature: A Point of Comparison between Thomistic and Scotistic Metaphysics," *Mediaeval Studies* 19: 1–14.

"The Number of Terms in the Suarezian Discussion on Essence and Being," *The Modern Schoolman* 34, no. 3 (Mar.): 147–191.

Review of *Der Mensch als Mitte*, by Josef Endres. *The Modern Schoolman* 34, no. 1 (Nov.): 144–146.

Reviews of Books by Owens

Bastable, J. D. Review of *St. Thomas and the Future of Metaphysics*, by Joseph Owens. *Philosophical Studies* 7: 199–200.

DeVries, Josef. Review of *St. Thomas and the Future of Metaphysics*, by Joseph Owens. *Scholastik* 32: 440.

Díaz, D. Review of *St. Thomas and the Future of Metaphysics*, by Joseph Owens. *Revista de Filosofía* 17: 316–317.

Langlois, Jean. Review of *St. Thomas and the Future of Metaphysics*, by Joseph Owens. *Science et Esprit* 9: 193.

Petty, M. Review of *St. Thomas and the Future of Metaphysics*, by Joseph Owens. *Ciencia y fe* 13: 376.

Ognio, Hiroyuki. Review of *The Doctrine of Being in the Aristotelian Metaphysics: A Study in the Greek Background of Mediaeval Thought* (1951), by Joseph Owens. *Journal of Classical Studies* (Kyoto) 5: 154–157.

Critical Studies

Beach, John D. "Separate Entity as the Subject of Aristotle's Metaphysics," *The Thomist* 20, no. 1 (Jan): 75–95.

Eslick, Leonard J. "What Is the Starting-Point of Metaphysics?" *The Modern Schoolman* 34, no. 4 (May): 247–263.

Moraux, Paul. "L'évolution d'Aristote," in *Aristote et Saint Thomas d'Aquin. Journées d'études internationales*, ed. Paul Moraux, Suzanne Mansion,

Daniel A. Callus and André Thiry, 9–41. Louvain-Paris: Publications Universitaires de Louvain.

1958

"The Accidental and Essential Character of Being in the Doctrine of St. Thomas Aquinas," *Mediaeval Studies*: Etienne Gilson Anniversary Studies 20: 1–40.

"Ignorance and Existence," *The New Scholasticism* 32, no. 2 (Spring): 210–219.

Reviews of Books by Owens

Beach, John D. Review of *St. Thomas and the Future of Metaphysics*, by Joseph Owens. *The Thomist* 21, no. 2 (Apr.): 215–220.

Clarke, W. Norris. Review of *St. Thomas and the Future of Metaphysics*, by Joseph Owens. *The New Scholasticism* 32: 264–266.

Coreth, E. Review of *St. Thomas and the Future of Metaphysics*, by Joseph Owens. *Zeitschrift für Katholische Theologie* 80: 459.

Hayen, André. Review of *St. Thomas and the Future of Metaphysics*, by Joseph Owens. *Nouvelle Revue Théologique* 80: 427–428.

J. E. B. Review of *St. Thomas and the Future of Metaphysics*, by Joseph Owens. *Convivium* 15–17: 224–225.

Schlüter, D. M. Review of *St. Thomas and the Future of Metaphysics*, by Joseph Owens. *Freiburger Zeitschrift für Philosophie und Theologie* 5: 336–337.

Critical Studies

Beach, John D. "The Notion of Being," *The Thomist* 21, no. 1 (Jan): 29–43.

1959

A History of Ancient Western Philosophy, xv–434 pp. New York: AppletonCenturyCrofts.

"Thomistic Common Nature and Platonic Idea," *Mediaeval Studies* 21: 211–223.

Reviews of Books by Owens

Bobik, Joseph. Review of *St. Thomas and the Future of Metaphysics*, by Joseph Owens. *The New Scholasticism* 33: 68–85.

Van Steenberghen, Fernand. Review of *St. Thomas and the Future of Metaphysics*, by Joseph Owens. *Revue Philosophique de Louvain* 57: 474–475.

Wright, John H. Review of *St. Thomas and the Future of Metaphysics*, by Joseph Owens. *Gregorianum* 40: 387.

Critical Studies

Bobik, Joseph. "Some Remarks on Father Owens's *St. Thomas and the Future of Metaphysics*," *The New Scholasticism* 33: 68–85.

1960

"Aristotle on Categories," *The Review of Metaphysics* 14, no. 1 (Sept.): 73–90.

"Diversity and Community of Being in St. Thomas Aquinas," *Mediaeval Studies* 22: 257–302.

"The Reality of the Aristotelian Separate Movers," in *Readings in Ancient and Medieval Philosophy*, ed. James Collins, 75–81. Westminster: Newman Press.

Review of *Aristotle*, by John H. Randall. *The New Scholasticism* 34, no. 4 (Oct.): 520–523.

Review of *Aristotle: The Growth and Structure of His Thought*, by Geoffrey E. R. Lloyd. *International Philosophical Quarterly* 9: 299–301.

Review of *An Approach to the Metaphysics of Plato through the Parmenides*, by William F. Lynch. *The New Scholasticism* 34, no. 1 (Jan): 134–136.

Reviews of Books by Owens

Gerardo, J. Review of *St. Thomas and the Future of Metaphysics*, by Joseph Owens. *Pensamento* 16: 248.

Vandenbroucke, F. Review of *St. Thomas and the Future of Metaphysics*, by Joseph Owens. *Recherches de théologie ancienne et médiévale* 27: 187–188.

1961

"St. Thomas and Elucidation," *The New Scholasticism* 35, no. 4 (Oct.): 421–444.

"Unity and Essence in St. Thomas Aquinas," *Mediaeval Studies* 23: 240–259.

Reviews of Books by Owens

Cleve, Felix M. Review of *A History of Ancient Western Philosophy*, by Joseph Owens. *The New Scholasticism* 35, no. 3 (July): 391–396.

Collins, James. Review of *A History of Ancient Western Philosophy*, by Joseph Owens. *Cross Currents* (Spring): 145.

Unknown. Review of *A History of Ancient Western Philosophy*, by Joseph Owens. *Catholic School Journal* 61: 50.

1962

"Analogy as a Thomistic Approach to Being," *Mediaeval Studies* 24: 302–322.

"Aquinas on Infinite Regress," *Mind* 71, no. 282 (Apr.): 244–246.

Reviews of Books by Owens

Pérez Ruiz, Francisco. Review of *The Doctrine of Being in the Aristotelian Metaphysics: A Study in the Greek Background of Mediaeval Thought* (1951), by Joseph Owens. *Pensamiento* 18: 205–211.

Critical Studies

Wallace, William A. "Metaphysics and the Existence of God," *The New Scholasticism* 36: 529–531

Nielsen, Harry. "Father Owens on Elucidation – a Comment," *New Scholasticism* 36: 233–236.

1963

An Elementary Christian Metaphysics, xiv–384pp. Houston, Texas: Center for Thomistic Studies, University of St. Thomas. [Reprinted 1985]

"Matter and Predication in Aristotle," in *The Concept of Matter in Greek and Medieval Philosophy*, ed. Ernan McMullin, 99–115. Notre Dame, Ind.: University of Notre Dame Press.

"Concept and Thing in St. Thomas," *The New Scholasticism* 37, no. 2 (Apr.): 220–224.

"Elucidation and Causal Knowledge: Rejoinder to J. Bobik," *The New Scholasticism* 37, no. 1 (January): 64–70.

"Existential Act, Divine Being, and the Subject of Metaphysics," *The New Scholasticism* 37, no. 3 (July): 359–363.

"St. Thomas Aquinas and Modern Science," *Transactions of the Royal Society of Canada* 4, no. 1: 283–293.

"The Unity in a Thomistic Philosophy of Man," *Mediaeval Studies* 25: 54–82.

"Discussion with Wilfrid Sellers," in *The Concept of Matter*, ed. Ernan McMullin, 275–276. Notre Dame, Ind.: University of Notre Dame Press.

"An Aquinas Commentary in English," *Review of Metaphysics* 16, no. 3 (Mar.): 503–512.

Review of *Metaphysics and the Existence of God*, by Thomas C. O'Brien. *The New Scholasticism* 37, no. 2 (April): 244–246.

Review of *Le problème de l'être chez Aristote: Essai sur la problématique aristotélicienne,* by Pierre Aubenque. *Gnomon* 35: 459–462.

Reviews of Books by Owens

W. G. E. Review of *The Doctrine of Being in the Aristotelian Metaphysics: A Study in the Greek Background of Mediaeval Thought* (1963), by Joseph Owens. *The Review of Metaphysics* 17, no. 1 (Sept.): 308.

Critical Studies

Yardan, John L. "Some Remarks on Metaphysics and the Existence of God," *The New Scholasticism* 37 (Apr.): 213–219.

Lobkowicz, Nikolaus. "Comment on (Joseph Owens) "Matter and Predication in Aristotle" in *The Concept of Matter*, ed. Ernan McMullin, 96–99. Notre Dame, Ind.: University of Notre Dame Press.

Bobik, Joseph. "Some Disputable Points Apropos of St. Thomas and Metaphysics," *The New Scholasticism* 37: 411–430.

Bobik, Joseph. "Some Remarks on Fr. Owens' 'St. Thomas and Elucidation,'" *The New Scholasticism* 37: 59–63.

1964

"The 'Analytics' and Thomistic Metaphysical Procedure," *Mediaeval Studies* 26: 83–108.

"The Aristotelian Conception of the Sciences," *International Philosophical Quarterly* 4: 200–216.

"The Limitation of Being by Essence," in *Readings in Metaphysics,* ed. Jean R. Rosenberg, 276–278. Westminster: The Newman Press.

"The Causal Proposition: Principle or Conclusion," in *Readings in Metaphysics*, ed. Jean R. Rosenberg, 188–199. Westminster: The Newman Press.

"Up to What Point Is God included in the Metaphysics of Duns Scotus," *Proceedings of the American Catholic Philosophical Association* 21: 165–172.

"Interrogation of Paul Weiss," in *Philosophical Interrogations*, ed. Sidney Rome and Beatrice Rome, 266; 287–288; 301–302; 311. New York: Holt, Rinehart and Winston.

Review of *Il concetto di filosofia prima e l'unità della Metafisica di Aristotele*, by Giovanni Reale. *The New Scholasticism* 38, no. 2 (Apr.): 254–256.

Reviews of Books by Owens

DeFinance, Joseph. Review of *The Doctrine of Being in the Aristotelian Metaphysics: A Study in the Greek Background of Mediaeval Thought* (1963), by Joseph Owens. *Gregorianum* 45: 414.

T. C. Review of *The Doctrine of Being in the Aristotelian Metaphysics: A Study in the Greek Background of Mediaeval Thought* (1963), by Joseph Owens. *The Heythrop Journal* 5: 233–234.

Turiel, B. Review of *The Doctrine of Being in the Aristotelian Metaphysics: A Study in the Greek Background of Mediaeval Thought* (1963), by Joseph Owens. *Studium* 4: 397–398.

Azar, Larry. Review of *An Elementary Christian Metaphysics*, by Joseph Owens. *The Modern Schoolman* 41, no. 3 (Mar.): 292–297.

Giannini, Giorgio. Review of *An Elementary Christian Metaphysics*, by Joseph Owens. *Aquinas* 7, no. 1: 133–134.

May, William E. Review of *An Elementary Christian Metaphysics*, by Joseph Owens. *Catholic School Journal* 64 (Sept.): 70.

Murphy, Thomas. Review of *An Elementary Christian Metaphysics*, by Joseph Owens. *The Heythrop Journal* 5, no. 2 (Apr.): 198–199.

O'Brien, Thomas C. Review of *An Elementary Christian Metaphysics*, by Joseph Owens. *The New Scholasticism* 38, no. 2 (Apr.): 270–273.

Critical Studies

Hunter, J. F. M. "Note on Father Owens' Comment on Williams' Criticism of Aquinas on Infinite Regress," *Mind* 73: 439–440.

1965

"Aristotle," in *The Catholic Encyclopedia for School and Home*, ed. John H. Harrington, 388–393.

"The Ethical Universal in Aristotle," *Studia Moralia* 3: 27–47.

"Comment on Czeslaw Lewjewski: "The Concept of Matter in Pre-Socratic Philosophy," in *The Concept of Matter in Greek and Medieval Philosophy*, ed. Ernan McMullin, 57–58. Notre Dame, Ind.: University of Notre Dame Press.

"Quiddity and Real Distinction in St. Thomas Aquinas," *Mediaeval Studies* 27: 1–22.

"The Real Distinction of a Relation from its Immediate Basis," *Proceedings of the American Catholic Philosophical Association* 39: 134–140.

"Abstract, Owens, Joseph, *The Doctrine of Being in the Aristotelian Metaphysics* (1963)," *The Monist* 49, no. 4 (Oct.): 670.

Review of Zum Ursprung der Analogie bei Parmenides und Heraklit, by Ebehard Jüngel. *The Modern Schoolman* 43, no. 1 (November): 78–80.

Review of *Aristotle and the Problem of Value*, by Whitney J. Oates. *The New Scholasticism* 39, no. 3 (July): 376–379.

Review of *Aristotle's System of the Physical World: A Comparison with his Predecessors*, by Friedrich Solmsen. *The New Scholasticism* 39, no. 4 (Oct.): 545–547.

Reviews of Books by Owens

R. de D. Review of *The Doctrine of Being in the Aristotelian Metaphysics: A Study in the Greek Background of Mediaeval Thought* (1963), by Joseph Owens. *La Ciencia Tomista* 92: 339.

Langlois, Jean. Review of *An Elementary Christian Metaphysics*, by Joseph Owens. *Sciences ecclesiastiques* 17: 561–564.

1966

"Aquinas and the Proof from the Physics," *Mediaeval Studies* 28: 119–150.

"The Dissolution of an Eclecticism," *Pacific Philosophy Forum* 5, no. 1 (Sept.): 80–84.

"Scholasticism: Then and Now," *Proceedings of the American Catholic Philosophical Association* 40: 1–12.

"The Grounds of Universality in Aristotle," *The American Philosophical Quarterly* 3, no. 2 (Apr.): 162–169.

"Abstract, Owens, Joseph, *An Elementary Christian Metaphysics,*" *The Monist* 50, no. 2 (Apr.): 304.

Review of *Early Thomistic School*, by Frederick J. Roensch. *International Philosophical Quarterly* 6: 144–145.

Critical Studies

Cahalan, John C. "Remarks on Father Owens' "The Causal Proposition Revisited," *The Modern Schoolman* 44: 152–160.

1967

"Actuality in the Prima Via of St. Thomas," *Mediaeval Studies* 29: 26–46.

"Aristotle," in *The New Catholic Encyclopedia*, 809a–814a. Washington, D.C.: The Catholic University of America Press.

"The Causal Proposition Revisited," *The Modern Schoolman* 44, no. 2 (Jan): 143–151.

"The Range of Existence," in *Proceedings of the Seventh Inter-American Congress of Philosophy* 1967, 44–59. Québec: Les Presses de l'Université. Laval.

"Greek Philosophy," in *New Catholic Encyclopedia*, 733–736. Washington, D.C.: The Catholic University of America Press.

"Heraclitus," in *New Catholic Encyclopedia*, 1046–1047. Washington, D.C.: The Catholic University of American Press.

"Recent Footnotes to Plato," *The Review of Metaphysics* 20, no. 4 (June): 648–661.

"The Starting Point of the Prima Via," *Franciscan Studies* 27, no. 5: 249–284.

"This Truth Sublime," in *Speaking of God: Essays on Belief and Unbelief*, ed. Denis Dirscherl, 128–156. Milwaukee: Bruce Publishing Company.

"Parmenides," in *New Catholic Encyclopedia*, 1027. Washington, D.C.: The Catholic University of America Press.

"Matter and Predication in Aristotle," in *Aristotle: A Collection of Essays*, ed. J. M. E. Moravcsik, 191–214. Modern Studies in Philosophy. Garden City, New York: Doubleday and Company.

"This Truth Sublime," in *Towards a Christian Philosophy*, 189–206. *Studies in Philosophy and the History of Philosophy*. Washington, D.C.: The Catholic University of America Press.

"Dewart's View of Christian Philosophy and Contemporary Man," *The Ecumenist* 5 (Jan.-Feb.): 19–22.

Review of *The Giants of Pre-Sophistic Greek Philosophy: An Attempt to Reconstruct Their Thought*, by Felix M. Cleve. *The New Scholasticism* 41, no. 1 (Winter): 132–135.

Review of *Le Thomisme et la Pensée Italienne de la Renaissance*, by Paul O. Kristeller. *Dialogue: Canadian Philosophical Review* 6, no. 3: 455–459.

Reviews of Books by Owens

Treptow, Elmar. Review of *The Doctrine of Being in the Aristotelian Metaphysics: A Study in the Greek Background of Mediaeval Thought* (1963), by Joseph Owens. *Philosophisches Rundschau* 14, no. 1: 62–64.

Critical Studies

Chambers, Connor J. "Prime Movers and Prime Provers," *The Thomist* 31, no. 4 (Oct.): 465–507.

Fontinell, Eugene. "Postscript to Father Owens' "This Truth Sublime," in *Speaking of God: Essays on Belief and Unbelief*, ed. Denis Dirscherl, 156–158. Milwaukee: Bruce Publishing Company

Quine, Willard. "Thoughts on Reading Father Owens," in *Proceedings of the Seventh Inter-American Congress of Philosophy* 1967, 60–63. Québec: Les Presses de l'Université Laval.

Cahalan, John C. "On the Proving of Causal Propositions," *The Modern Schoolman* 44, no. 2 (Jan): 129–142.

1968

An Interpretation of Existence, vii–153pp. Houston, Texas: Center for Thomistic Studies, University of St. Thomas. [Reprinted 1985]

"The Universal in Physics I, 1," in *Mélanges â la mèmoire de monsieur Charles de Koninck*, ed. Lucien Zérounian, 301–315. Québec: Les Presses de l'Université Laval.

Joseph Owens and Eugene Freeman, eds. *The Wisdom and Ideas of Saint Thomas Aquinas*, 160 pp. Greenwich, Connecticut: Fawcett World Library.

"Immobility and Existence for Aquinas," *Mediaeval Studies* 30: 22–46.

"The Study of Knowledge – Natural Philosophy or Metaphysics?" *The New Scholasticism* 42, no. 1 (Winter): 103–106.

"Teleology of Nature in Aristotle," *The Monist* 52, no. 2 (Apr.): 159–173.

"The Universality of the Sensible in the Aristotelian Noetic," in *Mélanges à la mèmoire de monsieur Charles de Koninck*, ed. Lucien Zérounian, 301–315. Québec City: Les presses de l'Université Laval.

Review of *The Cambridge History of Later Greek and Early Medieval Philosophy,* ed. Arthur H. Armstrong. *Phoenix* 22: 177–180.

Reviews of Books by Owens

Kuhn, Helmut. Review of *The Doctrine of Being in the Aristotelian Metaphysics: A Study in the Greek Background of Mediaeval Thought* (1963), by Joseph Owens. *Gnomon* 40: 139–147

Colombo, E. Review of *The Doctrine of Being in the Aristotelian Metaphysics: A Study in the Greek Background of Mediaeval Thought* (1963), by Joseph Owens. *Sapientia* 88: 159.

Critical Studies

Klubertanz, George P. "Theory of Knowledge – A Reconsideration (Joseph Owens, "The Study of Knowledge – Natural Philosophy or Metaphysics?")," *The New Scholasticism* 42: 107–111.

LaPlante, Harry. "The Characteristics of Existence," *Philosophical Studies* (Maynooth) 17: 95–109.

1969

"Aquinas – Existential Permanence and Flux," *Mediaeval Studies* 31: 71–92.

"The Aristotelian Argument for the Material Principle of Bodies," in *Naturphilosophie bei Aristoteles und Theophrast.* Verhandlungen des 4. Symposium Aristotelicum veranstaltet in Göteborg. August 1966, ed. ingemar Düring, 193–209. Heidelberg: Lothar Stiehm.

"The Grounds of Ethical Universality in Aristotle," *Man and World* 2, no. 2 (May): 171–193.

Review of *Aristotle: The Growth and Structure of His Thought,* by Geoffrey E. R. Lloyd. *International Philosophical Quarterly* 3: 635–636.

1970

"Judgment and Truth in Aquinas," *Mediaeval Studies* 32: 138–158.

"Nature and Ethical Norm in Aristotle," in *Akten des XIV internationalen Kongresses für Philosophie*, Wien, 2–9 September 1968, 442–427. Vienna: Herder.

"Scholasticism and Metaphysics," in *The Future of Metaphysics,* ed. Robert E. Wood, 14–31. Chicago: Quadrangle.

"Value and Metaphysics," in *The Future of Metaphysics*, ed. Robert E. Wood, 204–228. Chicago: Quadrangle Books.

"The Notion of Catholic Philosophy," *The Antigonish Review* 1: 112–140.

Review of *Logic and Metaphysics in Aristotle: Aristotle's Treatment of Types of Equivocity and its Relevance to His Metaphysical Theories*, by Walter Leszl. *Journal of the History of Philosophy* 15: 331–314.

Reviews of Books by Owens

Lefèvre, Charles. Review of *The Doctrine of Being in the Aristotelian Metaphysics: A Study in the Greek Background of Mediaeval Thought* (1963), by Joseph Owens. *Revue Philosophique de Louvain* 68: 249–250.

Binnie, Donald. Review of *An Interpretation of Existence*, by Joseph Owens. *Dialogue: Canadian Philosophical Review* 9, no. 1: 120–124.

Kane, William H. Review of *An Interpretation of Existence*, by Joseph Owens. *The Thomist* 34, no. 1 (Jan): 151–152.

1971

"Aristotle's Definition of Soul," in *Philomathes. Studies and Essays in Humanities in Memory of Philip Merlan*, ed. Robert B. Palmer and Robert Hamerton Kelly, 125–145. The Hague: Martinus Nijhoff.

"God in Philosophy Today," in *God, Man and Philosophy: A Symposium*, ed. Carl W. Grindel, 41–51. New York: St. John's University Press.

"Cause of Necessity in Aquinas' Tertia Via," *Mediaeval Studies* 33: 21–45.

"The Universality of the Sensible in the Aristotelian Noetic," in *Essays in Ancient Greek Philosophy I*, ed. John P. Anton and George L. Kustas, 462–477. Albany, N.Y.: State University of New York Press.

"Common Nature: A Point of Comparison Between Thomistic and Scotistic Metaphysics," in *Inquiries into Medieval Philosophy: A Collection in Honor of Francis P. Clarke,* ed. James F. Ross, 185–209. Westport, Conn.: Greenwood Publishing Company.

Review of *Aristotle, Aristotle's Physics Books I and II*, by William Charlton. *Phoenix* 25: 279–282.

Reviews of Books by Owens

Teske, Roland J. Review of *An interpretation of Existence*, by Joseph Owens. *The Modern Schoolman* 48, no. 2 (Jan): 184–185.

Critical Studies

Smith, John E. "Comments on "God in Philosophy Today" (Joseph Owens)," in *God, Man and Philosophy: A Symposium*, ed. Carl W. Grindel, 55–61. New York: St. John's University Press.

1972

"Reality and Metaphysics," *The Review of Metaphysics* 25, no. 4 (June): 638–658.

"'Ignorare' and Existence," *The New Scholasticism* 46, no. 2 (Spring): 210–219.

"Metaphysical Separation in Aquinas," *Mediaeval Studies* 34: 287–306.

"Author's Abstract: *An Interpretation of Existence,*" *The Monist* 56, no. 1 (Jan): 144–145.

"Medalist Address: A Non-Expendable Heritage," *Proceedings of the American Catholic Philosophical Association* 46: 212–218.

"Foreword in Leo Sweeney, *Infinity and the Presocratics, A Bibliographical and Philosophical Study*," in *Infinity and the Presocratics, A Bibliographical and Philosophical Study*, xvii–xix. The Hague: Martinus Nijhoff.

Critical Studies

Boullart, Karel. "Metaphysische Problemen – Metaphysische Methoden," *Philosophica Gandensia* 10: 90–96.

Leszl, Walter. "Knowledge of the Universal and Knowledge of the Particular in Aristotle," *The Review of Metaphysics* 26, no. 2 (Dec.): 278–313.

1973

"Comment – Effects Precede Causes," *Technology and Culture* 14: 19–21.

"The Content of Existence," in *Logic and Ontology*, ed. Milton K. Munitz, 21–35. New York: New York University Press.

Review of *Theophrastus, De igne*: *A Post-Aristotelian View of the Nature of Fire*, by Victor Coutant. *The Classical World* 66, no. 8 (May): 468–469.

Translations

Carrière, Bernard, and Roger Carrière, trans. "Owens, Joseph, Aristote – Maître de ceux qui savent," in *La philosophie et les philosophes*, 45–68. Montréal: Bellarmin/Desclée.

1974

"Soul as Agent in Aquinas," *The New Scholasticism* 48, no. 1 (Winter): 40–72.

"Aquinas as Aristotelian Commentator," in *St. Thomas Aquinas 1274–1974: Commemorative Studies I*, eds. Armand A. Maurer, Étienne Gilson, Joseph Owens, Anton Charles Pegis, Edward Synan, John F. Quinn, and James A. Weisheipl, 213–238. Toronto, Ontario: Pontifical Institute of Mediaeval Studies.

"Aquinas on Cognition as Existence," *Proceedings of the American Catholic Philosophical Association* 48: 74–85.

"Aquinas and the Five Ways," *The Monist* 58, no. 1 (Jan.): 16–35.

"The Primacy of the External in Thomistic Noetics," *Église et Théologie* (Ottawa) 5: 189–205.

"The Physical World of Parmenides," in *Essays in Honour of Anton Charles Pegis*, ed. J. Reginald O'Donnell, 378–395. Toronto: Pontifical Institute of Mediaeval Studies.

"Realism," in *The New Encyclopedia Britannica*, 539–543.

Joseph Owens, Armand Maurer, Étienne Gilson, Anton C. Pegis, John F. Quinn, and James A. Weisheipl, eds. *Saint Thomas Aquinas, 1274–1974: Commemorative Studies, I–II*, 488; 526. Toronto, Canada: Pontifical Institute of Mediaeval Studies.

Critical Studies

Clark, Ralph W. "St. Thomas Aquinas's Theory of Universals," *The Monist* 58, no. 1 (Jan): 163–172.

Croteau, Jacques. "Comments on Father Owens' Paper," *Église et Théologie* (Ottawa) 5: 207–211.

1975

"Naming in Parmenides," in *Kephalaion: Studies in Greek Philosophy and its Continuation Offered to Professor C. J. De Vogel*, ed. J. Mansfield and Lambertus Marie De Rijk, 16–25. Assen: Van Gorcum.

"Maritain's Three Concepts of Existence," *The New Scholasticism* 49, no. 3 (Summer): 295–309.

Review of *Die logischen Fragmente des Theophrast*, by Andreas Graeser. *The Classical World* 69, no. 2 (Oct.): 135–136.

Review of *New Light on His Life and on Some of His Lost Works*. 2 Vols. *Vol. 1: Some Novel Interpretations of the Man and His Life; vol. 2, Observations on Some of Aristotle's Lost Works*, by Anton Hermann Chroust. *The New Scholasticism* 49, no. 2 (Spring): 244–246.

Review of *Die transzendentalienlehre der alten ontologie, 1: Die transzendentalienlehre im corpus Aristotelicum,* by Karl Bärthelein. *Archiv für Geschichte der Philosophie* 77, no. 2: 217–222.

1976

"A Note on Aristotle: *De Anima* 3.4.429b9," *Phoenix* 30, no. 2: 107–118.

"Aquinas: 'Darkness of Ignorance' in the Most Refined Notion of God," *The Southwestern Journal of Philosophy* 5, no. 2 (Summer): 93–110.

"Aquinas on Knowing Existence," *The Review of Metaphysics* 29, no. 4 (June): 670–690.

"Aristotle: Cognition a Way of Being," *Canadian Journal of Philosophy* 6, no. 1 (Mar.): 1–10.

"Aquinas: 'Darkness of Ignorance' in the Most Refined Notion of God," in *Bonaventure and Aquinas: Enduring Philosophers*, ed. Robert W. Shahan and Francis J. Kovach, 69–86. Norman, Oklahoma City: University of Oklahoma Press.

"Aristotle on Empedocles Fr. 8," in *New Essays on Plato and the Pre-Socratics,* ed. Roger A. Shiner and John King-Farlow, 87–100. Guelph: Canadian Association for Publishing in Philosophy.

"Foreword to Giovanni Reale's The *Concept of First Philosophy and the Unity of the Metaphysics of Aristotle*, Translated by John R. Catan," in *The Concept of First Philosophy and the Unity of the Metaphysics of Aristotle*, xi–xii. Brockport, N.Y.: State University of New York.

Review of *San Tommaso e il pensiero Moderno*, by Pontificia Accademia di S. Tommaso d'Aquino. *The Thomist* 40, no. 1 (Jan): 153–160.

Review of *Der Aristotelismus bei den Griechen: Von Andronikos bis Alexander von Aphrodisias. T. II: Der Aristotelismus im I und II. Jahrhundert nach Christi,* by Paul Moraux. *The Classical World* 69, no. 7 (Apr.-May): 489–491.

Review of *Franz Bentano: On the Several Senses of Being in Aristotle*, Rolf George (tr.). *The Review of Metaphysics* 30, no. 1 (Sept.): 122–123.

Critical Studies

Husain, Martha. "The Question 'What Is Being?' and its Aristotelian Answer," *The New Scholasticism* 50, no. 3 (Summer): 293–309.

1977

"Aristotelian Ethics, Medicine, and the Changing Nature of Man," in *Philosophical Medical Ethics: Its Nature and Significance*, eds. S. F. Spicker and H. T. Engelhardt, 127–142. Dordrecht, Holland: D. Reidel Publishing Company.

"Aristotle on God," in *God in Contemporary Thought: A Philosophical Perspective,* ed. Sebastian A. Matczak, 415–442. New York/Paris: Learned Publication/Nauwelaerts.

"Jacques Maritain – Toronto Recollections," *Notes et documents de l'institut international Jacques Maritain* 3, no. 7 (Apr.June): 12–15.

Critical Notice of *Reason and Human Good in Aristotle*, by John M. Cooper. *Canadian Journal of Philosophy* 7, no. 3 (Sept.): 623–636.

Review of *Aristotle's Metaphysics Books M and N*, by Julia Annas. *The Review of Metaphysics* 31: 310–311.

Review of *Aristotle's Conception of Ontology*, by Walter Leszl. *Journal of the History of Philosophy* 15, no. 3 (July): 331–334.

Review of *St. Thomas Aquinas' Philosophy in the Commentary on the Sentences,* by Battista Mondin. *The Review of Metaphysics* 30: 532–523.

Critical Studies

Sontag, Frederick. "Reality and its Expressions," *The Modern Schoolman* 54: 259–269.

1978

The Doctrine of Being in the Aristotelian Metaphysics: A Study in the Greek Background of Mediaeval Thought, xxxi–539 pp. Toronto, Ontario: Pontifical Institute of Mediaeval Studies. [Reprint of 1951 edition]

"Aristotle: Motion as Actuality of the Imperfect," 3 in *Paideia.* Special Aristotle Issue. ed. George C. Simmons, 120–132. Brockport, N.Y.: State University of New York.

"Being in Early Western Tradition," in *The Question of Being*, ed. Mervyn Sprung, 17–30. University Park, Pa.: Pennsylvania State University Press.

"Philosophy's Role in Thanatology," in *Philosophical Aspects of Thanatology*, ed. Florence M. Hetzler and Austin, H. Kutscher, 163–70. New York: Arno Press.

"Value and Person in Aquinas," in *Atti del Congresso internazionale Tommaso d'Aquino nel suo settimo centenario*, Roma-Napoli, 17–24 Aprile 1974, 56–62. Naples: Edizione Domenicane Italiane.

"Anton Charles Pegis," *Royal Society of Canada: Proceedings and Transactions* 16: 101–104.

Review of *Studies in the History of Philosophy and Religion,* by Harry A. Wolfson. *International Journal for Philosophy of Religion* 9: 260–261.

Review of *Aristotele: Dalla dialettica alla filosofia prima,* by Enrico Berti. *The Review of Metaphysics* 31, no. 3 (Mar.): 471–472.

Review of *Metaphysik und Sprache: Eine sprachphilosophische Untersuchung zu Thomas von Aquin und Aristoteles*, by Hermann Weidemann. *The Review of Metaphysics* 32, no. 2 (Dec.): 373–374.

Review of Thearchia: Die Frage nach der Sinn von Gott bei Pseudo-Dionysius Areopagita und Thomas von Aquin, by Walter M. Neidl. *The International Journal for Philosophy of Religion* 9: 124–125.

Critical Studies

Dewan, Lawrence. "Being Per Se, Being Per Accidens and St. Thomas' Metaphysics," *Science et esprit* 30: 169–184.

1979

"The Relation of God to World in the Metaphysics," *Études sur la Métaphysique d'Aristote*: Actes du VI Symposium Aristotelicum, 1972 Cerisy-la-Salle, ed. Pierre Aubenque, 207–228. Bibliothèque d'Histoire de la Philosophie. Paris: J. Vrin.

"The Notion of Actuality in Aquinas," *Proceedings of the Patristic, Mediaeval and Renaissance Conference* 4: 13–23.

"Existence as Predicated," *The New Scholasticism* 53, no. 4 (Autumn): 480–485.

"Knowledge and Katabasis in Parmenides," *The Monist* 62, no. 1 (Jan): 15–29.

The Philosophical Tradition of St. Michael's College, Toronto, Canada: St. Michael's College Archives.

Review of *Images of Man in Ancient and Medieval Thought*, by D. DeNachter, J. Ijsewijn, G. Maertens, G. Vanhumel, G., and D. E. Verhelst F. Bossier. *Archiv für Geschichte der Philosophie* 61, no. 1: 112–115.

Review of *Introduction to Aristotle's Theory of Being as Being*, by Werner Marx. *Classical World* 73: 190.

Review of *Aristoteles' allgemeine und spezielle Metaphysik,* by Klaus Brinkmann. *The Review of Metaphysics* 33, no. 2 (Dec.): 414–416.

Reviews of Books by Owens

Bourke, Vernon J. Review of *The Doctrine of Being in the Aristotelian Metaphysics: A Study in the Greek Background of Mediaeval Thought* (1978), by Joseph Owens. *Speculum* 54, no. 2 (Apr.): 412–413.

Critical Studies

Miller, Barry. "'Exists' and Other Predicates," *The New Scholasticism* 53, no. 4: 475–479.

1980

St. Thomas Aquinas on the Existence of God: Collected Papers of Joseph Owens, C.Ss.R., xii–291, ed. John R. Catan. Albany, N.Y.: State University of New York Press.

Papers Included:

"Foreword to John Catan's *St. Thomas Aquinas on the Existence of God: Collected Papers of Joseph Owens*, by Catan, John R," vii–viii.

"Aquinas as Aristotelian Commentator," 1–19.

"Aquinas on Knowing Existence," 20–33.

"Judgment and Truth in Aquinas," 34–51.

"The Accidental and Essential Character of Being in the Doctrine of St. Thomas Aquinas," 52–96.

"Diversity and Community of Being in St. Thomas Aquinas," 97–131.

"Aquinas and the Five Ways," 132–141.

"The Conclusion of the Prima Via," 142–168.

"The Starting Point of the Prima Via," 169–191.

"Actuality in the Prima Via of St. Thomas," 192–207.

"Immobility and Existence for Aquinas," 208–227.

"Aquinas on Infinite Regress," 228–230.

"Form and Cognition in Aristotle," *Ancient Philosophy* 1, no. 1 (Fall): 17–27.

"Diversificata in Diversis: Aquinas in I Sent. Prol. 1. 2," in *La scolastique. Certitude et recherche. En hommage à Louis-Marie Régis*, ed. Ernest Joós, 113–129. Montréal: Les Éditions Bellarmin.

"Quandoque and Aliquando in Aquinas' Tertia Via," *The New Scholasticism* 54, no. 4 (Autumn): 447–475.

"Existence and the Subject of Metaphysics," *Science et Esprit* (Montréal) 32 (Octobre Septembre): 255–260.

"Philosophy: An Est and Quid Est," *Proceedings of the American Catholic Philosophical Association* 54: 37–48.

"An Appreciation of Blanshard's Views on Catholicism," in *The Philosophy of Brand Blanshard,* ed. P. A. Schilpp, 1015–1039. La Salle, Ill.: Open Court.

"La filosofía cristiana de la *Aeterni Patris*," *Revista de filosofía* (México) 13: 229–246.

Review of *Struttura e fine: La Logica della teleologia Aristotelica*, by Angelo Capecci. *The Review of Metaphysics* 33, no. 3 (Mar.): 622–623.

Review of *From a Realist Point of View: Essays on the Philosophy of Science,* by W. A. Wallace. *The Review of Metaphysics* 33, no. 3 (Mar.): 650–651.

Reviews of Books by Owens

Mansion, Suzanne. Review of *The Doctrine of Being in the Aristotelian Metaphysics: A Study in the Greek Background of Mediaeval Thought* (1978), by Joseph Owens. *Revue Philosophique de Louvain* 78, no. 37 (février): 138–140.

Reix, André. Review of *The Doctrine of Being in the Aristotelian Metaphysics: A Study in the Greek Background of Mediaeval Thought* (1978), by Joseph Owens. *Revue Philosophique de la France et de l'Étranger* 105: 90–92.

1981

Aquinas on Being and Thing, 33 pp.. *Niagara University Publications in Honor of Jacques and Raissa Maritain*. Niagara Falls, N.Y.: Niagara University Press.

Aristotle, The Collected Papers of Joseph Owens, vii–264pp, Ed John R. an. Albany, N.Y.: State University of New York Press.

Papers Included:

"Foreword" vi–vii.

"Aristotle on Categories," 14–22.

"The Aristotelian Conception of the Sciences," 23–34.

"Matter and Predication in Aristotle," 35–47.

"The Grounds of Universality in Aristotle," 48–58.

"The Universality of the Sensible in the Aristotelian Noetic," 59–73.

"Aristotle: Cognition a Way of Being," 74–80.

"Aristotelian Soul as Cognitive of Sensibles, Intelligibles and Self," 81–98.

"A Note on Aristotle: *De Anima* 3.4.429b9," 99–108.

"Aristotle's Definition of Soul," 109–121.

“The Aristotelian Argument for the Material Principle of Bodies,” 122–135.

“Teleology of Nature in Aristotle,” 136–147.

“The Grounds of Ethical Universality in Aristotle,” 148–164.

“Nature and Ethical Norm in Aristotle,” 165–168.

“Aristotelian Ethics, Medicine, and the Changing Nature of Man,” 169–180.

“The Kalon in the Aristotelian Ethics,” in *Studies in Aristotle*, ed. Dominic J. O’Meara, 261–277. Studies in Philosophy and the History of Philosophy, vol. 9. Washington, D.C.: Catholic University of America Press.

“Actuality in Aristotle and Aquinas,” in *Proceedings of the World Congress on Aristotle* (Thessaloniki, August 7–14, 1978). II, 192–196. Athens: Publication of Ministry of Culture and Sciences.

“Aristotle on Leisure,” *Canadian Journal of Philosophy* 11, no. 4 (Dec.): 713–723.

“Stages and Distinction in *De Ente*: A Rejoinder,” *The Thomist* 45, no. 1 (Jan): 99–123.

“The Future of Thomistic Metaphysics,” in *One Hundred Years of Thomism: A Symposium,* ed. Victor B. Brezik, 142–161. Houston, Texas: Center for Thomistic Studies, University of St. Thomas.

Review of *Form and Universal in Aristotle*, by A. C. Lloyd. *The Review of Metaphysics* 35, no. 2 (Dec.): 395–396.

Review of *Möglichkeit und Notwendigkeit bei Aristoteles und heute,* by Ursula Wolf. *The Review of Metaphysics* 34, no. 3 (Mar.): 625–626.

Review of *Grundbegriffe der Scholastik*, by Josef de Vries. *The Review of Metaphysics* 35, no. 2(Dec.): 380–381.

Review of *Le jugement par inclination chez Saint Thomas d’Aquin*, by RafaelTomas Caldera. *The Review of Metaphysics* 35, no. 2 (Dec.): 369–370.

Review of *Quellenkritische und logische untersuchungen zur Gegensatzlehre des Aristoteles*, by Osvaldo Norberto Guariglia. *The Review of Metaphysics* 35, no. 2 (Dec.): 390–392.

Reviews of Books by Owens

Langston, Douglas C. Review of *St. Thomas Aquinas on the Existence of God: Collected Papers of Joseph Owens,* C.SS.R., ed. John R. Catan. *Religious Studies Review* 7: 146.

Critical Studies

Catan, John R. 1981. "Two Views on the Completeness of the Metaphysics of Aristotle," *Rivista de Filosofia NeoScolastica* 73: 388–398.

Translations

Peters, Wenzel, trans. "Owens, Joseph, 'Wissen und Realdistinktion bei Thomas von Aquin,'" in *Thomas von Aquin*, ed. Klaus Bernath, 239–265. Darmstadt: Wissenschaftliche Buchgesellschaft.

Peters, Wenzel, trans. "Owens, Joseph, 'Metaphysische Trennung bei Thomas von Aquin,'" in *Thomas von Aquin*, ed. Klaus Bernath, 339–365. Darmstadt: Wissenschaftliche Buchgesellschaft.

DeLaGarza, M. Teresa, trans. "Owens, Joseph, Los tres conceptos de existencia en Maritain," *Revista de filosofía* (México) 14 (Septiembre-Diciembre): 399–414.

1982

"Aristotelian Soul as Cognitive of Sensibles, Intelligibles and Self," in *Ancient and Medieval Philosophies of the Soul*, ed. Parvitz Morewedge.

"Aristotle on Common Sensibles and Incidental Perception," *Phoenix* 36: 215–236.

"The Doctrine of Being in the Aristotelian Metaphysics: Revisited," in *Philosophies of Existence: Ancient and Medieval*, ed. Parviz Morewedge, 33–59. New York: Fordham University Press.

"Maritain on Aristotelian Ethics," *Notes et documents de l'institut international Jacques Maritain* 7, no. 27 (Apr.-June): 20–23.

"Material Substance: Temporal or Eviternal?" *The New Scholasticism* 56, no. 4 (Fall): 442–461.

"Natures and Conceptualization," *The New Scholasticism* 56, no. 3 (Summer): 376–380.

"The Relevance of Thomistic Metaphysics for Christian Life," in *Actas del tercer congresso nacional de filosofia*, Buenos Aires, 13 al 18 de octobre de 1980, 413–418. Buenos Aires: Universidad de Buenos Aires.

"Foreword to *The Object of Moral Philosophy According to St. Thomas Aquinas*," by Richard P. Geraghty, ix–x. Albany, N.Y.: State University of New York Press.

Review of *Aristotle and His Philosophy*, by Abraham Edel. *Ancient Philosophy* 2, no. 2 (Fall): 152–156.

Reviews of Books by Owens

O'Brien, Thomas C. Review of *St. Thomas Aquinas on the Existence of God: Collected Papers of Joseph Owens,* C.SS.R., ed. John R. Catan. *The Thomist* 46, no. 4 (Oct.): 644–653.

Spade, Paul V. Review of *St. Thomas Aquinas on the Existence of God: Collected Papers of Joseph Owens,* C.SS.R., ed. John R. Catan. *Dialogue: Canadian Philosophical Review* 21, no. 4 (Dec.): 772–773.

Stump, Eleonore. Review of *St. Thomas Aquinas on the Existence of God: Collected Papers of Joseph Owens,* C.SS.R., ed. John R. Catan. *International Studies in Philosophy* 14, no. 2 (Fall): 114–115.

Weber, Stephen L. Review of St. *Thomas Aquinas on the Existence of God: Collected Papers of Joseph Owens,* C.SS.R., ed. John R. Catan. *Philosophy Books* 23 (Oct.): 205–206.

Roccaro, Giuseppe. Review of *Aquinas on Being and Thing*, by Joseph Owens. *Giornale di Metafisica* 4, no. 4: 606–610.

Bodéüs, Richard. Review of *Aristotle: The Collected Papers of Joseph Owens*, by John R. Catan. *Les Études classiques* 50: 178.

Brumbaugh, Robert S. Review of *Aristotle: The Collected Papers of Joseph Owens*, ed. John R. Catan. *Classical World* 75: 377–378.

Turnbull, Robert G. Review of *Aristotle: The Collected Papers of Joseph Owens*, ed. John R. Catan. *Phoenix* 36: 366–370.

Critical Studies

Miller, Barry. "Existence and Natures," *The New Scholasticism* 56: 371–5.

Dewan, Lawrence. "St. Thomas, Joseph Owens, and Existence," *The New Scholasticism* 56, no. 4 (Autumn): 399–441.

1983

"Aristotle's Contribution on the Nature of Ethical Norms," *Listening: Journal of Religion and Culture* 18 (Fall): 225–234.

"Is Philosophy in Aristotle an Ideology?" in *Ideology, Philosophy and Politics*, ed. Anthony Parel, 163–178. Waterloo, Ontario: Wilfrid Laurier University Press.

"Aquinas on Being and Thing," in *Thomistic Papers*, III, ed. Leonard A. Kennedy, 3–34. Houston, Tex.: University of St. Thomas, Center for Thomistic Studies.

Review of *A History of Greek Philosophy, Volume VI: Aristotle: An Encounter,* by William K. C. Guthrie. *Canadian Philosophical Reviews* 3 (June): 125–8.

Festschrift

Gerson, Lloyd P., ed. *Graceful Reason: Essays in Ancient and Medieval Philosophy Presented to Joseph Owens on the Occasion of his Seventy-Fifth Birthday and the Fiftieth Anniversary of his Ordination,* xiii–447. Papers in *Mediaeval Studies*, vol. 4. Pontifical Institute of Mediaeval Studies: Toronto, Ontario.

Review of Books by Owens

Konyndyk, Kenneth. Review of *St. Thomas Aquinas on the Existence of God: Collected Papers of Joseph Owens,* C.SS.R., ed. John R. Catan. *Religious Studies Review* 7 (Apr.): 146.

Zimmermann, Albert. Review of *St. Thomas Aquinas on the Existence of God: Collected Papers of Joseph Owens,* C.SS.R., ed. John R. Catan. *Archiv für Geschichte der Philosophie* 65, no. 3: 315–320.

Ackrill, John L. Review of *Aristotle: The Collected Papers of Joseph Owens*, ed. John R. Catan. *Classical Review* 33: 64–66.

Gerson, Lloyd P. Review of *Aristotle: The Collected Papers of Joseph Owens*, ed. John R. Catan. *Ancient Philosophy* 3: 72–81.

Grimaldi, William M. A. Review of *Aristotle: The Collected Papers of Joseph Owens*, ed. John R. Catan. *Philosophy and Rhetoric* 16, no. 4 (Fall): 275–277.

Ito, M. Review of *Aristotle: The Collected Papers of Joseph Owens*, ed. John R. Catan. *Journal of Classical Studies* 31: 143–145.

Konyndyk, Kenneth. Review of *Aristotle: The Collected Papers of Joseph Owens*, ed. John R. Catan. *The Philosophical Review* 92: 297–302.

Critical Studies

Gerson, Lloyd P. "The Aristotelianism of Joseph Owens," *Ancient Philosophy* 3, no. 1 (Spring): 72–81.

Veatch, Henry B. "A Non-Cartesian Meditation upon the Doctrine of Being in the Aristotelian Metaphysics," 4 in *Graceful Reason: Essays in Ancient and Medieval Philosophy Presented to Joseph Owens on the Occasion of His Seventy-Fifth Birthday and the Fiftieth Anniversary of His Ordination*, ed. Lloyd P. Gerson, 75–100. Toronto, Ontario: Pontifical Institute of Mediaeval Studies.

1984

"Being and Nature in Aquinas," *The Modern Schoolman* 61, no. 3 (Mar.): 157–168.

"The Present Status of Alpha Elatton in the Aristotelian Metaphysics," *Archiv für Geschichte der Philosophie* 66, no. 2: 148–169.

"How Flexible is the Aristotelian 'Right Reason'?" in *The Georgetown Symposium on Ethics: Essays in Honor of Henry Babcock Veatch*, ed. R. Porreco, 49–65. Lanham, Md.: University Press of America.

Review of *Das Prinzipienproblem in der Philosophie des Thomas von Aquin*, by Wilfried Kühn. *The Review of Metaphysics* 38, no. 1 (Sept.): 129–130.

Review of *Aquinas*, by Anthony J. P. Kenny. *Dialogue: Canadian Philosophical Review* 23, no. 2 (June): 352–353.

Reviews of Books by Owens

Husain, Martha. Review of *Aristotle: The Collected Papers of Joseph Owens*, ed. John R. Catan. *International Studies in Philosophy* 16, no. 3: 120–123.

Kachi, Y. Review of *Aristotle: The Collected Papers of Joseph Owens*, ed. John R. Catan. *Archives internationales d'Histoire des Sciences* 34: 269–271.

Van Rijen, Jeroen. Review of *Aristotle: The Collected Papers of Joseph Owens*, ed. John R. Catan. *Archiv für Geschichte der Philosophie* 66, no. 2: 216–7.

Reix, André. Review of *Graceful Reason: Essays in Ancient and Medieval Philosophy. Presented to Joseph Owens, C.SS.R., on the Occasion of his Seventy-Fifth Birthday and the Fiftieth Anniversary of his Ordination,* ed. Lloyd P. Gerson. *Revue Philosophique de la France et de l'Étranger* 109: 462–463.

Critical Studies

Dewan, Lawrence. "Saint Thomas, Joseph Owens, and the Real Distinction between Being and Essence," *The Modern Schoolman* 61, no. 3 (Mar.): 145–156.

1985

An Elementary Christian Metaphysics, xiv–384 pp. Houston, Texas: Center for Thomistic Studies, University of St. Thomas. [Reprint of 1963 edition].

An Iterpretation of Existence, vii–153 pp. Houston, Tex.: Center for Thomistic Studies, University of St. Thomas. [Reprint of 1968 edition].

Human Destiny: Some Problems for Catholic Philosophy, viii–117 pp. Washington, D.C.: The Catholic University of America Press.

"A Note on Aquinas, in Boeth. *de Trin.*, 2, 2 ad 1m," *The New Scholasticism* 59, no. 1 (Winter): 102–8.

"Need Philosophy Hold that Nature Is Something Complete?" in *Essays Honoring Allan B. Wolter*, ed. William A. Frank and Girard J. Etzkorn, 221–244. Bonaventure, N.Y.: Franciscan Institute.

"Tenent Philosophi Perfectionem Naturae," in *Essays Honoring Allan B. Wolter,* ed. William A. Frank and Girard J. Etzkorn, 221–244. Franciscan Institute Publications: Theology Series, vol. 10. St. Bonaventure, N.Y.: Franciscan Institute.

"The Acratic's "Ultimate Premise" in Aristotle," in *Aristoteles: Werk und Wirkung,* I, ed. Jürgen Wiesner, 376–392. Berlin: Walter de Gruyter.

" Note on Aquinas, *in Boeth. de Trin.* 2, 2 ad 1m," *The New Scholasticism* 49, no. 1 (Winter): 102–108.

"An Appreciation of Professor Turnbull's Views on Aristotle," *Philosophical Inquiry* 7, no. 3–4 (Summer-Fall): 158–76.

Review of *Essays in Ancient Greek Philosophy* II, by John P. Anton and Anthony Preus. *Ancient Philosophy* 5, no. 1 (Spring): 153–6.

Reviews of Books by Owens

Ewbank, Michael B. Review of *Aquinas on Being and Thing*, by Joseph Owens. *The New Scholasticism* 59, no. 2 (Spring): 238–243.

Leroux, Georges. Review of *Graceful Reason: Essays in Ancient and Medieval Philosophy. Presented to Joseph Owens,* C.SS.R., *on the Occasion of his Seventy-Fifth Birthday and the Fiftieth Anniversary of his Ordination*, ed. Lloyd P. Gerson. *Philosophiques* 12 (printemps): 229–231.

Madigan, Arthur. Review of *Graceful Reason: Essays in Ancient and Medieval Philosophy. Presented to Joseph Owens,* C.SS.R., *on the Occasion of his Seventy-Fifth Birthday and the Fiftieth Anniversary of his Ordination*, ed. Lloyd P. Gerson. *Ancient Philosophy* 5, no. 1 (Spring): 136–140.

Critical Studies

Turnbull, Robert G. "Fr. Owens on Nature, Matter, and Immateriality," *Philosophical Inquiry* 7, no. 3–4 (Summer-Fall): 146–157.

1986

Towards a Philosophy of Medieval Studies, 22. *The Etienne Gilson Series*, vol. 9. Toronto, Canada: Pontifical Institute of Mediaeval Studies.

"Ideology and Aquinas," in *Thomistic Papers* I, ed. Victor B. Brezik, 135–152. Houston, Tex.: Center for Thomistic Studies, University of St. Thomas.

"Aquinas and Philosophical Pluralism," in *Thomistic Papers,* II, ed. Leonard A. Kennedy and Jack C. Marler, 133–158. Houston, Tex.: Center for Thomistic Studies, University of St. Thomas.

"Aquinas' Distinction at *De Ente et Essentia* 4. 119–123," *Mediaeval Studies* 48: 264–287.

"Further Thoughts on Knowledge of Being and Truth," *The New Scholasticism* 60, no. 4 (Autumn): 454–470.

"Is There any Ontology in Aristotle?" *Dialogue: Canadian Philosophical Review* 25, no. 4 (Winter): 697–707.

"The Distinguishing Feature in Catholic Philosophy," in *The Papin Gedenkschrift: Dimensions in the Human Religious Quest – Essays in Memory of Joseph Papin*, ed. Joseph Armenti. Ann Arbor, Mich.: University Microfilms International.

Review of *Die Metaphysik des Thomas von Aquin in historischer Perspektive* I, by Leo J. Elders. *The Thomist* 50, no. 3 (July): 463–465.

Reviews of Books by Owens

Brague, Rémi. Review of *Aristotle: The Collected Papers of Joseph Owens*, ed. John R. Catan. *Archives de Philosophie* 49, no. 2 (avril-jeune): 311–313.

Freudenthal, Gad. Review of *Graceful Reason: Essays in Ancient and Medieval Philosophy. Presented to Joseph Owens, C.SS.R., on the Occasion of his Seventy-Fifth Birthday and the Fiftieth Anniversary of His Ordination*, ed. Lloyd P. Gerson. *Isis* 77: 183–184.

Kretzmann, Norman. Review of *Graceful Reason: Essays in Ancient and Medieval Philosophy. Presented to Joseph Owens, C.SS.R., on the Occasion of his Seventy-Fifth Birthday and the Fiftieth Anniversary of His Ordination*, ed. Lloyd P. Gerson. *Dialogue: Canadian Philosophical Review* 25, no. 3 (Autumn): 564–566.

Peña, Lorenzo. Review of *Graceful Reason: Essays in Ancient and Medieval Philosophy. Presented to Joseph Owens, C.SS.R., on the Occasion of his Seventy-Fifth Birthday and the Fiftieth Anniversary of His Ordination*, ed. Lloyd P. Gerson. *Philosophia: Philosophical Quarterly of Israel* 19, no. 1 (May): 73–79.

Whiteny, Barry. Review of *An Elementary Christian Metaphysics* (1985), by Joseph Owens. *Studies in Religion* 15, no. 1: 98–100.

Penna, James V. Review of *Human Destiny: Some Problems for Catholic Philosophy*, by Joseph Owens. *Canadian Philosophical Review* 6: 240–242.

Critical Studies

Wilhelmsen, Frederick D. "Response to Joseph Owens' "Aquinas and Philosophical Pluralism." in *Thomistic Papers*, II, ed. Leonard A. Kennedy, 159–163. Houston, Tex.: Center for Thomistic Studies, University of Saint Thomas.

1987

"Es La 'Sustancia Primera' en las Categorías Aristotélicas una causa primera y un primer principio del Ser?" *Revista de filosofía* (México) 20: 208–211.

"Aquinas on Being and Thing," in *Thomistic Papers, III*, ed. Leonard A. Kennedy, 3–34. Houston, Tex.: Center for Thomistic Studies, University of St. Thomas.

"Aquinas on the Inseparability of Soul from Existence," *The New Scholasticism* 61, no. 3 (Summer): 249–270.

"Aristotle's Notion of Wisdom," *Apeiron* 20: 1–16.

"Confronto fra la coscienza cristiana e la retta ragione Aristotelica," in *La coscienza morale oggi: omaggio al prof. Domenico Capone*, ed. M. Nalepa and T. Kennedy, 109–143. Rome: Accademia Alfonsianae.

"Metaphysics – The Fulfillment of a Natural Desire," *The Modern Schoolman* 65, no. 1 (Nov.): 1–13.

"Christian Conscience vs Aristotelian Right Reason," in *La coscienza morale oggi: omaggio al Prof. Domenico Capone*, ed. M. Nalepa and T. Kennedy, 109–143. Rome: Editiones Accademiae Alphonsianae.

"Es la sustancia primera en *las Categorías* aristotélicas (5.2a11–b6) una causa primera y un principio del ser?" *Revista de filosofía* (México) 20, no. 58–59: 208–211.

"Christian Conscience vs. Aristotelian Right Reason, in *Towards a Christian Philosophy*, 150–173. *Studies in Philosophy and the History of Philosophy*. Washington, D.C.: The Catholic University of America Press.

"Aristotle and Aquinas on Cognition," 103–123. Calgary: University of Calgary Press.

Reviews of Books by Owens

Ashley, Benedict M. Review of *Graceful Reason: Essays in Ancient and Medieval Philosophy. Presented to Joseph Owens, C.SS.R., on the Occasion of his Seventy-Fifth Birthday and the Fiftieth Anniversary of His Ordination*, ed. Lloyd P. Gerson. *The Modern Schoolman* 64: 124–125.

Dewan, Lawrence. Review of *An Interpretation of Existence* (1985), by Joseph Owens. *Dialogue: Canadian Philosophical Review* 26, no. 3 (Autumn): 572–576.

Wilhelmsen, Frederick D. Review of *An Interpretation of Existence* (1985), by Joseph Owens. *Faith and Philosophy* 4, no. 3 (July): 348–350.

Dewan, Lawrence. Review of *An Elementary Christian Metaphysics* (1985), by Joseph Owens. *Dialogue: Canadian Philosophical Review* 26, no. 3 (Autumn): 572–576.

Centore, Floyd F. Review of *Human Destiny: Some Problems for Catholic Philosophy*, by Joseph Owens. *Dialogue: Canadian Philosophical Review* 26, no. 1 (Spring): 216–219.

Desharnais, Richard P. Review of *Human Destiny: Some Problems for Catholic Philosophy*, by Joseph Owens. *International Studies in Philosophy* 20: 135–136.

Veatch, Henry B. Review of *Human Destiny: Some Problems for Catholic Philosophy*, by Joseph Owens. *Ethics* 97, no. 3 (Apr.): 709–710.

1988

"The Self in Aristotle," *The Review of Metaphysics* 41, no. 4 (June): 707–722.

"Aristotle and Modern Epistemology," in *Philosophy and Culture* IV, ed. Venant Cauchy, 848–851. Montréal: Montmorency.

"The Neoplatonic Leaven in Western Culture," in *Philosophy and Culture* V, ed. Venant Cauchy, 181–185. Montréal: Ed Montmorency.

"Thomas Aquinas: Dimensive Quantity as Individuating Principle," *Mediaeval Studies* 50: 279–310.

"Medieval Studies Fifty Years After," *Medieval Studies* 50: xi–xvi.

Review of *Lex et Libertas: Freedom and Law According to St. Thomas Aquinas*, by Leo J. Elders and K. Hedwig. *The Thomist* 52, no. 3 (July): 539–542.

Review of *Parmenides: Being, Bounds, and Logic*, by Austin Scott. *Canadian Journal of Philosophy* 18, no. 3 (Sept.): 609–620.

Review of *Knowing the Unknowable God,* by David B. Burrell. *International Journal for Philosophy of Religion* 23, no. 2 (Mar.): 119–121.

Reviews of Books by Owens

Burrell, David B. Review of *Graceful Reason: Essays in Ancient and Medieval Philosophy. Presented to Joseph Owens, C.SS.R., on the Occasion of his*

Seventy-Fifth Birthday and the Fiftieth Anniversary of His Ordination, ed. Lloyd P. Gerson. *The New Scholasticism* 62: 239–241.

Ewbank, Michael B. Review of *An Interpretation of Existence* (1985) by Joseph Owens. *The New Scholasticism* 62, no. 4 (Autumn): 474–479.

Harper, Albert W. J. Review of *An Interpretation of Existence* (1985), by Joseph Owens. *Irish Philosophical Journal* 5: 121–126.

Henle, Robert J. Review of *Human Destiny: Some Problems for Catholic Philosophy*, by Joseph Owens. *The Modern Schoolman* 65, no. 2 (Jan): 142–145.

1989

"Faith, Ideas, Illumination, and Experience," in *The Cambridge History of Later Medieval Philosophy: From the Rediscovery of Aristotle to the Disintegration of Scholasticism, 1100–1600*, ed. Norman Kretzmann, Anthony Kenny and Jan Pinborg, 440–459. Cambridge; New York: Cambridge University Press.

"The Actuality of *The Thomistic* Distinctions between Essence and Existence," in *Être et savoir. En hommage au professeur Jacques Croteau*, ed. Jean-Louis Allard, 161–173. Ottawa: Les Presses de l'Université d'Ottawa.

"An Ambiguity in Aristotle, *EE* VII 2 1236a23–4," *Apeiron* 22, no. 2: 127–237.

Review of *Middle Platonism and Neoplatonism*, by Stephen Gersh. *International Journal for Philosophy of Religion* 26, no. 2 (Oct.): 126–128.

Review of *Die Transformation des klassischen Seinsverständisses*, by Rolf Schonberger. *Journal of the History of Philosophy* 27, no. 3 (July): 470–471.

Review of *Die Metaphysik des Thomas von Aquin in historischer Perspektive* II, by Leo J. Elders. *The Thomist* 53, no. 2 (Apr.): 337–339.

Reviews of Books by Owens

Harper, Albert W. J. Review of *An Interpretation of Existence* (1985), by Joseph Owens. *Indian Philosophical Quarterly* 16: 237–244.

Bodéüs, Richard. Review of *Human Destiny: Some Problems for Catholic Philosophy*, by Joseph Owens. *Revue Philosophique de Louvain* 87: 101–102.

Critical Studies

Dewan, Lawrence. "St. Thomas, Metaphysical Procedure, and the Formal Cause," *The New Scholasticism* 63, no. 2 (Spring): 173–182.

1990

Towards a Christian Philosophy, x–332 pp. *Studies in Philosophy and the History of Philosophy,* vol. 21. Washington, D.C.: The Catholic University of America Press.

Papers Included:

"Introduction," 1–59.

"The Christian Philosophy of *Aeterni Patris*," 63–75.

"Is Nature Something Complete?" 76–96.

"The Notion of Catholic Philosophy," 97–118.

"The Distinguishing Feature in Catholic Philosophy," 119–136.

"The Objectives of the American Catholic Philosophical Association," 137–149.

"Christian Conscience vs. Aristotelian Right Reason," 150–173.

"God in Philosophy Today," 177–189.

"This Truth Sublime," 189–206.

"Aquinas: "Darkness of Ignorance" 207–224.

"Cause of Necessity in Aquinas' Tertia Via," 225–249.

"The Special Characteristic of the Scotistic Proof that God Exists," 250–265.

"Soul as Agent in Aquinas," 266–290.

"Aquinas on the Inseparability of Soul from Existence," 291–306.

"Epilogue," 307–326.

"Aquinas on the Intimacy and Contingency of Existence," *The American Catholic Philosophical Quarterly* (formerly *The New Scholasticism* 64, no. 2 (Spring): 261–264.

Review of *Mind and Imagination in Aristotle*, by Michael V. Wedin. *Classical World* 84: 235.

Review of *A History of Ancient Philosophy*, Volume IV, by Giovanni Reale. *Review of Metaphysics* 44, no. 1 (Sept.): 164–166.

Review of *The Schools of the Imperial Age*, by Giovanni Reale. *The Review of Metaphysics* 44, no. 1 (Sept.): 164–166.

1991

"Moral Reasoning: Value and Practical Knowledge in Aristotle," in *Essays in Ancient Greek Philosophy*, IV: Aristotle's Ethics, ed. John P. Anton and Anthony Preus, 143–157. Albany, N.Y.: State University of New York Press.

"The Aristotelian Conception of the Pure and Applied Sciences," in *Science and Philosophy in Classical Greece*, ed. Alan C. Bowen and Francesca Rochberg-Halton, 31–42. Institute for Research in Classical Philosophy and Science: *Sources and Studies in the History and Philosophy of Classical Science*, vol. 2. New York: Garland Publishing Inc.

"Human Reason and the Moral Order in Aquinas," *in Historia memoria futuri: mélanges Louis Vereecke*, ed. R. Tremblay and D. J. Billy, 159–177. Rome: Editiones Academiae Alphonsianae.

"Aristotle and Aquinas on Cognition," *Canadian Journal of Philosophy*, Supplement 17: 103–123.

1992

Cognition: An Epistemological Inquiry, viii–373 pp. Houston, Tex.: Center for Thomistic Studies: University of St. Thomas.

"Two Consequences of the Object's Priority in Aristotle's Episteme," in *Philosophies of Being and Mind: Ancient and Medieval*, ed. James T. H. Martin, 103–112. Delmar, N.Y.: Caravan Books.

"The Relevance of Avicennian Neoplatonism," in *Neoplatonism and Islamic Thought,* ed. Parviz Morewedge, 41–50. *Studies in Neoplatonism: Ancient and Modern,* vol. 5. Albany, N.Y.: State University of New York Press.

"The Keystone of the Aristotelian Metaphysics," *Journal of Neoplatonic Studies* 1, no. 1 (Fall): 125–131.

"Deo intus Pandente (Augustine, *De Magistro*, 40, *CSEL*, LXXVII, 6.4.49)," *The Modern Schoolman* 69, no. 3–4 (Mar.-May): 369–378.

Reviews of Books by Owens

Centore, Floyd F. Review of *Towards a Christian Philosophy*, by Joseph Owens. *The Review of Metaphysics* 45, no. 3 (Mar.): 628–630.

1993

"Aristotle and Aquinas," in *The Cambridge Companion to Aquinas*, ed. Norman Kretzmann and Eleonore Stump, 38–59. New York: Cambridge University Press.

"The Problematic of the Active Mind's Causation in Aristotle, *De Anima* 3.5," *The Journal of Neoplatonic Studies* 1, no. 2 (Spring): 181–193.

"Analytic and Continental Philosophies in Overall Perspective," *The Modern Schoolman* 70, no. 2 (Jan): 131–142.

Reviews of Books by Owens

Centore, Floyd F. Review of *Towards a Christian Philosophy*, by Joseph Owens. *Dialogue: Canadian Philosophical Review* 32, no. 4 (Fall): 820–827.

1994

"Preface: The Necessity of a Pluralistic Approach to Philosophy," in *Greek and Medieval Studies in Honor of Leo Sweeney, S.J.*, ed. William J. Carroll and John J. Furlong, xviiii–xxviii. New York: Peter Lang Publishing.

"Thomas Aquinas (b. 1225–d. 1274)," in *Individuation in Scholasticism: The Later Middle Ages and the Counter-Reformation* 1150–1650, ed. Jorge J. E. Gracia, 173–194. Albany, New York: State University of New York Press.

"Neo-Thomism and Christian Philosophy," in *Thomistic Papers*, ed. John Knasas, 29–52. Notre Dame, Ind.: Notre Dame University Press.

Reviews of Books by Owens

Centore, Floyd F. Review of *Cognition: An Epistemological Inquiry*, by Joseph Owens. *Philosophia Perennis* 1, no. 2 (Fall): 131–137.

1996

Some Philosophical Issues in Moral Matters: The Collected Ethical Writings of Joseph Owens, i–500pp. Questiones Morales, vol. 8. eds. Billy, Dennis J. and Terence Kennedy. Roma: Editones Accademiae Alphonsianae.

Papers Included:

"Introduction," 13–23.

"The Kalon in the Aristotelian Ethics," 27–44.

"Value and Practical Knowledge in Aristotle," 45–62.

"Value and Metaphysics," 63–88.

"Value and Person in Aquinas," 89–97.

"Is Philosophy in Aristotle an Ideology?" 99–114.

"Ideology and Aquinas," 115–130

"Maritain on Aristotelian Ethics," 133–138.

"The Ethical Universal in Aristotle," 139–158.

"The Grounds of Ethical Universality in Aristotle," 159–183.

"Nature and Ethical Norm in Aristotle," 185–189.

"Teleology of Nature in Aristotle," 191–207.

"How Flexible is the Aristotelian "Right Reason?" 209–230.

"Christian Conscience vs. Aristotelian Right Reason," 231–259.

"Human Reason and the Moral Order in Aquinas," 261–280.

"Aristotle's Contribution on the Nature of Ethical Norms," 283–294.

"An Appreciation of Blanshard's Views on Catholicism," 295–326.

"The Acratic's "Ultimate Premise" in Aristotle," 327–343.

"*Lex et Libertas*," 345–348.

"The Relevance of Thomistic Metaphysics for Christian Life," 351–357.

"Neothomism and Christian Philosophy," 359–378.

"Aristotle on Leisure," 379–390.

"Philosophy's Role in Thanatology," 391–401.

"Aristotelian Ethics, Medicine, and the Changing Nature of Man," 403–421.

Review of *Reason and Human Good in Aristotle*, by John M. Cooper. 423–438.

"Aquinas and Philosophical Pluralism," 439–458.

"An Ambiguity in Aristotle, *EE* VII 2 1236a23–4," 459–470.

"Aristotle's Notion of Wisdom," 471–487.

Review of *Lex et Libertas: Freedom and Law According to St. Thomas Aquinas*, by Leo J. Elders and K. Hedwig, 345–348.

Reviews of Books by Owens

Lekka Kowalik, Agniez. Review of *Some Philosophical Issues in Moral Matters: The Collected Ethical Writings of Joseph Owens*, eds. Billy J. Dennis and Terence Kennedy. *Revue de Théologie et de Philosophie* 128, no. 3: 297–298.

Wilder, Alfred. Review of *Some Philosophical Issues in Moral Matters: The Collected Ethical Writings of Joseph Owens*, eds. Billy J. Dennis and Terence Kennedy. *Angelicum* 73, no. 4: 616–619.

1997

"Aristotle's Conceptualizations of Thing, Existent, and Unit at *Metaphysics* 4.2.1003b22–29," in *Beiträge zur antiken Philosophie: Festschrift für Wolfgang Kullmann*, ed. Hans-Christian Günther and Antonios Rengakos, 125–134. Stuttgart: Steiner.

Review of Books by Owens

Flannery, Kevin L. Review of *Some Philosophical Issues in Moral Matters: The Collected Ethical Writings of Joseph Owens*, eds. Billy J. Dennis and Terence Kennedy. *Gregorianum* 78, no. 1: 190–191.

Goldin, Owen. Review of *Some Philosophical Issues in Moral Matters: The Collected Ethical Writings of Joseph Owens*, eds. Billy J. Dennis and Terence Kennedy. *Canadian Philosophical Review* 17, no. 3 (June): 196–198.

McInerny, Daniel. Review of *Some Philosophical Issues in Moral Matters: The Collected Ethical Writings of Joseph Owens*, eds. Billy J. Dennis and Terence Kennedy. *The Review of Metaphysics* 52, no. 1 (Sept.): 164–166.

1999

Critical Studies

Dewan, Lawrence. "St. Thomas and the Existence of God: Owens vs Gilson, and Beyond," in *God and Argument*, ed. William Sweet. Ottawa: University of Ottawa Press. pp. 115–41.

Dewan, Lawrence. "The Individual as a Mode of Being according to Thomas Aquinas," *The Thomist* 63, no. 3 (July): 403–424.

2000

Dann, G. E. Review of *Some Philosophical Issues in Moral Matters: The Collected Ethical Writings of Joseph Owens*, eds. Billy J. Dennis and Terence Kennedy. *American Catholic Philosophical Quarterly* 74, no. 4 (Fall): 671–674.

2002

Critical Studies

DeNys, Martin J. "If Everything Can Not-Be There Would Be Nothing: Another Look at the Third Way," *The Review of Metaphysics* 56, no. 1 (Sept.): 99–122.

2003

Critical Studies

Brown, Montague. "Aquinas and the Individuation of Human Persons Revisited," *International Philosophical Quarterly* 43, no. 2 (June): 167–185.

Foreword

In the course of the last few years, Book Zeta of the Aristotelian *Metaphysics* has been given extensive coverage. It has furnished the subject matter for some full-length monographs, and has received continuous attention in the current periodical literature. Zeta's close and readily recognizable connection with book Eta places it naturally in the grouping that is traditionally known as the "central books" of the *Metaphysics*. From another important viewpoint, however, Zeta offers a parallelism with the first chapter of book Epsilon, the book that immediately precedes it in the accepted order of the metaphysical treatises. This parallelism is striking enough to suggest a unified theme for philosophical investigation into Aristotle's procedure in reasoning from secondary instances of being to primary beingness or *ousia* with promise of welcome light upon the nature and function of the Aristotelian *ousia* in its various philosophical contexts.

The parallelism lies in the gradations of being that emerge in Epsilon and Zeta. The opening chapter of Epsilon, in seeking the first principles or causes of beings, works upwards from the composite things of the perceptible world to the role that is played by separate or immaterial substance in its functioning as the primary instance of being in the macrocosmic structure. Book Zeta, on the other hand, works inwards from those composite perceptibles to their basic intrinsic constituents. It finds that the primary instance of being in each of the composites is the form that causes the things and their material components to be what each of them is. The result is that from the macrocosmic viewpoint the primary instance of being, in the sense of primary *ousia*, is the intrinsic formal cause of the material thing.

This means, obviously enough, that primary *ousia* has different though comparable meanings in those two metaphysical treatises. Further, the situation becomes more complicated because of the fact that the *ousiai* from which our philosophical thinking commences are the individual composite substances confronting us in the perceptible world. From that standpoint, those individual composite substances are regarded in the *Categories* (5.2a11–14) as the primary *ousiai*. In the sphere of logic, the singular composite substance has the primacy. The familiar Aristotelian problem of manifold meaning looms large at the entrance into this inquiry.

In facing the manifold meaning of primary *ousia* in Aristotle, one might well keep in mind the adage that the best source for the interpretation of Aristotle is Aristotle himself – *Aristoteles ex Aristotele.* This saying is regularly understood to mean that a text in Aristotle is to be interpreted according to other texts of his own that throw light upon the points at issue. But the saying may also have a deeper implication, in the sense that Aristotle's philosophical reasoning is to be understood and judged in the light of its own starting-points, which are the real things of the perceptible world. These external things themselves, and not our ideas of them or our language about them, are the principles and norms by which human thought and human language are to be gauged. Aristotle can use the same term "principle" with equal ease to denote either the things in themselves or the mental propositions by which they are understood.[1] Both of these are starting-points for human reasoning but the external perceptible things are the absolutely basic norm. This factual status of Aristotle's philosophy seems to be tacitly acknowledged by those who refer to his notion of cognition as a "naive realism." But it is in fact Aristotle's philosophical procedure, and his explanation of it merits close attention.

In regard to the present investigation, then, Aristotle's text calls for understanding from its own viewpoint, if the richness of his philosophical thought is to be appreciated. On account of the way in which that thought was actually developed, it requires fully conscious interpretation in virtue of what the things themselves reveal. The things are not to be gauged according to our clear and distinct ideas about them or according to our linguistic structures in expressing them. Rather, the concepts and the language are to be understood and adjudicated in the light of what the things themselves make manifest. Accordingly this inquiry bears primarily upon being that is seen in all its various ways in those things. Only secondarily and in accompanying fashion is the investigation concerned with the multisignificance of the concept of being or of the word "being."

A translation of the opening chapters of each of the two treatises, Epsilon and Zeta, should be sufficient to illustrate the way in which the text may be read from this viewpoint. Fine English translations of the text, notably those of Ross, Tredennick, Hope, and Apostle, are readily available. What is important is to stress the necessity of understanding the translations in the light of Aristotle's procedure from things in themselves to human thought and language, instead of allowing ideas or language to function as the basic norm for judging things.

1 On this twofold sense of "first principle" for Aristotle, see Terence Irwin, *Aristotle's First Principles* (Oxford: Clarendon Press, 1988), 3–4.

Part One (Book Epsilon): Macroscopic Overview

E I (English Translation)

The principles and causes of beings, and obviously of them qua beings, are the subject of the inquiry. For there is a cause of health / and of fitness and there are principles and elements and causes of the mathematical objects; and in general every science that is intellective, or shares to some degree in intellection, is about causes and principles either more finely detailed or of simpler type. But all these sciences, marking off some particular being and particular genus, deal with this genus but not with being / simply or qua being. Nor do they give any account of a thing's whatness, but from it – some of then making it clear by sense perception and others taking the whatness as a supposition – they demonstrate either more rigorously or more loosely the attributes proper to the genus of which they are treating. Therefore it is clear that from an approach of this kind there is no demonstration of / beingness or of whatness, but some other way of clarification. Likewise they say nothing about whether the genus with which they are dealing has being or does not have being, since it belongs to the same intellective act to make clear *what* something is and *if* it has being. Now since even the science of nature happens to be about a particular genus of being (for it is about the kind of beingness in / which the origin of motion and rest is in the beingness itself, clearly it is neither practical nor productive science. For the origin of things produced is in the producer – either intuition or art or some faculty; and the origin of things done is in the doer, namely choice – for "something done" and "something chosen" are the same thing. So if all intellection / is either practical or productive or theoretical, the science of nature will have to be a theoretical science. But it is theoretical about the kind of being that is able to undergo notion, and solely about the beingness that in notion is for the most part not separate.

Now the manner in which what is essentially a thing's being, or the thing's definition, is formulated should not escape notice, / for indeed without this the inquiry is vacuous – of things defined in the sense of quiddities, some are as the snub and others as the concave. The difference between these is that the snub is taken together with its matter (for

the snub is a concave nose), while concavity is taken without sensible
1026a1 matter. If then / all physical objects are meant in a way similar to the
snubs such as nose, eyes face, flesh, bone, and animal in general,
leaves, root, bark, and plant in general (for the definition of none of
them is without motion, but always contains matter), it is clear how the
a5 whatness is to be treated of and defined in physical objects, / and why
it belongs to the specialist on nature to treat theoretically even of some
of the soul, namely of as much as is not without matter. From these
considerations, then, it is evident that the science of nature is theoreti-
cal. Yet mathematics is also theoretical; but whether it is about things
immobile and separate is at present not clear; nevertheless that some
mathematics do treat of objects qua immobile and qua separate is clear.
a10 Now if there is something / eternal and immobile and separate, knowl-
edge about it evidently pertains to theoretical science, yet not indeed
to the science of nature (for the science of nature is about some mobile
things[1]) nor to mathematics, but to a science prior to both. For the sci-
ence of nature is about things non-separate but not immobile, and
a15 some kinds of / mathematics are about things immobile yet perhaps not
separate but as in matter, while the primary science is about things
both separate and immobile.

Now all the causes have to be eternal, but these most of all, for
these are causes of the observable instances of things divine. So there
a20 will be three theoretical philosophies, mathematics, philosophy / of
nature, and theological philosophy. For it is not unclear that if the
divine subsists anywhere it subsists in a nature of this kind, and that the
most honored philosophy should be about the most honored genus.
The theoretical, then, are more desirable than the other sciences, and
this science is more desirable than the other theoretical ones. For
someone might propose the difficulty whether indeed the primary phi-
a25 losophy / is universal or is about a particular genus and one particular
nature. For the same situation is not present even in the mathematical
sciences, but geometry and astronomy are about a particular nature
while the science treating universally of them all is common.[2] If then
there is no other substance beyond those constituted by nature, the sci-
ence of nature will be the primary science. But if there is an immobile
a30 substance, / this science is prior and is primary philosophy, and in this
way universal because primary; and it will belong to this science to
treat universally of being qua being, both of what it is and of its attrib-
utes qua being.

1 For the excision of this parenthesis, see note in Jaeger's text.

2 Cf. *Metaphysics* 4.2.1004a6–9.

Chapter One

The Role of Book Epsilon in the *Metaphysics*

From a careful reading of this opening chapter of book Epsilon three rather sharply etched positions emerge. The first is that a thing's beingness and whatness are grasped by the same intellectual activity, the same *dianoia* (1025b17–18). The second is that the science of beings qua beings, despite the all extensive universality of its object, leaves ample room for other sciences, theoretical and practical and productive. The third position is that this science of beings qua beings has as its specifying object a definite nature, namely the divine, an object whose primacy in the order of being enables the primary philosophy to treat universally of all beings in the context of focal meaning.

Further considerations will show that these three positions bring the philosophical doctrine of the *Metaphysics* into a specifically coherent whole, a whole quite distinct from medieval and modern Aristotelianisms. The three together seem to hold in place the thrusts of the various sections of this collection of treatises, allowing each section to rest firmly in its appropriate place within the one solid structure of doctrine. In a word, this short chapter in book Epsilon would appear to be the keystone for an understanding of the metaphysical thinking elaborated in the whole collection of the treatises.

Such, at least, is the prima facie impression given by reflection on these three positions outlined in the opening chapter of Epsilon. Obviously, a detailed study of the text and of the issues at stake is required in order to substantiate this initial reaction. In point of fact, the chapter is located not too far from the middle in the series of treatises handed down as the *Metaphysics*. Naturally, in view of the way the series of papers came to be assembled, mathematically exact location in this regard is not at all to be expected. But aside from that historical consideration, the two bases of the arch do not rest precisely on the same epistemological level. The basis from which all the reasoning commences in book Alpha (1–2.980a2lff.) is very obviously the things of the sensible world, animate as well as inanimate. These are things evident at once through sensible perception. They are the things constituting the world that had been studied from the time of Aristotle's earliest

Greek predecessors. The inspiration is drawn from the deep natural desire of all human beings to know the causes of the things perceived in the world around them. The quest for causes leads ultimately to an inquiry into the first and thereby highest causes of whatever is observed in the sensible world as well in human cognition of it. In that way one foot of the arch is based firmly on the things perceived through the senses. The charge of naive realism leveled by modern and postmodern thought against this approach did not at all come to the fore in Aristotle's own day. His elaborate philosophy of cognition in the *De Anima* precluded it doctrinally, by showing how in the actuality of cognition knower and thing known are thoroughly identical, and that the real external things are grasped in epistemological priority to the knower's awareness of the cognitive activity.

The purpose of the investigation, then, was in this way clearly stated. Its definite intent was an inquiry into the ultimate and thereby most universal causes of the things that make up the sensible world. The knowledge of the sensible things through their causes was at once equated with knowledge of them in universal fashion, in the way that knowing the causes of a disease enables the medical practitioner to treat the malady in any particular patient. The knowledge of the universal proceeds from acquaintance with the singular things, by discovering in them the nature of the disease or of any other object in question. The object that makes scientific knowledge possible, therefore, was seen in the particular sensible things. This aspect of universality introduced no further object, no object other than the sensible thing itself. But it did provide the means for going in scientific fashion to similar individuals. It kept the starting point of any reasoning about them firmly located within the particular sensible things grasped through intelligence as well as through sensation. It made the crucial difference between cognition by lower animals and cognition by human knowers. The parallel aimed at, obviously, was that the most universal aspect of all, namely being, might be grasped first in particular sensible things, and yet offer the ground for reasoning to still further things, things beyond the sensible world – in a word, to supersensible being. Be that as it may, this first basis of the arch is firmly grounded in the things that are immediately manifest in the sensible world.

The other basis of the arch, quite on the contrary, was not something immediately evident. That basis was the divine, something beyond the range of sensible substance. General acquaintance with it, however, was recognized by Aristotle (*Metaphysics*, 12.8.1074a38–b14) in his own interpretation of the gods that peopled the traditional mythologies. At core these gods were for him a very vague yet impressive version of the separate substances reached in his own philosophical reasoning. So one need not be surprised that the opening book of the *Metaphysics* (1.2.982b17–1.2.983a10) stresses the notion that the lover of myth is in a way a lover of wisdom, a philosopher, motivated as both are by wonder. There the science under consideration was described as divine, on account of its object as well as of its own intrinsic worth.

This opposite basis of the structure was accordingly envisaged from the start in Aristotle's metaphysical procedure. But it was brought forward as familiar in traditional religious belief. Its factual status will naturally call for strict philosophical demonstration, both of its existence and its positive nature. Separate substance, however, becomes philosophically established only in the last three books of the *Metaphysics*, through reasoning from sensible things and through comparison with the results of the inquiries undertaken by Aristotle's philosophical predecessors. Not until then does it become philosophically acceptable as a rational conclusion. Yet from the start it is placed actively in mind as something required for the integral pursuit of metaphysics. It is envisaged as something necessary for the completion of the philosophical account.

The same thrust illustrated in book Alpha's description of the science may be seen in the subsequent books. Book Alpha elatton (1.993b28–29) is concerned with the primary status of the originating principles of the eternal beings, that is, with the primacy of the first causes of what is observable in the heavens. Book Gamma asserts that nature, in this sense of things composed of matter and form, is only one genus of being, with the result that the science treating universally of all beings will be a higher science than the science developed by the philosopher of nature. This higher science, which treats of primary substance, will accordingly have the task of dealing with the universal axioms used in demonstration.[1] Even at this early stage of the investigation the supersensible object is seen as the ultimate ground for those absolutely universal axioms. People who question the absolute validity of the those axioms are to understand that there is among beings a kind of substance other than the sensible, a kind immune to change, destruction, or coming to be (4.5.1009a36–38). Those especially who argue against the first principle of demonstration, namely the principle of contradiction, are to be shown that there is in the universe an absolutely immobile nature (4.5.1010a33–35; cf. 4.8.1012b26–31). Though the axioms are immediately evident in sensible reality,

1 *Metaphysics* 4.3-5.1005al9-1010bl. Aristotle speaks as though he is understanding the basic axiom to mean that being contradicts not being. Hence in Scholastic parlance it could be "the principle of contradiction." With Leibniz it bore rather on essence. It became the principle "of essences, that is, the principle of identity or contradiction" - see *The Leibniz Clarke Correspondence*, ed. H.G. Alexander (New York: Philosophical Library, 1956), p. 57. In that Leibnizian setting the notion of this principle as "more correctly the principle of Non Contradiction," was suggested by Sir William Hamilton, *Lectures on Metaphysics and Logic*, ed. H. L. Mansel and John Veitch, 2nd. ed. (Edinburgh and London: William Blackwood and Sons, 1863.), I II, 368; cf. p. 524 for it as "Law, Principle or Axiom." With Aristotle the procedure is based upon the things themselves. Aristotle goes from the things to the mental principles, not from those principles to the things. Under the guidance of those mental principles, however, one reasons from the things immediately known to things about which one does not have immediate awareness.

their grounding in supersensible substance has to be brought forward in answer to those who question them.

In the first part of the *Metaphysics*, then, the basis of the science in supersensible substance is kept in view. In the books immediately following Epsilon the same attitude persists, with clear reminders that the present study of sensible substances is bearing upon the supersensible (1029b3–12; 1037a10–14; 104la7–9; 1046al–2). As Aristotle notes in the *Nicomachean Ethics* (1.4.1095a30–b4) when interpreting a saying attributed to Plato, the way is both from and to the judges' stand. There is simultaneous stress in opposite directions. As a pure fact, the principle of contradiction is of course immediately evident. Yet the ultimate reason for it is shown through demonstration. As in the case of the eclipse (*Posterior Analytics*, 2.2.90a7–18; cf. 1.13.78a22–b3l), one can know the fact immediately, but needs the reason in order to have a scientific explanation of it. Likewise in ethics, the moral choices of persons properly brought up are known at once and serve as the principles of good conduct. Still, the ultimate goal, known only through philosophical study, is also a principle (*Nicomachean Ethics*, 1.12.1102a4). Both types of principle, though remaining at opposite ends, are required for the philosophical understanding. The same seems to hold in metaphysics. Sensible things provide the basis for the unshakable efficacy of its axioms, but the basis for the philosophical explanation of this efficacy lies in the supersensible substance. The procedure has to maintain its thrusts in the opposed directions.

In the strictly demonstrative process, of course, the Aristotelian reasoning starts from the things better known to us and goes on to reach the things more intelligible in themselves.[2] As in conduct the ethical task is to make what is supremely good good for the individual, so in metaphysics the effort is to make what is most knowable in its own nature knowable to oneself, passing over from the less knowable to the most knowable. The notion of the highest instance is in this way present from the start. Both the primitive facts and the ultimate goal are kept concomitantly in Aristotle's mind throughout the whole procedure. The thrust bears on both of them simultaneously. An exactly fitting keystone is indispensable if the opposed thrusts are to be appropriately distributed and a solid structure achieved and maintained. The second base of the arch may be known only in the vaguest and most general way, but it has to be envisaged at least in that way if the progress and structure of the science is to be understood.

Does the first chapter in book Epsilon serve this purpose for the *Metaphysics*? Can it explain how the Aristotelian procedure is able to develop a science with the pressures running throughout in the opposed directions? Though the explanation in book Epsilon is disconcertingly brief, its account of the three different types of sciences (1025bl8–24) is informative enough to allow this question to be addressed to it. If the science now in question were essentially a type

2 *Metaphysics*, 7.3.1029b3–12; cf. *Nicomachean Ethics*, 1.4.1095b2–4.

of construction, the metaphor of a keystone would be incongruous. Each stone would have to be artificially supported in its place, till the final one was set. The demonstrative process by which the nature and existence of separate substance is reached would first have to be undertaken step by step before a role could legitimately be given this type of entity in the philosophical discussion. As a result the kind of scientific procedure here at issue demands attention. Epsilon's first chapter may legitimately be asked to provide it.

Likewise, Epsilon's doctrine that a thing's beingness and whatness are grasped by the same type of intellective activity, seems to play a key role in shaping the direction of the reasoning and its arrival at its distinctive conclusion. What precisely is the import of this combined cognition of being and thing in the same notion? Already in book Gamma (2.1003b22–33) a human person and a human person endowed with being were regarded as the same. The addition "endowed with being" did not add anything new to the meaning. Neither in their coming into being nor in their perishing is the one separated from the other. The substance of each thing is essentially a being.[3]

The text here is difficult. The point directly at issue was that being and unity are one and the same nature (b23–26), though the two aspects are not made manifest by the same definition. But it makes no difference, Aristotle interjects, if we may understand the two in the same fashion; rather, it would be more advantageous for the point he is driving home at the moment. These remarks, though bearing directly on unity and being, seem applicable also to being and thing. Though their concepts may be different, in reality the two are one and the same. For metaphysical reasoning, it would even be more advantageous to regard them as conceptually the same. However, this point is not pursued in book Gamma. It is left open. The doctrine of being in the first two chapters of that book, taken alone, could be used later for development in the direction of one supreme and infinite being or of a plurality of finite separate substances. One has to wait for the first chapter of Epsilon to see the procedure locked definitely in the latter setting.

There is also a problem of translation. Literally, the meaning of the text at 4.2.1003b26–27 is "a being man," in the sense of a person endowed with being. But that is not English idiom. The temptation is to translate it "an existent man." This translation, however, introduces a notion not explicit in the Greek and not

3 On these "transcendentals," or aspects that immediately follow upon being, see Karl Barthlein, *Die Transzendentalienlehre der alten Ontologie*, I. Teil (Berlin: Walter de Gruyter, 1972). The designation of them as "transcendentals," however, does not appear before the sixteenth century. The "real distinction" between two of them, namely, being and thing, becomes an acute problem after Avicenna's time. The reason lay in the Judeo-Christian doctrine that creatures received their being from God, even though they had to be regarded essentially as beings. For Avicenna the same thing could have different being in the mind from the being that it had in reality.

necessarily implicit in it. It is a translation made against the background of essence and existence. Essence is regarded as stating what a thing is, and existence as asserting that it actually is present in the real world or in cognition. The background, historically, is that of medieval thought, in which for Christian, Jewish, or Islamic writers the things of the finite world did not have their existence from themselves but had received it through creation out of nothing. The Greek background, in contrast, had been stated succinctly in the poem of Parmenides (DK 8.6–13). Nothing could come from nothing, for there is no such thing as "nothing;" no process could be started by which anything could come from it, and the result would not be anything besides nothing itself. Through and through, thing was from the start identical with being. Even where in later Greek thought change was admitted, the matter for the change was already there and the problem was to explain how things could be new.

The radical difference between the Aristotelian approach and the essence–existence approach becomes sharply apparent when one asks if the notion of what a thing is tells anything about its presence in reality or in cognition. The medieval answer was no. You could be aware of what a phoenix is, or what a mountain of gold is, without thereby knowing if either of them ever existed in reality or in anyone else's cognition. For Aristotle (*Post. An.*, 2.7.92bl7-18; 8.93a18-20), on the contrary, it is impossible to know what a thing is without thereby knowing that it is.

In this latter context the Greek verb for "is" cannot be translated by the English "exists" without giving a wrong impression. The meaning is, rather, that you cannot know what a thing is without thereby knowing that it is a being. The question is not concerned with its existence either in reality or in cognition.[4]

Against this general background the text of Epsilon's first chapter may be asked if it definitely determines the course of the *Metaphysics* in the direction of a plurality of finite separate substances as the second base upon which the structure rests. Does it at all permit reasoning to the one supreme and provident being in whom the medieval thinkers believed? If not, how could these later thinkers make such abundant use of the Aristotelian reasoning processes in working toward so different a goal?

Finally, the third position noted in the chapter needs careful scrutiny. It concerns the kind of universality required by the science that treats of being qua being. The universality has to extend to all beings without exception, yet has to bear upon one definite nature, the nature of immobile substance. The universal had been introduced in book Alpha (98la5–12) as an object seen in a number of similar individuals marked off "according to one form" (*kat eidos hen,* a10). The Greek expression *katholou* is adverbial, meaning that the object is taken in the

4 On the difficulties in the translation of Aristotle's term for "being," see Myles Burnyeat, *Notes on Book Zeta of Aristotle's Metaphysics* (Oxford: Sub Faculty of Philosophy, 1979), 1.

way it applies to the whole group. So in knowing what a disease is in universal fashion, the physician can apply that knowledge to any individual suffering from the malady. That was the example given by Aristotle in book Alpha. Any other example, e.g., book, tree, house, will illustrate it equally well. It is an object seen in the individuals one by one, as identical with each in turn. That is the way it is explained in book Delta: "by all of them, e.g. man, horse, god, being severally one single thing, because all are living things" (*Metaphysics*, 5.26.1023b3l–32; Oxford trans., 2nd ed., 1928). These instances are identical one by one with the universal object "living thing," but only severally or in turn. Because a man and a horse are each a living thing they do not become identical with each other as singular things. They remain different as singulars, even though each is severally a living thing. The crucial point at issue is that each becomes identical, though severally, with the object expressed by the universal. In predication the singular is asserted to be the universally conceived object. The man and the horse are each a living thing. The universal object, though, has no real existence outside the individuals.

That is the model used by Aristotle for universality. The predication is *kath' hen* (981a10), as noted in the preceding paragraph. But at the beginning of book Gamma a different type of universality is introduced. This is the type that explains the universality of being qua being. The universality is that of the highest causes and principles, the text states, so these have to be the per se causes and principles of a certain definite nature (*phuseōs tinos*, 4.1003a27). This is taken as evident, since any accidental character here would presuppose a nature to which they belonged per se and thereby keep them from being the highest principles and causes. They are the principles and causes that from Aristotle's viewpoint his Greek predecessors had been pursuing all along when dealing universally with being qua being. But instead of a universality *kath' eidos hen*, as universality had been explained at Alpha 1.981a10, the universality is now *pros hen*, in the sense of relation to a certain definite nature (*mian tina phusin,* 4.2.1003a34).

The importance of understanding this extension of universality can hardly be exaggerated in one's study of the Aristotelian *Metaphysics*. The type of meaning involved has been neatly described in English as focal.[5] In both kinds of universality a certain definite nature is the basis of the predication. But in the ordinary type of universality the identity of the subject with the object predicated is asserted.[6] Socrates is said to be a man and an animal and a living thing. But in the second type a relation to the basic definite nature is meant, such as cause or effect or

5 See G. E. L. Owen, "Logic and Metaphysics in Some Earlier Works of Aristotle," in *Aristotle and Plato in the Mid Fourth Century*, ed. I. During and G. E. L. Owen (Göteborg: Studia Graeca et Latina Gothoburgensia, XI, 1960), 163-190.

6 On the identity involved in essential predication, see Jaakko Hintikka, "The Varieties of Being in Aristotle," in *The Logic of Being*, eds. S. Knuuttila and J. Hintikka (Dordrecht, Holland: D. Reidel Publishing Co., 1986), 93–96.

sign of that nature. In a word, in the ordinary type of universality the basic nature is intrinsic to the subject of which it is predicated. In the second type, the nature is extrinsic to secondary instances at least as far as the setting in book Gamma is concerned.

Aristotle immediately illustrates this second type of universality with two examples, namely, of healthy and of medical. Healthy is predicated always in relation to health, the appropriate disposition of a bodily organism. The basic nature involved in this predication is the disposition of the living animal or plant. Nourishment is healthy because it sustains this disposition, care because it safeguards it, color because it is a sign of it, a person because she or he enjoys it. Cooked spinach may be healthy for the person who eats it, but the health thereby referred to is that of the person, not that of the spinach. As regards its own bodily disposition, the cooked spinach is in anything but a healthy state. The basic nature so involved is identified only with the disposition of the human organism. The other instances of which the notion is predicated are merely related to health as to a thing outside their own intrinsic natures.

The same situation may be seen in regard to medical. The basic nature there involved is the art in the mind of the medical practitioner. Even the practitioner is medical only on account of the possession of that art. The nature basically involved is identical with an accident in the category of quality, and not with anything in the category of substance. So anything naturally helpful for medical art, or any of the effects its practice brings about, is medical only through the respective relation to that basic nature, and not through identity with it.

Even just in themselves, these two illustrations indicate that a science can be based upon this second type of universality. The science of hygiene is based upon it; the science of medicine likewise. In these sciences the basic nature studied will be identical only with the basic nature to which all the other instances are related. It will not be identical with any of these other instances, and in that sense will remain outside them. Nevertheless it will be the object of the science, and will give the science its specification, as in the case of medicine and hygiene. It will be universal to all the instances, even though it does not become identical with them one by one, or severally. In its own way, then, it is universal. The ordinary type of universality, in which all the instances are severally one with the common object, remains the model for scientific procedure. But in a certain way the instances of predication through reference to a common object are all made in accordance with that object, so that these *pros hen* predications are "in a certain sense *kath' hen*" (4.3.1003bl4–15). The ordinary type of predication remains the model, but the *pros hen* type conforms sufficiently to it to satisfy the demands of scientific procedure.

It is in this framework of focal meaning that Aristotle introduces the science of being qua being. The primary instance will be substance, and all other instances will be beings because of their relation to substance, either as accidents of it such as qualities and quantities, or as processes toward or destructive of substance, or in the denials of these instances as when "nothing" is asserted by way of a denial of being. All of them come in one of these ways under the universal notion of being. In consequence the study of beings qua beings will be the work of this science. But everywhere the science of the primary instance will be dominative. On it the other instances depend, and through it they are understood as beings. In this case the primary instance is substance. Accordingly the principles and causes of substances should be had by the philosopher (4.2.1003bl5–19). Here "substances" is in the plural.

These statements outline clearly enough the manner in which the science of the highest causes and principles of things faces its object. The nature that specifies it extends to all things without exception, but by way of focusing upon a primary instance and seeing all other things in their respective relations to that primary instance. Here the primary instance is located in substance. In the Greek, merely the neuter singular "proton" is used to designate the instance. No noun like "instantiation" or "token" seemed necessary. Aristotle was approaching focal reference against the background of ordinary universality, in which the one universal object is seen in a number of singular instances. He has introduced focal meaning in this context as modeled upon the ordinary type of universality. There seems to be no reason, then, why the current term "instance" should not be used in this context to designate the individual things to which the object extends through focal reference. In the present context the primary instance of being is repeatedly (1003a27; a34; b14; b23) called a "nature." The instances in which it is seen through focal reference do not instantiate it in exactly the same way, as would be done in ordinary universality. Nevertheless they instantiate one and the same nature, though in various ways or grades. They all may be safely regarded as instances of which the primary nature is predicated, even though in themselves they stay unchanged in their own distinct natures. In Aristotle's illustration of "healthy," therefore, food or exercise or color will each have its proper nature predicated univocally of its own instances. But through focal reference they all have in common the nature of health, a nature found univocally only in living organisms.

In regard to the relation to substance in the case of the instances of being, Aristotle mentions that the other instances *depend upon* the primary instances and are called beings on account of it. The phrasing here resembles the way the heavens and the natural world in book Lambda (7.1072b13–14) depend upon (*ērtētai*) the absolutely changeless primary movent. If that impression is correct, the notion of the divine as one of the two bases upon which the whole of the philosophical construction rests is being kept in mind just as in the cases already noted. It would indicate that the divine is included among the principles and causes of substances that are being sought in the present inquiry.

For the moment, however, this topic is not pursued further. Book Gamma is content with enumerating instances, as in the case of the ordinary universal. Here the instances enumerated are substance and accidents, processes and privations and negations. No attempt is made to investigate the gradations within the order of substance itself, as is done later in Book Zeta. Mention is merely made of the requirement to seek the principles and causes of substance. Shortly after in book Gamma (3.1005a35) the primary wisdom is said to treat universally of beings and of the primary substances in a way in which the unemended text would suggest that the phrase "of the primary substance" is explicative of "universally." But for the present no inquiry into the principles and causes of substance is undertaken.

In regard to the question whether the nature of being remains outside the secondary instances, however, one might note here that all the illustrations given by Aristotle leave it outside those other objects. The notion of healthy is not intrinsic to the food or the exercise that are the cause of health, nor is it intrinsic to color as the sign of health. As a nature it occurs only in the disposition of the living organism. Similarly medicine is an art that is found intrinsically only in a human quality. Other things are medical only insofar as they are related to that quality. In these sharp illustrations the nature in question is not seen in any of the secondary instances. Yet what one would expect from the introduction in Alpha elatton (993b4–31) is that being is present in everything and missed by nobody, regardless of how difficult its explanation may be. What was offered there was the conception that the thing possessing the characteristic in the highest degree will be the cause of that same characteristic in lesser degrees in all the other instances. The conclusion is then drawn that the principles of the eternal beings have truth in the highest degree. They are not just sometimes true, sometimes not. Nor is anything a cause of their being, but they are the cause of being for other things. Aristotle then closes with the overall inference that everything partakes of truth in the same manner that it partakes of being.

In this passage of Alpha elatton, the background is the way truth and being had been equated in the poem of Parmenides.[7] Being is regarded as the unchangeable, in contrast to the doxastic world of becoming. Yet, like the physical quality of heat, being is looked upon as present in lesser degrees in things other than the eternal beings, and as caused in the things by those eternal beings quite as heat is caused in other things by the heat present in fire. Despite difference in degree, it remains the same characteristic. That means, obviously, that the nature in question is the same nature seen throughout all the gradations.[8]

A like conclusion could be drawn from the passage in Gamma (1.1003b22–33) in which the substance of everything is regarded as essentially a

7 Parmenides, Fr. 8–50–52; DK, 1, 239. 6–8.

8 In this respect, one may compare the gradations seen in the various kinds of courage (*Nicomachean Ethics*, 3.6–8.1115a6–1117a28) and in those of friendship (8.1–8.1155a3–1159b24).

being, even though substance and being are explained in different ways. There being is looked upon as intrinsic to each thing. Yet in the same context the illustrations given by Aristotle for focal meaning place the predicated nature in the primary instance only. It would seem that Aristotle has some special motive for proceeding in this way. It would suggest a doctrine of being in which the nature of being is found in a primary instance only, yet is seen in the references to that primary instance in all other cases. At least what has been said as far as Delta in the *Metaphysics* may open the way to different thrusts. Does the first chapter of Epsilon lock the procedure definitely in one of the directions? That is surely a question that may be asked of the text itself along with those about the other two positions outlined at the start of the present discussion.

The next step, then, will be to confront the text itself with the questions regarding the three positions seen emerging from it. In subsequent chapters each of the positions can be discussed in the wider context of Western philosophy in general, and in the light of the controversies that have arisen in the efforts to interpret correctly the Aristotelian doctrine itself and the issues with which it deals.

* * * * * * * * * *

The first of the three positions outlined in book Epsilon is concerned with the identity of a thing and its being. The problem is at once placed in the setting of book Alpha's quest for the principles and causes of things, presented in book Gamma (1.1003a21–32; b15–16) as the science of being qua being or beings qua beings. The contrast with the other sciences was then emphasized in Gamma. Each of the other sciences deals with a particular genus or kind of being, as may be seen for instance in the various branches of mathematics. These deal explicitly with their particular kinds of being, but not with being that is taken simply or qua being (1.1003a22–26).

What does this mean? In the Greek text, the "qua being" seems to be explicative of "simply." With Aristotle all human cognition has its origin in sensible things, things that become identical with the percipient in the actuality of the cognition. As in the opening chapter of Gamma (1.1003a23–24), none of the other sciences deals universally with being qua being, but only with a section of it marked off in accord with some other feature that accrues to it (*to sumbebēkos*, a25). This seems to describe the situation quite neatly. The science that treats of the highest causes of the things in the universe has to bear upon all those things in the most universal fashion, and not deal just with a certain section of them. The things are all beings, and when their being is viewed simply as such without addition of any other notion they confront the intellect with a readily discernible object for scientific investigation. The objects of the other sciences are set up by addition of further and narrowing aspects, over and above the notion of being. The description of this object as "qua being" is accordingly explained by its status as a simple notion, in contrast to the objects of other sciences. The other sciences bear upon beings insofar as these particular beings are specified by further notions added to their basic characterization as beings. So in mathematics the things counted or measured have the further specification of quantity, over and above their basic characterization of being.

These considerations serve also to clarify the understanding of the Greek term "being" as used in the neuter singular with the definite article in the way met in the present texts. *To on* covers being in universal fashion, in any or all of its instances. It can mean "a being" or "all beings" insofar as each and all of them come under the notion of "being." Likewise, in accord with the Greek use of the neuter singular of an adjective to signify in abstract fashion the quality expressed by the adjective, it can mean the being of the thing, quite as the Greek neuter singular to leukon can mean whiteness as well as something white.[9]

In point of fact, the theme brought forward in Epsilon (1.1025b3–4) is the causes of *beings*. Obviously enough, this means concrete things taken in their most universal extent. In consequence the phrasing "beings qua beings" in the plural, or "being qua being" in the singular, can be used indifferently. Gamma preferred the singular, though with the plural occurring at 1003b15–16 and at 1005a27 and b10. But in the present context the use of "being" in an abstract sense is not brought in, even where the contrast is with a thing's whatness at 1025a14. The temptation to understand the second occurrence of the term "being" in an abstract sense in the phrase "being qua being" is prohibited by the way the plural is used indifferently with the singular version. In the plural the second occurrence of the term "beings" has to be taken in the same sense as the first. It cannot be understood abstractly.

The parallelism requires that the phrasing in the singular be taken in the same way. The second cannot be interpreted as though it were expressing a characteristic of the subject. Grammatically, of course, *to on* in Greek can denote the notion of being in abstract fashion. Whereas in Gamma (2.1003b20–34) *to on* is contrasted with *to hen*, translators do not hesitate to render the Greek terms as "being" and "unity" in abstract fashion. But in the present context the parallelism with the plural phrasing shows definitely enough that the second "being" in the singular phrasing has to be understood in the sense of a concrete being.

Further, the particular sciences do not give any explanation of a thing's what-

9 In English the use of the present participle as a noun is normal, e.g., "the fighting lasted thirty days." With verbs other than "being," however, the participle just alone does not stand for the subject that exercises the actuality. One has to add explicitly the subject, e.g. "the fighting rebels," to denote the subject in question. This points to a significant difference in the predicate "being" from the bearing of other verbal predicates. On the topic, see Etienne Gilson, *Being and Some Philosophers*, 2nd ed. (Toronto: Pontifical Institute of Mediaeval Studies, 1952), 217–227, in an "Appendix" replying to L.M. Regis.

ness. Rather, they take the whatness as evident through sensation or else just presuppose it (1.1025b10–12). The Greek expression translated here by "whatness" (*to ti estin*) means the answer to the question "What is the thing?" The Greek idiom uses the definite article *to* to signify that the question is being answered. English does not require the article when the interrogative pronoun is taken over into the answer. We answer by stating what the thing is, or its whatness, while the Greek phrases it as "the what is" of the thing. Aristotle's point is that just as the task of explaining beings qua beings belongs to the highest science, so likewise the explanation of them from the viewpoint of their whatness is undertaken by none of the particular sciences. These sciences accept both the *ousia* and the whatness without being able to demonstrate either. Likewise, Aristotle continues, the particular sciences do not say anything about whether the genus with which they deal is or is not, since it belongs to the same *dianoia* to make known what the thing is and if it is (b14–18).

The exact meaning of the assertions in this condensed and difficult passage is not easy to attain. The objects specifying the particular sciences are being contrasted with the object that specifies the most universal science. The first point of contrast is with the simplicity of being qua being. None of the particular sciences attempt to explain that aspect in the things with which they deal. Secondly, the particular sciences do not give any account of the whatness in those things. Each, indeed, of the things is a "what" or a "something." But the particular sciences merely recognize this at once, as in the case of earth, air, fire, or water, or of composite bodies. What each of these things is, is thus grasped in sensation. Other objects, such as mathematical entities like a point, are taken as presuppositions. The particular sciences do not have to demonstrate that each is a "something." That seems clearly enough to be the contrast here. So when the text goes to draw the conclusion that obviously there is in these sciences no demonstration of either *ousia* or of whatness, the term *ousia* should be expected to signify the qua being aspect, the beingness in contrast to the whatness.

Yet there are difficulties. "Beingness" is recognized without restrictions as an English word by the second edition of the Oxford English Dictionary. Morphologically it corresponds to the Greek word *ousia*, formed from the feminine participle *ousa* quite as "beingness" from "being." Yet in current Greek speech *ousia* meant property. It meant one's possessions, what one owned, the things that made one socially what one was. The image it evoked was that of concrete material things. In this way it was taken over philosophically to signify the substance of each thing, for instance the metal, the plant or tree, the ox or the human person. It was the substance that allowed all the other characteristics of the thing to be, for they had their own being as the size, the color, the activities, or other modifications of the substance their basic subject. Hence for purposes of logic the *Categories* (2.2a11–26) could regard the individual human being or the individual horse as the primary instance of *ousia*. One's property, including slaves, consisted of individual things. But the overtones of beingness in the Greek *ousia* made themselves felt. For predication in logic the individual man Socrates was a human being, was an animal, was a substance, and was as well a number of accidental predicates. The individual was the primary instance of beingness for all these. He was his individual self first of all, and was the other predicates in secondary fashion. Hence the universal predicates in the category of substance were from the logician's viewpoint secondary substances. The logician had no need to analyze the individual substance philosophically into matter and form.[10] The most basic entity for logic was the individual subject. It was the basic beingness with which the logician was concerned. It was for him the primary *ousia* in the sense of beingness.

In the *Metaphysics* (1.3.983a27), however, *ousia* is introduced as the formal cause in the sense in which form had been contrasted with matter in the *Physics* (2.3.194b16 ff.) Here, in the *Metaphysics*, *ousia* is presented as that which constitutes the being of the thing. Yet only a few lines later (983b10) *ousia* is used for the substance that changes in its accidents, quite as it occurs in the categories. Aristotle seems entirely at his ease in passing from the one meaning to the other. He writes as though the Greek *ousia* conveys both senses simultaneously, the popular sense of concrete property and the abstract sense of being that its morphology insinuates. It does not seem possible to find an English word that does just that. "Entity" may be used consistently for every instance in which *ousia* occurs in Aristotle.[11] But the word is not very expressive, and does not carry any overtone of material property that would give it a vivid image. To appreciate the implications, one would have to keep mentally translating it back to the original Greek term *ousia*. "Substance," the now generally accepted English equivalent, can be made to function in the sense of what basically constitutes a thing, as well as in the sense of substrate. But in a case like the present, where the being simply as such of a thing is expressed in direct contrast to the thing's whatness, a translation that brings out sharply the notion of being seems required. It need not be surprising, then, that an increasing number of present day writers prefer to leave the Greek *ousia* untranslated and to use it as an English word. But if "beingness" is now acceptable, it serves the purpose neatly enough in instances like that of the present text. It cannot, of course, be used in general as a translation of *ousia*, since you cannot speak of a tree or dog as a "beingness" in the way each is referred to

10 On the observation that "the term for 'matter' appears nowhere in the *Organon*," see Daniel W. Graham, *Aristotle's Two Systems* (Oxford: Clarendon Press, 1987), 157. Cf. W. D. Ross, *Aristotle's Prior and Posterior Analytics* (Oxford: Clarendon Press, 1949), 639.

11 On "entity" for the translation of *ousia*, see Philip Merlan, "Aristotle's Unmoved Movers," *Traditio*, 4 (1946), 8. Its use is appropriate only in a very general study of *ousia* in Aristotle, in which a single term that will cover all its occurrences in the *Corpus Aristotelicum* is required. Elsewhere the English term that corresponds to the meaning in the particular instance is in order.

in Greek as an *ousia*. Later one may show that Aristotle reasons to the identity of being and whatness in the thing. Yet his reasoning starts from a contrast between these two aspects. In order to follow his thought, a translation of *ousia* in terms of being is helpful.

The text of Epsilon (1.1025b16–18) adds that the particular sciences in similar fashion say nothing about whether the genus with which they deal does or does not have being. Again there is a problem of translation. Literally, the rendition would be "whether the genus is or is not." But this hardly seems English idiom, unless one italicizes the *is*. It is unlikely that the contrast here is between the whatness mentioned in the preceding sentence and the simple aspect of being from which it was there distinguished. That contrast was already treated, and a new contrast similar to it is being introduced.

The meaning, rather, is that a particular science does not have the task of showing whether or not the genus with which it deals comes under the order of beings. That is all. The reason is given. To know whether a thing has being, in this most general sense, belongs to the same intellective activity as the knowledge of that thing's whatness. In knowing what a thing is, you thereby know that it is, as had been maintained in the *Posterior Analytics* (1.8–93a20; cf. 7.92bl7–18).

The "if it is," then, refers to the general designation of being, over and above all the categories. The "what it is" bears on the particular genus or category in which the object is located. But the significant statement here is that both the "if it is" and the "what it is" are grasped by the same type of intellection. Whatever "intellection" (*dianoia*) may mean, the assertion definitely excludes a new mental act for the grasp of the "if it is" over and above the "what it is." This excludes the interpretation of the "if it is" in the medieval sense of existence as distinct from essence.[12] In the medieval approach you can know what a thing is, for instance a phoenix, without knowing whether the thing exists or ever existed. Even in the ordinary use of "exist" in English today, the question about what a thing is calls for its definition. The answer to that question does not inform you whether or not the thing exists. The two answers belong to different types of intellection.

In book Epsilon, then, the question whether a genus is or is not is different from the question whether or not the science of being qua being is specified by a particular genus. It is likewise different from a question of essence and existence. But what is asserted in Epsilon is that the science of being qua being has the task, in contrast to the particular sciences, of dealing with the whatness and the beingness of things, and that these two features in things are grasped by the same mental act. This stand has far reaching consequences. It may well lock the Aristotelian

12 E.g.: "Now, every essence or quiddity can be understood without knowing anything about its being. I can know, for instance, what a man or a phoenix is and still be ignorant whether it has being in reality." Aquinas, *On Being and Essence*, 4.5, trans. Armand Maurer, 2nd ed., (Toronto: Pontifical Institute of Mediaeval Studies, 1968), 55.

procedure into the course it takes for reaching separate substance, the other basis upon which the arch rests. That is a problem that will be left for discussion in detail in the next chapter.

In like fashion the second position emerging from the text of Epsilon, namely the theoretical character of the science of being qua being, prompts a question. It is about how the divine, something not immediately known in a theoretical way, can be regarded from the start as a basis for the science. Epsilon explains how the theoretical, practical, and productive sciences have different types of starting points. The starting points for the practical and productive sciences are in the knower. The objects envisaged do not exist till the cognition itself brings them about. But those of the theoretical sciences are already there in the things themselves. The model used is the science of nature. Its starting points are embedded in sensible matter, as snubness in a nose. Yet its study of cognition reaches out to intellectual soul, which functions on the immaterial level. In the theoretical order, the science itself as well as its object is spread before the mind's eye for consideration as a whole. This aspect may be investigated from the angle of solidity in a structure resting simultaneously on both bases of the arch.

Finally, the opening chapter of Epsilon faces the question whether the science that is specified by the primary instance of being is the science that treats of all other beings universally. Book Gamma (1003bl5–17) had emphasized that everywhere in predication by focal reference the science is dominantly of the primary instance, and shortly afterwards (1005a35) had described the science of beings qua beings as universal in scope and as dealing with the primary substance. Book Epsilon takes up this situation as meaning that the primary philosophy bears on a certain definite nature and yet is universal in its coverage of beings (1026a23–32). The definite nature had just been specified as the object of theological science (a19). Even in the mathematical sciences the situation is not paralleled. Geometry and astronomy are each concerned with a definite nature, but general mathematics is common in regard to all mathematical objects.[13]

13 On the understanding of "general mathematics" in this context as a study of quantity in general, see Bertrand Dumoulin, *Analyse génétique de la Métaphysique d'Aristote* (Montreal: Bellarmin, 1986), 142–143. Cf. W. D. Ross, Aristotle's *Metaphysics* (Oxford: Clarendon Press, 1924), 1, 356–357. The question is whether the primary philosophy is universal in the sense of not bearing specifically upon a particular genus or a particular nature (*Metaphysics*, 6.1.1026a24–25). Aristotle (a25–27) notes that in the mathematical sciences, geometry, and astronomy deal with particular kinds of quantitative subjects, while general mathematics treats of all quantitative subjects in universal fashion. Accordingly there cannot be the same kind of universality in both these general coverages, because the primary philosophy bears upon a particular type of being, namely separate substance, while "general mathematics" does not deal with any particular kind of quantity as such. Dumoulin (p. 142) remarks, "Il y a donc disparité entre le cas des mathématiques et celui de la philosophie première." The point is that in the case of general mathematics the universality is *kath' hen*, while for the primary philosophy it is *pros hen*.

Epsilon presents this difficulty with the full contrast given it in modern times by Natorp and Jaeger. The primary philosophy is specified by a definite nature, the divine. That nature is one genus of being, namely, the supersensible. Specification by the divine should therefore make the primary philosophy a particular science. Yet that philosophical science has to deal universally with all beings. For Natorp and for Jaeger, and to a wide extent for commentators in recent times, this seems to be a glaring contradiction. Most of today's writers would like the Aristotelian metaphysics to be some kind of an ontology, in the sense of the *metaphysica generalis* in the Wolffian tradition. Yet book Epsilon, far from seeing any real clash between the opposed alternatives, finds in the specific nature of the primary instance the reason for the universal coverage given by the science. The science treats universally of being qua being precisely because its object is the primary instance of being. The framework is that of focal meaning.

In a word, Epsilon looks upon the primary philosophy in the straightforward setting described at the beginning of book Gamma. It is the science of the primary instance of being, and thereby the universal science of being qua being. It treats of all beings in their reference to the nature of being that is located in the primary instance. The implications of this stand will call for careful discussion against the broader background of Western philosophy as a whole, the background against which it has in fact been placed by the modern controversies that have developed around it.

* * * * * * * * * *

The rest of book Epsilon discusses briefly the various ways in which being is divided when it is taken simply as being, in the manner explained in the opening chapter of Gamma. When it is understood simply as such, it is taken without the further determinations that accrue to it in sensible things. These added determinations are left out of consideration. Book Delta (7.1017a7–b9) had outlined the four ways in which being in that overall coverage may be considered. This fourfold division is now given fresh consideration.

As in Delta, the first kind of being that is mentioned is the division into the per se and the accidental. The reason for listing it in first place seems to lie in the emphasized conclusion that the accidental is to be barred from the function of specifying any science whatever. It occasions sophistries, yet it gives the explanation why in actual life all things do not follow of necessity or even for the most part.[14] Accordingly it is given a somewhat detailed discussion in Epsilon 2–3.

The second way in which being, simply as such, may be understood is in the sense of the true. Here it is opposed to non-being in the meaning of the false. The

14 For Aristotle (*Nicomachean Ethics*, 1.3.1094b11-27) things that happen "for the most part" exhibit their own type of universality, with each type appropriate to the nature of the subject matter under discussion.

true is what is, the false is what is not. This is concerned with a synthesis of subject and predicate that takes place in the mind. Since truth and falsity in this sense pertain to human judgments about things rather than to the things themselves, they are primarily characteristics of human thought about things, and like accidental being they do not manifest any nature (*phusin*, 1028a2) that would be present in things over and above the being of the categories. The concern, in consequence, is with the nature of being as such. This is left for study in its categories and in its actual and potential instances, a study undertaken in the central books of the *Metaphysics*.

Chapter Two

Pure Actuality and Primacy in Being

The opening chapter of book Epsilon, as the preceding investigation has shown, identifies the nature of being, namely being qua being, with separate substance. In the context, separate substance meant substance that is not composed of matter and form. There can be no matter in its nature. That kind of substance, then, is the primary instance of being. All other things are beings through the relation they have to it. Accordingly Aristotle's basic gradation in being stands out clearly. Separate substance is the primary instance. All other things are secondary instances of being.

But separate substance is not an immediate object of human cognition. It has to be reached by a process of reasoning that starts from immediately perceived sensible things. This reasoning process is outlined in book Lambda of the *Metaphysics* (6.7.1071b3–1073a13). Proceeding by way of actuality and potentiality, book Lambda finds that motion and time are eternal, and that they are sustained in being by perishable substances in a succession that had no beginning and will have no end. Basically, however, the motion has to be proceeding from a cause that is purely actual, without any potentiality at all that would demand or allow further actuation. This basic cause would exclude all matter from itself, since matter is something potential.

The primary instance of being is in this way presented by Aristotle in terms of actuality. It is a primary instance that causes motion by being loved and desired. It makes other things produce their own effects, with the result that the heavens and the world of nature depend upon it (1072a26–b14). But it itself remains unaware that it is producing these effects, for it has itself alone as the object of its knowledge (9.1074b33–35). It cannot be potential in regard to anything else, even by way of having something else as the object of its cognition. Its pure actuality allows it nothing else, even cognitionally. Such is its status in Aristotle himself.

The contrast with the pure actuality reached by medieval thinkers via this Aristotelian argument is startling. The difference may be seen at its sharpest in Thomas Aquinas. The starting point, as with Aristotle, remains in the things of the sensible world. Prima facie, the route is the same. Sensible things are potential in nature. For their actualization an efficient cause, already in actuality, is required. Even finite supersensible beings, though they have no matter in their essence, have their actuation from a creative cause. Because first, this cause has no potentiality for actuation by any prior cause. It is moreover infinite in nature, unique, all powerful and omniscient, and exercising providence and loving care in regard to all creatures. In a word, the pure actuality whose existence and nature are demonstrated by the Aristotelian argument coincided with the God of biblical revelation.[1] The question then arises about how the same argument could be understood in such radically different ways.

The medieval writers themselves were far from agreement in their own interpretations of the Aristotelian demonstration. A study of the argument in Duns Scotus vis-à-vis Aquinas illustrates this graphically.[2] Avicenna, Averroes, Maimonides, Henry of Ghent have different ways of understanding the proof from the actualization of sensible things. But for them all it reached in one way or another the creator accepted through religious faith. The problem for the present investigation is to find what determines the Aristotelian demonstration to proceed in the way it does. What sets it in the framework that makes it lead to finite and multiple separate substances, substances without knowledge of or providence over the sensible world? Does the notion of being that is presented in book Epsilon lock it into a structure inevitably requiring the conclusions found in book Lambda about separate substance?

Since the contrast is clear cut, when the procedure of Aquinas is compared with that of Aristotle, the point at issue can be best understood by examining the respective viewpoints of these two thinkers. Both find the origin of human cognition in the things of the sensible world. But for Aquinas the essence and the being of these sensible things are not known originally by the same kind of intellection. Under the aspect of what they are, that is, from the standpoint of their essence, they are known through an act of simple apprehension. This original act of simple apprehension does not give any knowledge of the thing's existence. As a result, one can know what a thing is without thereby knowing whether or not the thing really exists. One can know what a phoenix is, aside from whether or not there ever was one in the real world. The notion of a bird that rises rejuvenated from its own ashes does not give any knowledge that the bird exists. One is of course concomitantly aware that the phoenix exists in one's mind while one is thinking about it. But even that knowledge does not come from knowing what a

1 On this topic, see Etienne Gilson, *Christian Philosophy: An Introduction*, trans. Armand Maurer (Toronto: Pontifical Institute of Mediaeval Studies, 1993), 14–23.

2 A comparison of the reasoning of Duns Scotus with that of Aquinas may be found in my paper "The Special Characteristic of the Scotistic Proof that God Exists," reprinted in J. Owens, *Towards a Christian Philosophy* (Washington, D.C.: Catholic University of America Press, 1990), 250–265.

phoenix is. Whatness provides a type of knowledge that abstracts from all existence.[3] So Aquinas reasons.

The thing's existence, on the other hand, is known through a complex act of cognition that is expressed mentally in a proposition and verbally in a sentence. It is the knowledge that the desk in front of you does exist. We do not have that kind of knowledge about the phoenix. In sensation these two kinds of cognition are not distinguished from each other. The things that you are actually seeing or feeling in the sensible world are grasped concomitantly as things and as beings. Whatness and existence are not sensed separately. But the same human person who is perceiving them in sensation is knowing them intellectually. In that intellection the thing's whatness or essence is grasped through abstraction, making universal cognition possible. But thereby the individuality and the existence are left out of the concept. The existence has to be known through the complex act of judgment, in which the individual sensible thing that is perceived in sensation is known to be endowed with actual presence in the real world. The judgment is an act of apprehension, the apprehension that here the thing really exists.[4]

This epistemology reveals a distinctive constitution in sensible things. In them a twofold object of intellectual knowledge is made apparent. There is the essence or whatness of the thing, an object grasped through abstraction or simple apprehension. There is also the existence or being of the thing, an object grasped through the complex apprehension that the thing exists. When compared, these two objects stand in the relation of potentiality to actuality. What the thing is, is now seen as able to exist either in reality or in cognition or in both. The whatness or essence appears as potentiality for existence. The existence makes the essence actual, while the essence specifies the existence. But here the essence specifies only as potentiality. It has no actuality just of itself.[5]

3 See Aquinas, *On Being and Essence*, trans. Armand Maurer. 2nd ed. (Toronto: Pontifical Institute of Mediaeval Studies, 1968), 3.4; p. 47.

4 Cf.: "Moreover, Aristotle states that there are two acts proper to the intellect. The first is understanding a simple meaning, by which we simply grasp what a thing is, the second combines subject and predicate or divides them (*compositio et divisio*), judging that a thing is or is not." Aquinas, *Summa Theologiae*, II.2.83.1. arg. 3, trans. Blackfriars (New York: McGraw Hill Book Company, 1964–1980), vol. 39, p. 47. In the Latin text the same verb (*apprehendimus . . . apprehenditur*) is used for the English words "grasp" and "judge." From his earliest period of writing, in the *Scriptum* on the *Sentences* of Peter Lombard, Aquinas understood this "second operation" of the intellect as an *apprehension* of existence. E.g., *Scriptum super Libros Sententiarum,* I.19.5.2. Solut., ed. P. Mandonnet (Paris: Lethielleux, 1929), I.491; and 38.1.3. ad 2m, p. 904.

5 "Hence being is not determined by something else as potentiality by act but rather as act by potentiality." Aquinas, *On the Power of God*, 7.2. ad 9m, trans. English Dominican Fathers (London: Burns, Oates & Washbourne, 1934; rpt. Westminster Md., 1952), III.13.

One is now dealing with a metaphysics quite different from the Aristotelian. Its thrust is toward keeping the things of the finite world from having any actuality just of themselves. According to the biblical doctrine of creation, finite things have no being whatever just of themselves. All they are and have comes ultimately from their creator. Of themselves they are merely nothing. For Aristotle, on the other hand, the visible world always existed. Its things had their being through *what* they are. No outside cause could bring them out of nothing. The notion of "nothing," was in fact a subsequent concept, formed from the notion of thing by way of outright denial. In this perspective the whatness of a thing is readily seen as identical with its being, as in Gamma 2. The two may differ in concept, since what a thing is places it in a definite category while the notion of it as a being is supergeneric in scope. But that is not regarded as enough to require any real distinction between the two.

In book Epsilon, consequently, it is not surprising to find that what a thing is and whether it is pertain to the same intellectual grasp. Aristotle, of course, is well aware of the difference between a term and a proposition. In Epsilon (4.1027bl8–1028b2) as well as in the logical works he is careful in distinguishing them. But he speaks of the synthesis or division of the proposition as being only in the mind. To be true the proposition has to correspond to the way the subject and predicate are related in the thing. Yet with him it seems to be no more than a case of the relations of the one to the other. Hence the same type of cognition by which the other categories are known is here carried over in explaining predication. Knowing that the thing is pertains to the same type of cognition as knowledge of what it is. There is no explanation of existence as a synthesis in the thing itself, with the role of a further actuality over and above the natures listed in the categories.

In Aquinas, on the other hand, an actual synthesis in the thing itself corresponds to the synthesis in the mental judgment or proposition.[6] In actualizing a tree or an animal, existence synthesizes the matter and the accidents into the one living thing and thereby grounds the predication. The real difference between the existence and the thing, however, is not immediately evident. The existence cannot come from the finite thing itself, because it is not contained within the thing's whatness. It has to come from something else already in existence, and ultimately from an existent that does not have its existence from anything else, but is itself existence. Here existence and essence coincide. "That it is" is "what it is," in this primary efficient cause. Its very nature is existence. There is no nature distinct from existence to play the role of a limiting factor within it. Pure actuality is now existence alone. That is the conclusion Aquinas draws.

The effects of basing the procedure on the existential actuality of sensible things is in consequence far reaching. What is thereby attained is a pure actuality that allows no formal limitation by a potency within itself. Not only matter as

6 See texts cited supra, n. 4.

a potentiality is excluded, but even a limiting immaterial essence is rendered impossible in its case. Purely spiritual creatures, the angels, can receive existence from it. But though purely spiritual, none of them can be pure actuality. Each angelic nature functions as a potentiality that limits the existence it receives. Pure actuality, as reasoned from the existence of sensible things, has to be unique. There can be only one God.

In this respect the contrast with the original Aristotelian procedure becomes apparent. The entire actuality of sensible things comes from their own intrinsic forms. In them the form is the cause of being, the cause of their whatness, the cause of their unity.[7] An efficient cause is necessary for bringing the sensible thing into actuality. But once the thing is brought into being, the form is actual of itself. It does not have the role of a potentiality to the thing's existence, as is the case with Aquinas. The form makes the thing the kind of a being it is, whether earth, water, air, fire, a plant, an animal, or a person. It makes the being a definite, limited thing. All that it specifies, it specifies by way of actuality. It does not specify as a potentiality to existence. This is the situation in Aristotle.

The result of this difference in the procedure is that the pure actuality reached in Aristotle is a limited or finite form. Each form means a definite nature. As known to us in sensible things, these natures are multiple. When in the Aristotelian reasoning one reaches form without matter, there is no apparent reason why form should not follow the pattern of multiplicity as seen in sensible things. Hence after having demonstrated the existence and immaterial nature of supersensible form, Aristotle in Lambda 8 can ask the question whether this type of substance is one or many. He has no immediate access to separate substance. His reasoning had been just that cosmic motion requires immaterial substance as its cause. To answer his question he has recourse only to the astronomers who determine the number of original or irreducible motions in the heavens. He finds they disagree upon the number. But according to the number you accept on their authority, you will have your number of separate substances.[8]

In any case, you will have a plurality of pure actualities. This is possible in Aristotle, because pure actuality means for him form without matter, and form as primary substance is its own actuality. With Aquinas, on the contrary, form is actual not by itself but by the existence that is other than the form. Form, as known on the model of its occurrence in sensible things, makes each thing a potentiality to existence, thereby specifying the existence by way of potentiality. What is functioning in this manner as a potentiality for Aquinas is functioning for Aristotle as ultimate actuality. For Aristotle formal actuality makes the thing def-

7 See Aristotle, *Metaphysics*, 7.17.104lb11–31. Cf. Aquinas: "*Esse* does follow per se upon form, but provided that God's causality is present, even as light results from the transparency of the atmosphere when light shines." *Summa Theologiae* I.104. arg. lm (trans. Blackfriars).

8 Aristotle, *Metaphysics,* 12.8.1073a14–1074bl4.

inite and limited to itself, but without interfering with the presence of other forms, each definite and limited to its own self. When form is understood in this fashion as actual of itself, there is no reason why pure actuality cannot be a multiplicity. It could be unique, but there is no intrinsic reason why it should be so. The universe can be one, even though the original causes of its motion are multiple. All that is required is that there be one type of motion dominating all the others, and, in this way, one first cause. There is not rule by many. For Aristotle there seems nothing strange in the notion of a universe that contains a multiplicity of pure actualities.

Quite different is the case when the notion of pure actuality is reached on the basis of the existence of sensible things, as in Aquinas. This existence is not attained originally through conceptualization, which is the way the natures of sensible things are grasped. These natures are limited, as has just been noted. When they form the model for the notion of actuality, the result will inevitably be the notion of something limited and finite, as in Aristotle. But when the existence of sensible things is understood as an actuality not grasped originally through conceptualization, the picture becomes radically different. The existence is not something that can be known immediately through a concept. The long controversies about the concept of existence in modern times show with sufficient clarity that when existence is approached in this perspective it soon fades away before our mental vision, leaving the alleged concept empty and meaningless. It finally becomes the equivalent of nothing, through the removal of all conceptual determinations.[9] But when it is approached as grasped through judgment, as in Aquinas, it appears as an actuality that strikes the intellect as first and foremost in the thing. Without it, all in the thing would be nothing. Nothing would be there. Existence is what actualizes everything else. Yet it is not grasped by way of a limiting nature. It is only that which makes the natures be. Later, by reflection on it, it can be conceptualized as an actuality or a perfection, and in this way made a subject of discursive thought.

But as originally attained it is not something that conforms to our notion of a "what." It is just an "is." When finally it is reached as a nature through reasoning that follows externally the Aristotelian format for procedure to separate substance, it does not carry with it the requirement of limitation and finitude that went with the Aristotelian notion of actuality. Rather, like the existence from which it started, it does not contain any of the determinations that are required for knowledge through conceptualization. The condition that has made the concept of existence appear to so many thinkers as empty and meaningless, now enables the existence reached as a nature in God to be understood as absolutely limitless and boundless in every perfection. Among these perfections is omnipotence, as required in creation.

9 See G. F. W. Hegel, *The Logic of Hegel*, trans. W. Wallace (Oxford: Oxford University Press, 2nd ed., 1892), §§86–87.

In this view, the existence met in the sensible things around us had to come originally through creation. Because omnipotent, subsistent existence can bring other things into being, things that in each case limit the imparted existence. But no second instance of subsistent being itself is at all possible. The alleged second instance would be something other than the first, something that would be functioning as a limiting nature. It would thereby introduce potentiality into what had been demonstrated to be pure actuality. In it the essence and the existence would no longer coincide. Only when pure actuality is modeled after the natures known through conceptualization can the question of pluralizing it enter into consideration. In Aristotle that question could and did arise, but for the metaphysical thinking of Aquinas it was inexorably banned. The radical difference between the starting points of the two philosophical procedures makes itself sharply felt in their respective conclusions about what pure actuality is.

Likewise the relations of pure actuality to other things vary profoundly in accord with the radical difference between these two notions of it. For Aristotle a separate substance knows only itself. It has no interest in or love for any other being. It enjoys life and happiness to the full, yet happiness all by itself. Not having knowledge of anything else it can exercise no concern or providence in regard to the sensible world. It cannot act upon anything outside itself, since for Aristotle the perfection of an efficient cause, as such, lies in the *passum*, the thing that is undergoing the motion.[10] If it could, it would no longer be its own self contained perfection, its own ultimate actuality. It would thereby be in potency to its action, quite as sensible things are. Yet all potentiality whatsoever is excluded from its nature, which is pure actuality in the Aristotelian setting. It cannot exercise any efficient causality at all. It can move the heavens only as final cause, as something known and loved and desired by the ensouled celestial spheres. From start to finish it has only itself as object of its knowledge and attention.

With Aquinas, in contrast, the pure actuality reached from the existence of sensible things carries no restrictions. This enables Aquinas to make his own the patristic dictum that God is the being of all things.[11] Here pure actuality, because it is subsistent existence, can be a nature only in the one infinite being. Yet existence is encountered in all the things of the sensible world, the things in which the philosophical reasoning to subsistent existence is grounded. These things are not their own existence. Their existence is not contained in any of their natures. It is something that comes to them from without, through efficient and not formal causality. In calling this existence "something," one is conceiving it as a nature, as a "what," and as a nature or a "what" existence is found only in God. Hence the patristic dictum, namely that God is the being of all things, called for the qualification that God is their being not in a formal but in a causal sense. Yet the say-

10 See Aristotle, *De Anima*, 3.2.425b25–426al7.

11 See Aquinas, *Scriptum super Libros Sententiarum*, I.8.1.2. Solut., ed. P. Mandonnet, I,198.

ing brought out strongly the conclusion that wherever existence is found outside of God, it has to be understood philosophically as a participation in an actuality present as a nature solely in its primary efficient cause.

Where existence subsists as a nature, it will have to contain within itself in the highest degree all the perfections that may be actuated in creatures, for it is what makes them exist. Among these perfections in the highest degree are omniscience, omnipotence, love, freedom, understanding, and providence. Hence the pure actuality reached via the philosophical route of existence knows everything that exists or can exist. Out of love, God can call them into being as he sees fit. Out of love he sustains them in existence, concurs in all their activities, and in the case of creatures endowed with freedom he asks their love and cooperation in return. But in all this he is supremely free. He does not have to create the best possible world, or to create any world at all. What he does in this regard he does freely and out of love. We cannot reason to creation from what we know of God's existence and nature, but from the sensible things observed in our universe we are able to reason to its creator and to understand philosophically the relations between them.

Into this conception of pure actuality a believer in biblical revelation should readily find the means for clarifying philosophically many of the important issues of her or his faith. One reads occasionally that the cold Aristotelian prime mover can never be an object of religious love or devotion. How could one pray to an Aristotelian separate substance, when that entity has no knowledge of what you are saying and no care for attending to it? The source of the misunderstanding becomes evident when one considers the two different kinds of actuality that may be reached with cogency by way of the Aristotelian argument from actuality and potentiality. If you identify potentiality with matter and actuality with form, you arrive at separate substance as finite actuality concerned only with itself and also able to be multiple in number. But if you start with essence as a potentiality to existence, the pure actuality you reach is an omniscient and omnipotent and supremely free being that has created us out of love and showers his provident attention upon us. There should be little difficulty in finding this subsistent existence endowed with all the qualities and perfections that are prized in religious practice. But awareness of the possibility of understanding in such opposed ways the reasoning from actuality and potentiality prompts the question of what causes the original Aristotelian development to take the course it did. Can the first chapter of book Epsilon in the *Metaphysics* provide the answer?

* * * * * * * * * *

As already hinted, the basis for the divergent interpretations of the argument from actuality and potentiality seems to lie in the way a sensible thing is related to its own existence. Yet even this phrasing, designed to cover the various approaches to the problem, is none too faithful to the Aristotelian setting. Aristotle's own contrast is between what the thing is and if it is. It reads as though the "is" carries the same meaning in both phrases, so that the difference is only between the "what" and the "if." This is not necessarily the same as the contrast between essence and existence. Aristotle did not have the two verbs "to be" and "to exist" to bring out the difference between those two notions. Later the accents placed in the third-person singular of the Greek *esti* could distinguish its use as a copula from its expression of existence or possibility. But that distinction did not confine its meaning to actual existence as opposed to what is possible. This latter distinction is the one at issue when essence is contrasted with existence. Essence expresses *what* the thing is, but not whether the thing is actually present in the real world or in anybody's cognition. A tree or a dog is something that can exist. Both the one and the other are potentialities for existence. But a goat stag or a square circle or a stick with only one end is not something that can exist. None of these is an essence. None of them can be conceptualized in positive intelligible fashion. But even the positive essences such as tree or dog when conceptualized abstract from individuality and from all existence. To know whether or not they exist, a further and complex act of apprehension is required, a cognitive act that is expressed mentally in a judgment and conveyed verbally in a sentence.

The distinction between essence and existence arose in a creationist setting. It was geared to the consideration that no creature could account for its own existence. From Aristotle's viewpoint, on the contrary, the things were taken as there in themselves, coming into being and perishing in the eternal succession of cosmic change. So they did not suggest to him any actuality over and above what they were in themselves, an actuality that made them exist. What they are included in this way their existence. They were not made to exist through a further actuality that was other than themselves. They were actual in virtue of what they were. Their actual presence in the universe could be stated by the verb *huparchein*, but did not require any new expression in terms of being.

Aristotle, nevertheless, was not unaware of a difficulty in this regard. He faced it in terms of what the thing is, on the one hand, and if it is, on the other hand. But he understood this distinction in a manner incompatible with the way essence was distinguished from existence in medieval times. He maintained that if one knew what a thing is one thereby knew if it is, an attitude contrary to the medieval stand that you could know what a thing is without knowing whether the thing did exist or ever had existed. Consequently what Aristotle had in mind with the "if it is," cannot be taken in the medieval sense of existence. What a thing is, Aristotle meant, placed it in a category. The thing was a substance, a quantity, a quality, a relation, or something in one of the other categories or postpredicaments. "If the thing is," on the other hand, referred to its status as a being. You answered the question "what" by giving the thing's category. You answered the question "if" by giving the thing's supergeneric status as a being, and not its particular category. The result was that in knowing what category the thing belonged to you knew it was a being, but by knowing that it was a being *tout court* you did not necessarily know its category. You could know that it was a being without thereby having the precise knowledge required for categorizing it. Knowledge itself for Aristotle was something immediately known, but whether it belonged to the category of quality or the category of relation or to both, was still open for discussion.[12]

This situation, however, is rather complicated. In the first chapter of book Zeta the respective priorities will be explained. "What" means primarily the thing's substance. But secondarily, it means any of the thing's accidents. Yet in focal reference to that primary instance, namely to substance, all are called beings. In this wider perspective the "what it is" and the "if it is" are seen ultimately to coincide. Aristotle can well say in Gamma that a person, and a person has being, are the same. He can imply that it is more advantageous not to make even a conceptual distinction between the two. But this does cause a bit of uneasiness when viewed against the later developments in Western philosophy. Plotinus will significantly distinguish unity from being. Avicenna will show that a thing in itself, such as equinity, is neither one nor many, nor existent either in the sensible universe or in human cognition. The contrast between essential being (*esse essentiae*) and existential being (*esse existentiae*) will make itself felt throughout Scholasticism. Duns Scotus, because of his doctrine of the univocity of being in God and creatures, is not able to see identity of essence and existence as the distinguishing mark of the divinity on the metaphysical plane. But he is able to meet the situation by his formal distinction of individuality (*haecceitas*) from common nature in all finite beings, while the two are strictly identical in God.[13] The problem of reaching the unicity of the divine nature metaphysically has its roots in the philosophical starting points. The present issue is to probe the difference in the starting points of Aristotle from those of the later thinkers who claimed to be learning their metaphysics from him.

One observation, though, is clear enough. Aristotle is not at all denying existence. All the things that are actually in the world exist, as far as he is concerned. He is not facing the modern question whether or not existence is vacuous, an empty concept, or a surd. He fully acquiesced in what we today call the existence of things. The only question at stake is whether for him that existence is distinct from the things themselves. He denies any real distinction, while in one way he allows a conceptual distinction, between a thing and its being. Now, in book Epsilon, he is saying that it belongs to the same intellection to know what a thing

12 Aristotle, *Categories*, 8.11a37–38.

13 E.g., ". . . sicut deitas de se est 'haec,' ita Deus – qui est Deus deitate – est de se 'hic.'" John Duns Scotus, *Opera Omnia* (Vatican City: Polyglot Press, 1956), *Ordinatio*, I.4.2.1.11; IV. 5.5.6.

is and if it is. Even though this is not precisely an explicit denial of a distinction between the kind of cognition that grasps essence and the kind that apprehends existence, at least it rejects with sufficient clarity the need for any further kind of cognition to recognize that the thing is actual. It regards the thing as made actual by its essence, without requirement of a different kind of cognition to apprehend it as such. Cognition of being is cognition by way of whatness.

There is little difficulty, then, in drawing the firm conclusion that Aristotle has no recognition of existence as an actuality over and above what the thing is, and no hint of a real distinction between a sensible thing and its being. It is here that the advantage of contrasting Aristotle with Aquinas stands out as a means of understanding and appreciating the point at issue. Both recognize the difference between potentiality and actuality. For Aristotle, potentiality is known only through actuality.[14] The only potentiality acknowledged in the sensible substance is the absolutely undetermined matter, unknowable in itself, yet inferred through the reasoning process given in the *Physics*. But for Aquinas the sensible thing as a whole is a potentiality to existence. True, the thing has to be actualized by existence before it can be known in any way. But once actualized by existence the thing, though remaining a potency, is known by itself as a positive object of cognition. It is at once perceived not as a restriction of existence but as something with knowability of its own, a knowability different from that of existence. It is the positive object of simple apprehension, and different from the object of judgment. From the thing's existence, which is the object of the judgment, one reasons to subsistent existence as its first cause. Infinite and unique, subsistent existence brings into being things other than itself, things that are and remain potentialities to the existence they receive. Nevertheless these other things are and remain positive essences in themselves. They remain positively knowable, even though in a different way from their existential actualities.

The result is that what for Aristotle is of itself actual as a nature, has for Aquinas to receive its actuality from something else. For Aquinas every finite nature, no matter how positive it is in itself, needs actualization by an existence that remains really other than the nature or the thing. Some care is required in understanding the terminology here. Aquinas knows the term "existence" (*existentia*), and uses it on a number of occasions. But his usual term in this regard is the infinitive of the verb "to be" (*esse*). He acknowledges a current use of *esse* in the sense of essence, but in his own practice consistently avoids that use of the word. Essence for him is the thing understood insofar as it is a potentiality to being, with the result that his distinction between essence and existence may be more forcefully expressed in English as the distinction between a thing and its being. In a word, all the thing's being is on the existence side of the couplet essence–existence, while all the thing's whatness is on the essence side of it. The

14 See Aristotle, *Metaphysics*, 9.8.1049b4–17.

esse of the essence (*esse essentiae*) is in creatures not the essence itself but the existence that is really distinct from it. Being and existence coincide as other than essence.

This metaphysical outlook of Aquinas provides a very clear backdrop against which the import of the Aristotelian conceptions may be gauged. For Aristotle the lack of real distinction between a sensible thing and its being will mean that the thing's form is its highest actuality. But form in actuating matter is a limiting principle, insofar as it gives the thing definite specification. It is accordingly finite. If form is equated with actuality, it places finitude in the very notion of the actual. Matter, as potential to it, is indefinite and undetermined. Actuality, in contrast, will be definite, limited, finite. When pure actuality is reached through reasoning, it will in consequence remain something finite. Hence the question whether it is one or many may, with Aristotle in book Lambda, be legitimately placed. The model for actuality will be the form of sensible things. In these things being adds no real actuality over and above the whatness. Since their whatness is finite and limited, the being that is really identical with it will inevitably be conceived as likewise finite and limited. There is no intrinsic reason, then, why actuality in its pure status should not be multiple. It is open to plurality, not by reason of any material subject into which it might be received, but by virtue of its character as actuality in the sense in which actuality coincides with formal whatness.

The contrast with Aquinas allows this character in Aristotle to be sharply outlined. For Aquinas existence was the actuality of all actualities and the perfection of all perfections.[15] Nothing at all could be actual except through existence. For Aquinas this existence was not grasped by way of a limiting concept but by way of a judgment that the thing was there. Accordingly for him existence did not have any limiting character inherent in itself. When, through reasoning, existence was reached as pure actuality, it had nothing that could limit it or make it finite in any way. In this primary instance it subsisted as the actuality of all actualities, and accordingly with all actuality already in itself. It therefore could allow no possibility of plurification in this subsistent state. For Aquinas pure actuality, that is, actuality without any passive potentiality in its essence, was necessarily unique.

* * * * * * * * * *

This brings one's attention to the main problem of the inquiry. Does Epsilon's tenet of the same intellective act (*dianoia*) for the "what" and the "if" lock Aristotle's metaphysical procedure into a framework in which supersensible substance inevitably becomes finite in itself and aloof from all else? Certainly it

15 ". . . the actuality of all acts, and therefore the perfection of all perfections." Aquinas, *On the Power of God*, 7.2.ad 9m, trans. English Dominican Fathers (London: Burns, Oates & Washbourne, 1932–1934; rpt. Westminster Md., 1952), III.12; cf. Aquinas, *Summa Theologiae*, I.3.4.

excludes the Thomistic reasoning to an infinite and provident God, since that reasoning demanded a different mental act, judgment, for knowing the existential actuality of things. Existence was not contained in conceptualization, the abstraction by which the whatness of a thing is grasped. The two cognitive acts were distinct. The one could not be reduced to the other. The knowledge given through conceptualization was of finite things. The knowledge given through judgment, on the other hand, was a new and synthesizing awareness of an actuality that had escaped the limiting confines of the conceptualization and that had in itself none of the determining characteristics that would render it finite. Just of itself, the existential actuality had no quidditative determinations. But it did not immediately pass over in Hegelian fashion into Nothing and then, through Becoming, into quidditative specification. Rather, it was from the start of the cognition determined in creatures by a potentiality other than itself, a potentiality that was the thing's whatness.[16] As subsistent in God, on the other hand, existence had no quidditative limitation and in consequence was actual to the full extent of every perfection. What was reached in the demonstration of pure actuality was for Aquinas existence that was nothing other than itself. Only then was existence in its own way a nature and was shown to be the God revealed in the Scriptures. The existing was reached first, and what thereby was conceived was seen to be identical with the God already accepted through religious faith. Since no potentiality could specify subsistent existence, there were no subjects in which it could be multiplied in being. An alleged second instance would coincide entirely with the first. Subsistent existence had to be unique.

Returning to Aristotle, though, one is left without any different kind of intellection for the grasp of existence. His acquaintance with the "if it is" is placed under the same sort of cognition as that of the "what it is." This will keep it quidditative in character, even though just in itself it does not make definite the particular category in which the thing is located. As a supergeneric grasp of the thing's whatness it is not attaining anything distinct from the whatness, but only the whatness itself in the widest possible fashion. It does not express the exact category by defining the thing as a substance or as some one of the accidents. Yet it is still restricted to the grasp of the thing as a "what." It does not propose to offer any new knowledge that would assert an actuality over and above the whatness, as when one has explained what the Loch Ness monster is and then asks if it really exists. The Aristotelian question does not bear upon a further actuality that places the thing in existence. The "if" is a characteristic universally present in the "what." Hence in knowing what the thing is, one knows that it is, for in knowing what the thing is one knows that it is a being.

16 "Now being, as being, cannot be diverse, but it can be differentiated by something beside being; thus the being of a stone is other than the being of a man." Aquinas, *The Summa Contra Gentiles*, II.52; trans. English Dominican Fathers (London: Burns, Oates & Washbourne, New York: Benziger Brothers, 1924–1929), II, 122.

With the medieval essence, on the contrary, one could know what the thing was without knowing whether it existed in reality. It left room for a further type of actuality different from form. In Aristotle this was not so. The necessary involvement of the "if" in the "what" made sensible things the model for the notion of actuality even when applied outside the sensible order. The sensible thing is actual by reason of its form, and is known as actual when grasped through conceptualization. All knowledge of it is accordingly specified by sensible quiddity. But sensible quiddity is of its nature something limited. Not only does matter limit it to a singular thing in each of its occurrences, but its form too restricts it as limited to a particular species in contrast to other species of the same genus. When form is conceived as actuality on this model, it carries with it intrinsically the limitation to a specific nature as distinct from other natures. When on this model it is conceived as entirely without matter, as in the case of separate substance, it loses the possibility of multiplication in singulars of the same species. Yet it intrinsically retains the limitation to a specific kind all its own. There is in this setting no inherent reason why there should not be different kinds of separate forms, quite as in the cases where the form actuates matter within the multitudinous sensible species that it itself renders different from one another.

In this setting, then, is the issue at all forced when a decisive role is attributed to Epsilon's tenet of the same cognition for what a thing is and if it is? Does not the tenet rule out a further and different type of cognition for the thing's existential actuality? If that is the case, the fact that the thing has being is attained in the quidditative cognition of what it is. No room is left for the cognition in it of an actuality surpassing quidditative limitation. In consequence Aristotle's notion of actuality intrinsically involves limitation, and will carry that inherent requirement into the supersensible order. The metaphysical procedure will be set firmly in the course taken in the subsequent treatises of the series. If limited inevitably by the model of specifically determined form, the notion of actuality, when subsistent in itself does not exclude multiplicity. Just as sensible forms may be multiple in kind by their very natures, so immaterial forms may differ specifically from one another. Aristotle, having shown in book Lambda that form without matter is required in order to explain the eternity of the cosmic processes, can go on without the least hesitation to propose the question whether immaterial form is one or multiple. From this angle, Epsilon's tenet of a single cognition for the "what" and the "if" may well be regarded as at least contributing to the function of a keystone in a metaphysical structure that on the one side is based upon sensible things and on the other upon finite supersensible substance.

One might object that other types of medieval metaphysics, unlike that of Aquinas, did not recognize existence as something grasped originally through judgment. Yet they kept within the biblical tradition of a unique and omnipotent God. Each of these metaphysical procedures has to explain its meaning and defend its cogency. Having reached God as a creator, each has the task of showing how creative causality requires omnipotence and thereby entails infinity in every perfection, with no second instance possible. But with Aristotle there is no route via the reception of being through creation. Creation is bypassed against the Parmenidean background that nothing can come out of nothing. For him, form will be the primary *ousia* or beingness within the sensible thing, and a supersensible substance will be specifically limited in virtue of itself alone. Epsilon's tenet of the same kind of cognition for whatness and being will inevitably lock the Aristotelian procedure into the course it takes in the *Metaphysics*, regardless of the routes open to thinkers who accept creation.

The consequences of the inherent limitation of actuality for Aristotle to a thing's formal perfection has other profound consequences besides the possibility of plurality in separate substance. It means that each separate form will be limited strictly to itself. There are no recognizable means by which the form could reach out to anything else. No possibility of its acting upon something else through efficient causality would be open. It could not create anything out of nothing, and it has no powers for acting upon anything already in existence. Powers would be potentialities for doing something, and the Aristotelian separate form cannot have any potentiality at all. It is just actuality, pure and simple. All that it might be imagined as able to do is already there in actuality within itself. Aristotle (*Metaphysics*, 12.9.1074b18–35) develops this point only in regard to cognition. If separate substance knew anything other than itself, he reasoned, it would be receiving perfection from that thing as the object of its cognition. It would therefore not be perfect in virtue of itself only, for knowledge receives its perfection from the object. Explicit, though, is Aristotle's tenet that separate substance is essentially knowledge of itself, and that knowledge of anything else would mean change in its nature (b26–27).

In this way the whole actuality of a separate substance is to know itself eternally. That is how its nature is defined by Aristotle. It is a knowing of knowing. Subject, activity and object meld into one. There is no way in which separate substance can get outside itself. To do so would be to destroy its nature. But having no matter in its essence, it is not subject to destruction. The result is that separate substance is concentrated entirely upon itself, and forever.

Aristotle's reasoning is cogent, given his stand that actuality coincides with form. In Aquinas, on the other hand, where the form of a thing is made actual through existence, the situation is radically different. Form, though it actualizes matter, is itself made actual through a still higher perfection, existence. The existence is a different actuality from the form, is really distinct from the thing's nature or whatness, and is known through a different type of cognition, namely through judgment. Pure actuality reached from this starting point is subsistent existence, a creator who imparts existence to other things according to his own plan and down to the last detail. The creator accordingly knows everything he has created. His knowledge is not at all confined to himself, but extends to everything that exists in accord with his own design. He continues to sustain all creatures through continued conservation of them in being.

He imparts the existence of every activity in creatures, even of the free activity in intelligent agents. In this way he is acting most intimately within the activity of each of them.[17] He is ever aware of their needs, their emotions, their triumphs and their sufferings, and he is able to exercise continued providence over them.

All those aspects make subsistent existence a far cry from Aristotle's separate substance, even though both qualify as pure actuality in their respective settings. In this light the importance of understanding the cleavage between the two ways of gauging actuality is strikingly apparent. Yet their inspiration is surprisingly parallel, and the reciprocal aid they give for understanding the one and the other is indispensable. Aristotle is entranced by actuality. He becomes lyric as he describes (*Metaphysics*, 12.7.1072b14–30) its fullness in the eternal thinking of separate substance. The actuality of this thinking is life at its highest and best. The waking state is what we prize, and in it the best that we can possess and enjoy and strive for and hope for is but a fleeting and faraway glimpse of the full actuality in separate substance. Potentiality, in fact, is known only through actuality and in terms of its order to actuality. What we strive for in everything is in consequence actuality, and the actual is what we desire and love and seek for in every waking moment. Its culmination in the divine life of separate substance is the apex of goodness and beauty and enjoyment and of all that makes life worthwhile.

This notion of actuality needs to be understood against the vibrant background of Greek intellectual and artistic culture, in which form played the leading role in literature, painting, sculpture, music, and architecture. Form was what made a thing stand out, what gave it its highest appeal and desirability, and what ranked it among beings. In fact, it was the cause of being, as everywhere understood throughout the *Metaphysics*. It was the factor that made a thing more than nothing, and gave it its standing as a being. Potentiality had recognition and appeal only insofar as it could be made actual. Matter of itself was neither a "this" nor a quantity nor a quality nor a relation nor any other determined category. All its determination to being something came from the form. All productive activity was meant for bringing matter into a new form, all practical activity was meant to make right reason the form of specifically human conduct. From start to finish form dominated. Its majesty was so overwhelming that even the aloofness and self-centered and Narcissus-like enjoyment of its own self in its highest instance proved no deterrent to its acceptance by Aristotle. It was the culmination of being,

17 See Aquinas, *Summa Contra Gentiles*, III.66–67; ed. cit., III part 1, 158–162.

the initial and final perfection of the universe, and vitally present in the universe from the beginning. On its beauty and necessity depended the heavens and the world of nature (7.1072b10–14).

The astonishingly different notion of pure actuality reached by Aquinas in following what is externally the same philosophical procedure surely deserves close attention. Like Aristotle he starts the reasoning from the actuality and potentiality found in sensible things. Like Aristotle he sees the gradation from matter as pure potentiality to sensible substances as actual composites and as potentialities to their own accidental characteristics and activities. But throughout all this actuation he finds existence first and foremost to be the actuality of all actualities and the perfection of all perfections. Existence is what confronts the intellect by way of actuality in absolute fashion.[18] Without existence anything whatsoever would be merely nothing. If it does not exist either in the created world or in cognition or in the creative essence of God it cannot be anything at all.[19] When the reasoning process starts from this conception of actuality, it is already on a path that will lead ultimately to subsistent existence, the creative and provident God, as the unique instance of actuality without any potentiality at all. In all other things, even in purely spiritual creatures where no matter is present in their essence, their form itself acts as a potentiality in limiting existence. Angels will be immaterial creatures, but they will not be their own existence. Like Aristotle, Aquinas also can strike a lyric note here, when he refers to the "sublime truth" that God is his existence.[20]

When asked, therefore, how it is that so many people have found the Aristotelian argument from cosmic motion to lead only to a cold and distant cause, incapable of having any part in the emotional and religious lives of human beings, the answer is clear. If actuality is equated with form, as it was in Aristotle's original presentation of the reasoning process, the conclusion of the argument lies in aloof and self-contained separate substance. One has the satisfaction of knowing what the final cause of cosmic activity is, but is left without an object of religious interest. If, on the other hand, one approaches the argument with the biblical belief in creation, the actuality in which one is interested is the existence the world and especially human beings have received from their creator. Arguing with this existence as the starting point, the procedure found in the Aristotelian reasoning leads to subsistent existence, an infinite and omnipotent being who is capable of love and interest in regard to the world he has created, and indeed who overwhelms it with his love. Infinite in every perfection, he is

18 Aquinas, *Expositio Libri Peri Hermenias*, I.5.397–407, in *Opera Omnia* (Rome: Commissio Leonina, 1989), I 1, p. 31b.

19 On these three ways of existing for Aquinas, see his *Quaestiones quodlibetales*, 8.11. Resp., ed. R. Spiazzi (Turin: Marietti, 1956), 158.

20 See Aquinas, *Summa contra Gentile,* I.22; ed. cit., 1, 56.

love and tenderness as well as wisdom and justice, all in the highest degree. He can be prayed to, hoped in, and trusted. From the philosophical viewpoint, the objective is to understand why in Aristotle the demonstration from actuality and potentiality did not lead to monotheism, while in a thinker like Aquinas it does. The explanation may be found in Epsilon's stand that the same type of cognition grasps both whatness and being, while in Aquinas two different types, namely conceptualization and judgment, bear respectively on quiddity and existence. The end result of the latter procedure is a metaphysics in which a biblical adherent can feel perfectly at home.

This digression into medieval metaphysics has been laborious. Yet it has been necessary in order to counteract today's tendency toward expecting that the Aristotelian separate substance will coincide with a Judeo-Christian conception of God. Failure to keep aware of the radical difference in Aristotle's philosophical starting points will lead to interpretations of his conclusions in senses that involve obvious contradictions.

Chapter 3

Aristotelian Sciences and Their Starting Points (E 1.1025b3–1026a23)

The second notable position that emerges from Epsilon's opening chapter concerns the division and procedure of the sciences. At issue is the way the science of beings qua beings is related to the sciences that treat of particular beings and that mark off a certain kind of being as the subject with which each deals. The problem, obviously, is to see how the primary science can attain all objects universally without encroaching upon the independence of each particular science. How can the all embracing sweep of the highest science leave inviolate the separate status and the characteristic procedure of each of the others? How is it that the other sciences do not become branches of metaphysics in the same way that species remain differentiated within a genus? The other sciences, one might urge, seem to have developed in their own right, and prior to any organized assistance from metaphysics.

The notion of philosophy as a tree of which metaphysics is the roots with natural philosophy as the trunk and all the other sciences as the branches, goes back to Descartes.[1] Francis Bacon had already broken the traditional metaphysics into "Primitive or Summary Philosophy," which he made "a parent or common ancestor to all knowledge," and "Natural Theology" for dealing with God and the angels and spirits, and ultimately "metaphysic" for treating of formal and final causes.[2] The school tradition continued these notions in one way or another into the present century. In Neoscholasticism the framework was that of the three degrees of abstraction, with natural philosophy abstracting in the first degree

1 "Ainsi toute la Philosophie est comme un arbre, dont les raciness sont la Metaphysique, le tronc est la Physique, les branches qui sortent de ce tronc sont toutes les autres sciences . . ." Descartes, *Principes*, Preface, 26, eds. Charles Adam & Paul Tannery (Paris: Léopold Cerf, 1897–1910), IX^2, 14.23–27.

2 Francis Bacon, *The Advancement of Learning*, 2.7.1–7, ed. G. W. Kitchin (London: Dent & Sons, 1973), 91–98.

from individuality, mathematics in the second degree from sensible qualities, and metaphysics in the third degree from matter and corporeality.[3] The model was quite obviously the successively wider abstraction of generic notions from individuals and species. All the sciences were brought into this basic framework, each in its own way.[4]

Of particular importance for the study of the Aristotelian *Metaphysics* is Bacon's cleavage of natural theology from the primary philosophy. This became enshrined in the German school tradition. *Metaphysica generalis* treated of all things in their greatest universality. It did not deal with any beings as particular, not even the highest of beings. With Natorp, this came to spotlight a glaring contradiction in the *Metaphysics* as it has come down to us. In some places the *Metaphysics* sees the primary philosophy as the most universal of sciences. In other places, it regards the primary philosophy as dealing with a particular type of being, namely the divine. In the former passages, it would claim to be an ontology. In the latter passages, it presents itself as a theology. The contradiction was irreconcilable from the then-prevalent standpoint. The object of a science cannot be particular and universal at the same time. Hence Jaeger in his widely read *Aristoteles* came to a historical explanation. Aristotle, as a youth overawed by Plato's eminence, commenced his own thinking along Platonic lines. He looked upon his highest science as a study of the supersensible world, as it had been with the Platonic concern about the Ideas. Gradually he moved away from that position as he himself matured, finally concentrating his interest upon the sensible world, with the primary philosophy as the most universal science insofar as it was a study of being qua being.

Jaeger published his great work in the early 1920s, at the time when the world was still basking in the triumph of Einstein's relativity theory. Time had turned out to be a fourth dimension, a dimension that had to be taken into account in explaining a writer's thought. Aristotle was no exception. The problem, however, was peculiarly difficult in his regard, since the relevant texts were scattered throughout his works. He himself never seemed to give any indication that he was changing his thought. He was utterly undisturbed by close association of passages that to his twentieth century readers seemed open contradictions. Still more difficult was the problem of chronological order for his writings. External criteria were few and difficult. Ultimately, with rare exceptions, the treatises had to be dated

3 See Josef Gredt, *Elementa philosophiae aristotelico thomisticae*, no. 232, 7th ed. (Fribourg: Herder, 1937), II. 188–190.

4 Even ethics, or moral philosophy, was forced into the procrustean framework of the theoretical sciences; "Ex dictis deducitur Ethicam subalternari tertiae Philosophiae naturalis specialis parti, quae est de anima. . . . huic obiecto superaddit differentiart accidentalem, quae est moralitas, de qua agit per se." Gredt, *Elementa*, no. 879. II. 303.

according to the modern commentator's conception of Aristotle's philosophical development.

Here it was easy to turn Jaeger's order into reverse. Aristotle could be regarded as a brash young student absolutely sure of himself, unable to see any real good in the thought of his elders, and eager to argue against Plato at every step. Only gradually did he come to see that perhaps after all Plato was not so wrong, and in the latter part of his life he became a convinced Platonist. To the mid twentieth-century mind, with its lived experience of the revolt of youth against parental values, the throwing of the question into reverse gear did not seem entirely improbable. As it was, some forty years of controversy and intense research after the publication of Jaeger's *Aristoteles* totaled up to a laborious zero. The results canceled each other out. The Aristotelian reading public was quite ready for Guthrie's sage observation that there are more profitable ways of studying a great philosopher's works than by picking them apart in search of chronological indications in regard to development of his thought.[5]

Against this recent background, it should be advantageous to take a close look at Epsilon's concise doctrine about the sciences and their starting points. In particular, the way the primary philosophy is conceived demands special attention. Is it projected in such a way that its all extensive universality comes into conflict with its specification by a certain definite nature? Does its explicit characterization as a theological science interfere with its universal coverage of all beings? These two questions bear on one and the same problem. But they are framed today in the contrast between primary philosophy and natural theology that has been prevalent since the time of Francis Bacon. There were indeed grounds for facing a roughly parallel contrast in Aristotle himself, as the immediately following section in Epsilon's first chapter makes evident. Also the medieval commentators saw a somewhat corresponding difference in the respective approaches of Avicenna and Averroes. These later viewpoints should not be allowed to determine one's attitude today toward the original Aristotelian conception of the problem. Rather, Epsilon's clearly etched description of the sciences and their objects should be allowed to stand on its own merits, without coloring from subsequent philosophical notions.

Precisely, the passage in Epsilon divides the sciences into three basic kinds, namely the theoretical, the practical, and the productive. Further, it subdivides the theoretical sciences into three types, namely, philosophy of nature, mathematics, and theological philosophy. The divisions are not made on any widening degrees of abstraction, but on the different sorts of starting points from which each science proceeds.

5 W. K. C. Guthrie, *Aristotle: An Encounter* (Cambridge: Cambridge University Press, 1981), 4–17 (vol. VI in *A History of Greek Philosophy*, Cambridge University Press).

The theoretical sciences have their starting points in the beings or things themselves, in contrast to the knower. The instance given (1.1025bl8–21) is the philosophy of nature, in which the starting point of movement and rest is in the sensible substance itself. The starting point for the productive sciences, on the other hand, is in the artisan or artist, the producer. It consists in some mental conception, or art, or skill. This means evidently enough that the starting point of productive science, as in an art or craft, is the plan or design in the producer's mind. From that plan proceeds the work of production, in which the mental form is wrought into external material, as the figure of Hercules or Athene into the marble or bronze. The third type listed in the text is practical science, today referred to usually as ethics or moral philosophy. Like productive science, it has its starting points in the knower, who is in this case the moral agent. It proceeds from free choice, the choice of rational conduct that accords with right desire. It is action according to right reason. This point, developed throughout the Aristotelian *Ethics*, is passed over in Epsilon with that brief description. Yet the passage etches sharply enough the differences between the three basic types of sciences, and also shows that the really fundamental difference lies in the consideration that the starting points of the theoretical sciences are located in the things themselves, independently of the knower. This means that none of the other sciences can be reduced to the theoretical, no matter how much they make use of the conclusions of theoretical science in their own procedures.[6]

The importance of this basic division between the theoretical and the other sciences can hardly be overestimated. The superiority of the theoretical over the other types was illustrated in Greek philosophical tradition by the story that seems to have originated in the fourth century B.C. in the context of Pythagoras. Of those who went to the Great Games, some competed for prizes, others sold wares, but the most fortunate were the spectators.[7] Aristotle himself, at the beginning of the *Metaphysics* (1.1–2.98la24–982b10), showed how the science he was there introducing was theoretical and occupied the highest place in the order of knowledge.

The roots for this preeminence of the theoretical lie deep in Aristotle's conception of human knowledge. With him, cognition is understood in terms of being, and not in terms of having. To be aware of a thing, or to know a thing, is to be that thing through immaterial reception or possession of the thing's form. You have the thing's form, you have the concept of it, but what you become and are in the actuality of the cognition is the thing itself. Through material reception of a form, as in generation or alteration or growth or local motion, a third thing,

6 For Aristotle, ethics or practical science has its starting points or principles in the correct habituation of the moral agent, with its conclusions in the actions that proceed from those principles. See *Nicomachean Ethics*, 1.1.1095a3–6; 2.1.1103b3–25; 7.4.1147al8–28.

7 Diogenes Laertius, *Lives of Eminent Philosophers*, 8.8, ed. R. D. Hicks (Cambridge: Harvard University Press, 1958), II. 327–328.

namely the product, comes into being through the material reception of the new form into the abiding matter. But in immaterial reception no third thing is brought into being. The percipient and the thing perceived, the knower and the thing known, become one and the same in cognitional being. There are just the two things involved, now become identical in the actuality of the awareness. There is no third thing, no product. This may be called reception of form into form, in contrast to reception of form into matter. In that way the reception is immaterial instead of material, even though in sensation or perception the cognitive agent is physically a material being.

This explanation of cognition is elaborated in detail in Aristotle's *De Anima*.[8] It is stated succinctly in the *Metaphysics*: "And thought thinks on itself because it shares the nature of the object of thought, for it becomes an object of thought in coming into contact with and thinking its objects, so that thought and object of thought are the same."[9] Only through knowing other things is the human cognitive agent aware of herself or himself, and any other percipient is aware of itself in sensible cognition only concomitantly or reflexively in the direct awareness of other things. Cognitive agent and the thing attained are identical in the actuality of the cognition. The one could not be attained without the concomitant awareness of the other, for they are one and the same in that actuality.

This explanation of cognition presupposes, of course, Aristotle's general notion of being as multisignificant. Just as in direct cognition the being may be either substantial or accidental, as in substance or the other categories, so, in contrast to physical being, the new being is cognitional. To know a cow is to be the cow cognitionally, but not to be it physically. The physical nature of knower and thing known remain the same as they always were, physically distinct from each other. But cognitionally they become and are one and the same in the actuality of the awareness.

How this comes about is explained elaborately by Aristotle in the *De Anima*.[10] The form of the thing perceived is transmitted through the media by efficient causality that originates in the external sensible thing. That form is received by the sense organ, and in accord with the Aristotelian doctrine that form is the cause of being, it causes the recipient to be cognitionally the external thing itself. There is nothing more mysterious in this doctrine than in the material transmission of the form of the statue from the mind of the sculptor through nerves, muscles, hands, and chisel into the marble block. There is no question of a form as such traveling through the light waves and eye and nerves into the cortex. Just the signals are transmitted through the media, and through them the external thing impresses its own form immaterially upon the percipient, corresponding to the way the Olympic game is transmitted materially to the television sets throughout

8 See *De Anima*, 2.12.424a17–b18; 3.2.425b25–426a11; 3.4–5.429b5–430a20.

9 *Metaphysics*, 12.7.1072b20–21, Oxford trans.

10 *De Anima*, 2.7–12.418a26–424b18.

the distant continents of the world. There is color and shape and sound only on the playing field itself and on the television screens. In between are just the electronic signals that enable the events in the distant playing field to impress their form on the screen before your eyes. That of course is only material transmission. But it does illustrate the *process* by which a distant thing impresses its form immaterially upon a percipient. So impressed, the form causes the percipient to be that thing when the reception of the form is immaterial. Where the reception is material, as in procreation or alteration, the result is a third thing, but the form imparted by the efficient cause or causes makes the matter a new being or a new accidental combination of substance and accident. In every case the form is the cause of the thing's being and of its being what it is.

So thoroughgoing is the identity of the percipient with the thing perceived, that not only the distance barrier but also the time barrier disappears. The astronauts actually speaking from the moon were heard on earth just as they were talking then, despite the brief time lag in between. The three astronomers who witnessed the burst of Supernova 1987A were actually seeing the event as it took place in reality hundreds of millennia ago. What was being impressed upon their vision was precisely the form of the occurrence at the distant time. That form caused those astronomers to see the event immaterially as enacted then. In a word, the form impressed upon the percipient is the form as it was in the distant object at the time the efficient causality of that thing originated it. It stays individually the same form. It is not just specifically the same form, as in material reception such as procreation, but individually the same: for it is identically the form of the individual that is perceived or known.

This elaboration and illustration through modern examples seems required for the understanding of the Aristotelian doctrine of cognition today. The doctrine was tightly packed into the phrases that form known is the cause of being, that knower and thing known are identical in the actuality of cognition, and that the external thing acts upon the sense organ through the media of transmission. These tenets have been neglected in the tradition and have received very little attention in recent times. But they are essential for understanding the role attributed to theoretical philosophy in the *Metaphysics*, and for realizing how the brief statement in Epsilon about the starting points of the sciences locks the procedure into the definite groove followed by the treatises. As already seen,[11] awareness of oneself and one's cognitive activity takes place only through direct cognition of something else. Book Lambda repeats this tenet even more pointedly when contrasting it with the divine self-knowledge: "But evidently knowledge and perception and opinion and understanding have always something else as their object, and themselves only by the way."[12] This gives epistemological priority to the things that are

11 *De Anima*, 3.4.429b5–10; see supra, n. 8.

12 *Metaphysics*, 12.9.1074b35–36; Oxford trans.

external to the cognition. They are known directly, and they are the standard by which the truth or falsity of the cognition is judged.[13] The result is that the object of theoretical science can be surveyed just in itself, independently of anything brought to bear upon it through philosophical study. So in book Alpha the notion of the divine as the object of metaphysical interest could be introduced from mythologies or religious beliefs without having to wait for philosophical demonstration of the existence and nature of the deity. Likewise a theoretical science can be spread before the mind's gaze as something there in itself for consideration. What the theoretical science reaches only as conclusions can be examined and assessed in themselves before one has come to see the cogency with which they follow from the starting points. The object of theoretical science is not something that one is doing or making, but something that is already there before one's mental view.

The contrast may be seen through comparison with the practical and productive sciences. In practical knowledge one finds one's starting points in choice made according to right reason, and one reasons from these starting points to what one should do here and now. The practical conclusion is not there till one draws it. There is no way in which it can antecede one's practical reasoning, as long as one remains within the orbit of practical knowledge. One can of course later view it theoretically, when the whole process is held before one's mental vision reflexively as a *fait accompli*. But that type of knowing is no longer practical science. It is a reflexive theoretical consideration. It takes as its object something that is already there. Practical knowledge, on the other hand, is dealing with something yet to be done. It cannot take its conclusion as something already drawn, but has to be ready to veer this way or that way according to the incessantly changing circumstances faced by human conduct. Similarly in productive knowledge, though the design or plan is fixed and the rules remain determined, these have to be adapted to the matter on which one is working at the moment. Only when the whole process is brought to completion may it be held before the mind's eye as an object of theoretical study. Every kind of knowledge comes under the survey of epistemology, but in it the study is theoretical and no longer practical or productive.

In the nature of theoretical science, then, there is nothing to prevent an entire science as such from lying before one's gaze at any time as an object of consideration. Epsilon's understanding of the three basically different types of knowledge shows how metaphysics can have its starting points entirely in sensible things, and still, from the opening book on, can be speaking of the divine even

13 See *Metaphysics*, 6.4.1027b18–1028a2; 9.10.1051b3–1052a4. This epistemology makes possible for Aristotle what today is called a correspondence explanation of truth. He has the two separate terms for the comparison, the one directly known, the other reflexively attained in a different act of cognition. Both those terms are *immediately* known in the basic cognition of the object.

though the nature and existence of the divine have not as yet been demonstrated and are not taken as immediately evident. The notion that theoretical science deals with an object already there, antecedently to metaphysical interest, will allow all the things that serve as the bases for the study to be kept simultaneously in mind. In fact, the science developed in the metaphysical treatises rests on one side on the things of the sensible universe, and on the other side on separate substance. Epsilon's succinct account of the different types of knowledge helps fix it in a framework that carries the opposed thrusts and allows the erection of a solid philosophical structure.

Of prime importance in this regard, moreover, is the way a comprehensive view of the object of metaphysics shows how its specifying character is to be determined. The notion of being that the Aristotelian metaphysical treatises hold before one's eyes in the earlier books is that of sensible things. From the start in books Alpha through Epsilon it is graded as that of substances and accidents, as being in the real world, as being in human cognition, and as being in actuality and potentiality. These are indeed different ways of gradation in being. But in overall view the first chapter of Alpha elatton (1.993b24–31) found the notion of being in its supreme degree in the causes of the heavenly motions. The context was meant to stress the role of the highest instance as the origin of the characteristic in the other instances. This would mean that the notion of being is derived in all other instances from the separate substances described in book Lambda as the causes of the celestial phenomena. Book Gamma (3.1005a33–35) saw the specifying object of the highest theoretical science in the kind of being that was above the physical and was thereby universal in its scope. What seems envisaged in these passages is the highest kind of being, namely the separate substances, as the specifying object of the highest theoretical science. Yet the type of being that enables the human mind to commence the study that leads to separate substance is sensible being. Consequently the objection arises that in actual fact we are already deeply engaged in metaphysical study well before the separate substances are reached. Metaphysics, then, should not be regarded as specified by separate substance, since it is already at work without them. It should be specified by the being that is found in varying degrees in the substances and accidents of the sensible universe. The science of metaphysics has to be regarded as existing and operative before there is a question of dealing with immaterial substances. Separate substance, therefore, cannot be its specifying object. Such is the objection made against the conception of separate substance as the object that specifies Aristotelian metaphysics.

To this objection one may reply that against the background of Alpha elatton (1.993b24–31) the secondary instances of a characteristic are had in virtue of (*kath' ho*, b24) the primary instance. This can hardly mean anything else than that in itself the specifying trait when taken precisely as such is to be located in the nature of that supreme instance. Where there is gradation, the secondary instances do not contain this nature in a way that allows them to specify the science treating of them under its aspect. The natures of sensible substances are earth, water, tree, animal, and so on. The natures of accidents are quantities, qualities, relations, and the attributes listed in the other categories. Being, which contains its own differentiae, is not a still higher genus over them all. As spread throughout its secondary instances, it does not present a generic aspect ready to serve for specifying a science. With Aristotle it seemed really identical with the individual things, and able to be regarded as not even conceptually distinct from them. In this supergeneric identity with them it does not offer any distinct object with a content just its own, as the modern discussions about being as an empty concept illustrate only too clearly. Yet it is recognized as being, and according to the passage in Alpha elatton it has that characteristic through reference to the causes or principles of the eternal beings. It is known at once as being, even though this being has to be explained through its primary instance, separate substance. The being that is present in sensible things remains the starting point for the science of metaphysics, despite the specification of the science by a particular kind of being, namely the divine.

How is Aristotle enabled to look with consistency at metaphysics in this twofold perspective? The answer is to be sought in Epsilon's notion of a theoretical science. The object of the science, being, antecedes the epistemological consideration of the science itself. As its object, being is from Aristotle's viewpoint an object that extends through the substantial and the accidental, and through the sensible and the supersensible. Spread before the mind's gaze for theoretical study, this object is found to be graded in focal reference to a primary instance. Examined in that perspective, it is seen to be an object whose nature is found in separate substance, but is shared in lesser degrees in the other instances. When the epistemological questions are asked, the science that investigates it is likewise spread before the mind's reflective vision for theoretical consideration. If the science were specified by the being that is common to sensible substances and accidents, it would be restricted to those types of being. It could not be regarded as advancing its sway to a type that was above them. It would limit the notion of being to that of sensible or extended being, as the situation had been formulated so vigorously by Zeno.[14] This would be the world as later generations of materialists demanded it. On the contrary, specification by the supreme instance of being would permit the science to extend its scope to all the lesser degrees that, as shown in Alpha elatton (1.993b25), are named in accord with it. In cases of gradated perfections, as book Gamma (2.1003bl6–17) succinctly stated, the science that deals with them is the science of the primary instance.

Aristotle, then, is enabled to take this view of the specification of metaphysics because his notion of theoretical science allows the science as a whole to

14 See Zeno, Fr. 1, in Diels Kranz, *Die Fragmente der Vorsokratiker*, 5th ed. (Berlin: Weidmann, 1934–37), I. 255.13–14. In Plato's critique (*Sophist*, 247B-C), this position meant that unless a thing could be squeezed by the hands, it could not be in any way at all.

stand before his mental gaze as something complete in itself. He does not have to consider it as specified by its opening steps. It starts, indeed, from sensible things only. It reaches separate substance after a long and difficult demonstration. But when the whole science is made the object of epistemological consideration, the specification is seen to come from separate substance even though separate substance is reached philosophically only at a later stage of the discussion. Aristotle's notion of theoretical science, as given in the opening chapter of Epsilon, distinguishes it from doing or producing, and allows it to examine an object as already existent. In the present case, being is already there in its multifold though graded instances, and the science that studies it is also there as a whole for epistemological scrutiny. On that level the problem of its specification is faced and the sensible being from which the scientific procedure starts is shown to be different from the being that specifies the science. There is focal relation among the instances. But there is not even a trace of the notion that what the human mind first knows is the highest instance of being. That conception of the nineteenth-century ontologists cannot be read into Aristotle's assertion that the science of being qua being is the science of the primary instance.[15] Nor, in the light of Aristotle's notion of theoretical science, is there any clash with his stand that all our knowledge originates in sensible things.

A problem that does emerge from these considerations, though, is the exact way in which Aristotle is understanding the notion of being. It is not precisely existential, as has been already noted in regard to the existential approach of Aquinas.[16] With Aquinas the primary instance of being is subsistent existence. Since existence is not part of the nature of any created thing, the parallel between it and the Aristotelian primary instances located in health and medicine are easy enough to understand. Health is found as a nature in the appropriate disposition of a bodily organism, its primary instance. In the other instances, namely the diet or the exercise or the color, it is external to the nature of each. The relation is that of cause or effect or sign. Similarly in the second Aristotelian simile, medicine in its own nature is an art located in the mind of the practitioner. Remedies and cures are medical through their relations to it. These latter are external to the art. In the Thomistic explanation, existence is not contained within any finite thing's nature. Like the appropriate disposition of a bodily organism in the case of health, and the mental quality of medical art in the case of medicine, existence for Aquinas is an actuality over and above the natures of its secondary instances. In consequence it is aptly illustrated by the notions of health and medicine. But with Aristotle, being coincides for practical purposes with whatness. As presented in

15 A short coverage of the ontologists may be found in E. Gilson, T. Langan and A. Maurer, *Recent Philosophy* (New York: Random House, 1962), 251–265, 583–584. For a more detailed study, see A. Fonck's article in *Dictionnaire de théologie catholique*, 11.1.999–1062, s.v. *ontologisme*.

16 See supra, chapter 2, nn. 3–15.

Alpha elatton, being appears as intrinsically the same characteristic throughout primary and secondary instances. The only difference is in internal degree. The highest degree is in the separate movers of the celestial spheres. Lesser degrees are seen in sensible substances and accidents. Yet the characteristic of being remains internal to all these natures, in contrast to the Thomistic being which is found as a nature in subsistent existence only and is really distinct from all the other natures it actuates.

Aristotle could well have his motives for using health and medicine as illustrations for his own doctrine of being. He attributes a distinctive type of universality to the notion involved. This, as will be considered in the next chapter, suggests illustration by a primary instance whose nature is specifically different from the natures of the secondary instances. But even from what has been seen in the present chapter, an important though less decisive motive is brought forward. If being gives rise to what is intrinsically the same notion throughout all its instances, the substance of sensible things might easily be taken as its primary instances with Zeno; being would then have intrinsically a material character. Supersensible being would be ruled out. The highest type immediately attainable by human cognition would thereby be given the rank of primary instance. To forestall temptation toward this avenue of approach, illustrations that foreshadowed a primary instance outside the immediately knowable instances would seem in order. A primary instance whose nature was different from the natures of all the secondary instances would be suggested, even though qua being all the instances both primary and secondary could be in some way brought under one and the same notion. At least an alert to a problem in this regard would have been sounded.

Be that as it may, this difficulty makes today's reader face squarely the question of what being meant for Aristotle. It was obviously not the perfection known through the act of judgment, as it was with Aquinas. Production from nothing would have had to intervene for that approach, and this had been excluded against the Parmenidean background in which nothing could come from nothing. Existence was not at all eliminated. But it played no significant role in the understanding of being. It was absorbed into the thing's whatness, as far as philosophical consideration was concerned. Viewed from a medieval perspective, it added nothing to the content of the essence, the content that the medievals expressly distinguished from existence. This quidditative character of being is brought to the fore in Aristotle's account of the first principle of demonstration: ". . . each of the expressions 'to be' and 'not to be' has a definite meaning; so that not everything can be both so and not so."[17] To be, in this context, was to have a definite nature.[18]

17 Aristotle, *Metaphysics*, 4.4.1006a29–31, Apostle trans.

18 See Alexander of Aphrodisias, *In Aristotelis Metaphysica Commentaria*, 1.1, p. 275.1–36.

That is the way it had been understood by Plato (*Theaetetus*, 183 A-B) in contrast to change and becoming. It meant stability. Philosophically the background may be traced to Parmenides, where truth was found only in being, and where not being, mistakenly mingled with being, gave rise to the doxastic world of change. More remotely in Greek mythology the abode of the gods was characterized as immortal in contrast to the vicissitudes of earthly life.[19] The contrast was between stability on the one hand and change on the other.

Against that deeply entrenched background in Greek culture, being readily took on the meaning of a stable nature. But stability had its degrees. For Aristotle, a sensible thing was changeable in its size, qualities, position, and relations, while remaining the same in its substance. That greater degree of stability indicated a higher degree of being for the thing's substance. But sensible things were also perishable. They could change into other things, as wood, for instance, was burned into ashes. Their substance, in consequence, could not rank as being in the highest degree. Only pure actuality, in which there was no potentiality for any change whatever, could lay claim to the highest niche in being. The primary instance had to be separate substance.

These considerations are of help in showing how sensible things bring human cognition into immediate contact with being, and yet do not allow that immediately known being to specify the science that studies it qua being. Though sensible things are always in process of change, their substance remains stable under the accidental variations. As a result the human mind is from the start in immediate cognitional contact with something stable. Even color and figure and other such accidents show a relative stability in contrast to the sensible motion directly experienced in them. The human cognitive agent, in consequence, is in immediate contact with stability from the very beginning of any knowledge of sensible things. When in this way being is understood in terms of stability as opposed to change, it is obviously present to the mind's eye from that initial act of cognition.

But when being is taken in these immediately known instances, can it at all specify a science that bears upon being qua being? The answer to this question has to be negative. The science of being qua being, as the opening chapter of Gamma had made clear, has an object that is being and only being. This object was regarded as a nature just in itself. As an object it was not taken as modified by any added characteristics. In the manner in which it is immediately known, it is restricted by one or more of those superadded traits. Taken in that way, it could not specify the science of itself precisely qua being. Rather, it would specify the science of that restricted kind of being. When being is understood as stability and permanence, however, it allows one to see more readily that the science treating of it qua being cannot be specified by anything that is not essentially stable. But quite obviously the being that is encountered in sensible things does not enjoy that

19 See Pindar, *Nemean Odes,* 6.1–4.

essential permanence, since it can change or perish. The accidental being, no matter how stable it may appear during the time it is perceived, may be increased or diminished or altered. The substantial being of a sensible thing may perish. Only substance without any potentiality at all for change could from that standpoint rank as being qua being.

Under this aspect, then, separate substance is more easily seen as the sole object that could specify metaphysics. Even though separate substance is philosophically known only by reasoning from the starting point of the being that is known in sensible things, one can see more readily that it reserves to itself the right of specifying the science of being qua being. The science itself is already at work and has been vigorously pursued before its specifying object is explicitly known. It starts from the sensible things and carries its direct demonstrations to the end, without any epistemological worry in regard to its own specification. Only when the entire science is spread critically before the mind's reflective gaze does one see that it is in fact specified by separate substance. Aristotle's general conception of theoretical science as a procedure from starting points that are independent of the knower's action or production makes possible this way of viewing the specification of the science of being qua being.

The understanding of being in terms of stability, then, is a help in grasping the tenet that only something entirely unchangeable can specify the science of being as such. At least it is protection against the tendency to regard the being that specifies this science as an object that has been abstracted in supergeneric fashion from the particular instances of being. In ascending the Porphyrian tree there is a temptation to continue the abstraction of "animal" from humans and beasts, "living thing" from animal and plant, "body" from animate and inanimate, on into an abstraction of a general notion of being from the corporeal and incorporeal. The result is a head-on collision with the tenet that being contains all its differentiae. But there could hardly be a corresponding tendency to abstract a supergeneric concept of stability that would be common in this fashion to the stable and the changeable. Rather, you would have to take the first of these two notions, namely the stable, and show how it can serve to explain the changeable by way of diminution of its own intrinsic perfection, quite as it is able to account for privations and negations of being.

Care has to be taken, of course, to preserve positive content in the notion of stability when it is used to explain being. Stability in this perspective is not to be considered as merely an absence of motion. That would be making motion the typical instance of actuality, and rest or stability would be a derogation from its perfection. With Aristotle motion or change is an actuality, but only an imperfect actuality. The perfect actuality is found in the stable goal of the change or process. So in using the notion of stability to illustrate Aristotle's conception of being, the positive aspect of actuality has to glow through it at every step, and culminate in its highest instance. With this in mind, one can readily see that Aristotle's route to the nature and existence of the separate substances does not arrive at something that could today be dyslogistically referred to as "static." In fact, the substance reached in the conclusion of his demonstration will stand in vivid contrast to today's usual conception of that condition. In relation to our current estimation of the "static" it would have to be called "dynamic." "Dynamic," however, is derived from the Greek word for potentiality. On that account it could be misleading if applied to the Aristotelian separate substance, which is actuality without any potentiality whatever. Even the Platonic Ideas, though incorporeal and unchangeable and radiant with life and goodness and beauty (*Sophist*, 247B–249A), do not measure up to Aristotle's full understanding of actuality. In the course of his reasoning to separate substance, Aristotle (*Metaphysics*, 12.6.1071bl4–19) is able to regard the Platonic Ideas as in themselves merely potential to the actuality required for the primary mover of the universe. He envisages pure actuality as something much more intense and vital than even the Platonic world of Ideas, and as endowed with a beauty and goodness that correspond to this further elevation. Yet the beauty and goodness are regarded as coming from the thoroughgoing unchangeableness or stability of separate substance. This is stated concisely in the course of the reasoning in book Lambda: "This mover, then, exists of necessity; and if so, then nobly, and as such, it is a first principle."[20] The necessity is explained as meaning that which cannot be otherwise: that which is what it is in simple fashion. There is no other element in it that could serve as a condition for change. On account of that necessity of always remaining the same, this reasoning in book Lambda continues, the primary mover functions as the final cause of cosmic motion. In the Greek the term *kalōs* is adverbial. The meaning is that the essential stability of separate substance is what gives it the goodness and beauty and attractiveness that make it the ultimate principle upon which the heavens and the world of nature depend.

Aristotle is accordingly looking upon separate substance as having in itself all the actuality that motivates the celestial and sublunary processes. It is their ultimate final cause. Each thing is striving to imitate and attain as best it can the perfection of the immobile movers. That is the perfection that the notion of being qua being involves. No matter how low the being in any particular instance may rank, it is in its own way an expression of the supreme goodness and beauty and actuality of separate substance. That is what being means.[21] That is the way it specifies metaphysics. Each thing is given its nature by its own form. But it is made a being by its relation to separate substance, namely to substance that is actuality only. What it brings out qua being is the actuality that is life at its high-

20 Aristotle, *Metaphysics*, 12.7.1072bl0–11.

21 "Being for the metaphysician is no inert, static 'object' given in our perception for our analysis . . ." G. B. Phelan, "Being and the Metaphysicians," in *From an Abundant Spring*, ed. staff of *The Thomist* (New York: Kennedy & Sons, 1952), 437.

est and best, life that is beauty and goodness and thinking in the most exalted degree. That is what Aristotle sees focally in every instance of being, that is encountered in daily life, quite parallel to the way existence is for Aquinas what strikes the mind first and foremost in each sensible thing and that cannot be understood except as a participation of existence that subsists, existence divinely revealed as the "I am who am" of Exodus.[22]

There can be no doubt about the enthusiasm of either Aristotle or Aquinas in their respective encounters with the being of perceptible things. The eloquent difference of existence from nothingness in Aquinas, and that of actuality from potentiality for Aristotle, resounds continually throughout their discussions on being. For Aristotle, the real identity of whatness and being in real things does not interfere in the least with his tenet that the aspect of being is not expressed by the perceptible thing's nature taken just in itself. Rather, that aspect consists in the focal reference the perceptible things have to a nature not their own, the nature of separate substance, a nature that is life and beauty and goodness in the most sublime degree. Solely in that primary instance does being rank as "being qua being" or as something that is "simply being."[23] Only in virtue of that highest instance does being specify for Aristotle the procedure of metaphysics. On this latter point the perspective of Aquinas is very different. Not God, but common being is the subject of this science.[24] Yet the enthusiasm of Aquinas for the sublimity of existence is not at all thereby diminished. Existence is for him the actuality of all actualities and the perfection of all perfections.[25] As the actuality of everything throughout the categories and beyond the categories, it leaves no being on the opposite side of the existence essence couplet. The essences it actualizes abstract in this way from all being. Yet what specifies metaphysics for Aquinas is not just the existence in itself. What specifies the science is the composite that results from this actualization and is known as common being. Under common being God is not ranged, though he is its first cause and principle. The divine being, therefore, is not contained within the specifying object of the highest purely human science.

With Aristotle, on the contrary, the way lies open for the specification of the primary philosophy by divine being. Divine being is being qua being, for him, in the sense that it is actuality only. It lacks all potentiality for change. In this way it cannot be other than it is. When being is so understood in terms of whatness, it points to its highest instance as its specifying object. Its highest instance is a par-

22 *Exodus* 3:13–14. See Etienne Gilson, *Elements of Christian Philosophy* (Garden City, NY.: Doubleday, 1960), 113–115.

23 See *Metaphysics*, 6.1.1025b7–10 and 1026a3l

24 See Aquinas, *Commentary on the Metaphysics of Aristotle*, Prologue, trans. John P. Rowan (Chicago: Henry Regnery, 1961; South Bend, Ind.: Dumb Ox Books), I.2.

25 Aquinas, *On the Power of God*, 7.2. ad 9m; text supra, chapter 2, n. 15.

ticular nature, and leaves the way open for other particular natures to specify their own sciences independently of generic absorption.[26] The other sciences do not become branches of metaphysics. Metaphysics does not provide in Cartesian fashion the roots that nourish them.

Yet despite the particular nature of its object, the Aristotelian primary philosophy is universal in its scope.[27] How it is able to have that universality is explained in the final section of Epsilon's opening chapter. This is a problem still to be faced. But the doctrine of Epsilon that locates the starting points of theoretical science in the things themselves allows separate substance to be the specifying object of the science even though the being that is first attained in human cognition is the being of sensible things. By no means does this view require that separate substance be immediately known in human cognition.

26 This explains how Aristotle (*Metaphysics*, 6.1.1026a27–29) could make the assertion that if there were no separate substance, the primary philosophy would be the philosophy of nature. The philosophy of nature undoubtedly has a definite object, composite nature. In quite parallel fashion a definite object, namely separate substance, may be expected as the specifying object of the primary philosophy.

27 This extension of being to all its secondary aspects enables Aquinas himself to attribute a doctrine of creation to Aristotle. On this attribution by Aquinas see Mark F. Johnson, "Did St. Thomas Attribute a Doctrine of Creation to Aristotle," *The New Scholasticism* 63 (1989), 129–155. The background is Aristotle's tenet that the primary instance of being is the cause of all other being. See Johnson, 146–147. Accordingly, from the viewpoint of making something out of nothing creation cannot be attributed to Aristotle. But from the viewpoint of cause of being to both the matter and the form, the notion of creation is quite in accord with Aristotle's.

Chapter 4

The Universality of Being qua Being

Aristotle's notion of the universal is sketched succinctly in book Delta of the *Metaphysics* (26.1023b30–32). The universal is each of its instances, but only in turn. The second edition of the Oxford translation (1928) aptly renders the relevant text as ". . . it contains many things by being predicated of each, and by all of them, e.g. man, horse, god, being severally one single thing because all are living things." The existents that confront human cognition are all singular things – e.g., stones, trees, horses. They can be lined up in order, and distinguished in differing kinds as one definite object is seen in a number of similar instances. The same object "tree" is seen in this tree, that tree, and in an indefinite number of yet other trees. A further object, "living things," is seen in animals as well as in plants. The object "tree" is in this way a universal that is seen in each instance one by one. It can accordingly be predicated of each of the singulars, in saying "this is a tree." Each singular is "a tree," but only severally. The universal does not make one singular be the other singular. It merely renders each instance in turn a tree. It leaves the instances numerically and really distinct from one another. In this case the lowest universal is the species "tree." A broader universal would be "living thing," a universal in which trees coincide with other plants and animals and with human persons, though severally. The process continues up the Porphyrian tree.

This situation is described graphically in the rout simile at the end of the *Posterior Analytics* (19.100a12–b3), in which the singulars and the species and genera are lined up successively in ever-widening range, until the highest universals are reached. The governing principle is the same throughout. Each singular thing is seen to be the same specific object and the generic objects, as Socrates is seen to be a person, and then an animal, a living thing, a body. Socrates is each of those objects, but always severally.

When Aristotle is asked why the human mind thinks in this way, the answer he gives in the *Posterior Analytics* (19.100al3–14) is that the soul is so constituted that it is able to undergo this process. That is the way the human mind is built. The mind that becomes the thing in cognition is pure potentiality in the cognitive order (*De Anima*, 3.5.430al4–15). Prior to the thinking, it is actually none of the objects it knows (3.4.429a24). In consequence any actual structure it has comes from the things it grasps. This can only mean that somehow sensible things themselves are so structured. The same sensible thing is of its nature able to be known as singular and as a specific and a generic object. The advantage is that this condition in things makes scientific knowledge of them possible, as was stressed in the opening book of the *Metaphysics* (1.98la5–30). What is seen in the object "tree" in particular instances can be applied to other instances in which the same specific object is recognized. The way is thereby opened to the widening and deepening of knowledge, and to scientific prediction.

The universal object, in consequence, is located in the natures of sensible things. The original Greek expression, *to katholou*, is adverbial in the force given to its noun. It signifies that which is known in the fashion of a whole. The meaning, therefore, is that of a nature taken according to the nature's whole range, whether the nature be corporeal, living, sentient, or human. It bears on real things under various and successively widening aspects. The things themselves are real, and can exist as singulars in the sensible world. Universality, however, is a way in which they can be known by the human mind. As a result they exist as universals only in our cognition. But the things remain real even though they are known in universal fashion. In speaking of a universal, consequently, one has to keep in mind the adverbial bearing of the term. What it expresses is something that is now being taken universally, even though in itself it is something real. For this reason Aristotle (*Posterior Analytics*, 2.19.100a17) in explaining scientific knowledge can say that the sensation or perception is of the universal. From that viewpoint what is perceived in human cognition is not confined to the singular instance of Callias. It extends universally in intellection to other similar instances. Always, for our ordinary cognition, "intelligible objects . . . exist in the forms of sensible objects" (*De Anima*, 3.8.432a4–5, Apostle trans.). The nature that exists as singular is known as universal. A further way of looking at the nature's capability for indefinite instantiation may be found at the end of book Mu of the *Metaphysics* (10.1086b14–1087a25). There, against an Academic background, the problem is phrased in terms of real existence on the one side and knowledge on the other. Only singular things can exist in the real world, but knowledge has to be of the universal. The dilemma, then, is that what we know is not real and what is real cannot be known. The answer given is that knowledge as well as the act of knowing is twofold. One way is actual; the other is potential. Accordingly a nature may be grasped as actually something definite but as potentially open to presence in an indefinite number of other instances: "Potentiality, like matter, being universal and indefinite, is concerned with the universal and the indefinite; but actuality, being definite and a this, is concerned with some definite thing and some *this*" (1087a16–18, Apostle trans.).What actually exists then, is definite and determined, such as this tree or this stone. Likewise what is actually known is this tree or this stone. But the nature of tree or stone, actually seen in each, is able to be seen in indefinitely numerous other singulars. The same object, stone or tree, is always known in a phantasm and consequently in a singular. But it is an object that can also be seen actually in a second and a third instance, and so on indefinitely. What is known of it can accordingly be applied to the other instances, and in that way give rise to scientific knowledge and scientific prediction. In this fashion what is universal is like matter. It can be actualized repeatedly in new instances, while remaining the same nature on account of its intrinsic potentiality to receive new actualizations.

Aristotle goes on in the same passage (1087a19–23) to illustrate the issue with two examples. One is that of a color seen by the eye. This particular color that comes under its actual vision is "a color," and thereby a specific object capable of being seen in any other actual perception of color. In seeing the particular instance of color, the eye is incidentally seeing the specific object "color," quite as in the text considered above from the *Posterior Analytics* (2.19.100al7) Aristotle was able to say that the perception is of the universal. Likewise, he can state in book Alpha of the *Metaphysics* (1.98lal8–20), that the medical practitioner in curing Callias or Socrates cures "a man" incidentally, for these individuals happen to be men.[1] The other example given in the passage in book Mu is an alpha that is being considered by a grammarian. It is a particular alpha that he holds before his vision or writes on the board, but the grammatical norms seen in that particular instance are meant to hold for all other instances of alpha. They are universal principles, and ground demonstrative conclusions. In these ways the capacity or potentiality of sensible natures for universal application may be seen. In the real world the natures are always individual. What is actually known in any cognitive act is something individual. But what is thereby known can be applied indefinitely to similar individuals. The knowledge is potentially universal.

A final point to be noted in regard to Aristotle's general notion of universality is the way it extends to principles and conclusions that will hold only "for the most part" (*epi to polu*, *Posterior Analytics*, 1.30.87b22–25). Today the prevalent conception of universality seems rule out the possibility of exceptions. Aristotle, in contrast, distinguishes two kinds of universality, one that holds necessarily, the other that holds for the most part. In the moral order, the principles and conclusions are of the latter type (*Nicomachean Ethics*, 1.3.1094b19–22). Yet Aristotle has no difficulty in considering them to be universal. In the physical world, the

1 This does not at all imply that personhood is an accidental category in regard to the individual Callias. What is cured by the medical practitioner is the individual person, not the universal "person" as such. But the perception is thereby of the universal and is not restricted to the case of the individual person Callias (*Posterior Analytics* 2.19.100a15–b1). The scientific knowledge of the curing process bears accordingly on an object that is universal. From this viewpoint the universal personhood may be regarded as incidental to the actual occurrence. On the history of the Latin term *universale*, see infra, ch. 9, n.1.

natures of things on the specific level are known only through their accidents, and, as in the case of the soul (*De Anima*, 1.1.402b16–403a2), a considerable amount of play back and forth may be required to determine just what their nature is. Hence our knowledge of them in the universal is subject to continued modification and depth. The progress of the natural and life sciences makes this only too evident. But that does not interfere with the universality of our concepts. As long as the one specific object is seen in different instances, the cognition is universal as Aristotle understands the notion. As far as can be ascertained, the Greek term for "universal" is original with him, and likewise, presumably, the philosophical notion that it is meant to express. There need not be any hesitation, then, in accepting his use of the term "universal" in the way he himself has explained it. There was no previously established use of the word against which his understanding of it could be checked.[2]

When Aristotle comes to apply the notion of universality to being, he may be expected to require the identity of it as an object with every one of its instances in turn. Each instance will be severally a being. Whether a thing be a substance such as a tree, or a quality, a size, a relation, or a motion or change, it will in every case be something that is. Though supergeneric, the predicate here will conform to the condition of identity one by one with the things of which it is asserted. Each will in that way be a being. Otherwise there would be no universality as Aristotle understood the notion.

Further, the type of universality required here will be that in which the connection between subject and predicate holds for all cases. There can be no question of its holding only "for the most part." The meaning is not at all that for the most part things are beings. For Aristotle they all are. Being and thing are always really identical, and even if a conceptual distinction be placed between them it is more advantageous in metaphysics to do without that distinction.[3] Even the notion of "nothing," when conceived as an object of thought, has to be represented in terms of being by way of absolute denial. Whatever distinction lies between being and thing as objects of conception will need to be explored later on when the type of universality in the predication of being has been clarified. But for the present, where the metaphysical study of real things is at issue, the connection between being and thing is necessary, and not just something that holds for the most part. The universality required for the predication of being is clearly of the type that applies to all instances without exception, and not merely to most of them.

A difficulty with far reaching consequences does arise, however, when this Aristotelian conception of universality is applied to the predication of being. The nature predicated in the specific and generic universals is in every case identical with the instance of which it is asserted, even though the identity here is with one

2 On the intimations in Plato, see infra, ch. 9, n. 3.

3 Aristotle, *Metaphysics*, 4.2.1003b25–26; cf. discussion supra, ch. 1, nn. 3–4.

by one in turn. But, as seen in the preceding chapter, the nature of being, or being qua being, is identical only with the primary instance. In all secondary instances the nature of the thing is different from the nature of being, though focally related to it. When you predicate being of a color or of a relation or of a motion, you do not mean that any one of these is a separate substance. Yet you do mean to say that each is a being. The type of universality is in consequence very different from the ordinary type in which you say that Parmenides and Socrates and Plato are humans, or that plants and animals are living things. The universality remains intact, but the natures of the instances vary.

Aristotle had at hand examples to illustrate this further type of universality. “Healthy” meant possession of a particular quality, namely the appropriate disposition of the living organism. Only living organisms could be identical, severally, with the possession of this vital disposition. The tonic was not identical with it, the exercise was not identical with it, the good color was not identical with it. Yet all of these instances were healthy. They were healthy because of the different ways in which they were related to the organic disposition. But none of them was identical with that disposition, even though all were in fact healthy. Similarly “medical” referred primarily to the art cultivated and developed by the Hippocratic tradition. It meant a quality that existed in human minds. Only individual instances of that art in its practitioners could be identical severally with that accidental nature. Yet books, schools, cures, and instruments were medical, though none of these instances was identical with the human act. All were truly and properly medical, but through the relations they had to the art that existed in the minds of the practitioners.

What these two illustrations bring out is that in predication through focal reference the nature predicated is found in the primary instance only.[4] In all other instances it is present just through reference in various ways to the nature of the primary instance. There is no indication that this doctrine of focal meaning was developed in any notable way prior to Aristotle's formulation of it. Facing in book Nu of the *Metaphysics* (14.2.1089a1ff.) the general problem of being, Aristotle noted that in the immediate Academic background of his own time the relevant *aporia* was still being framed "in archaic fashion" (*archaikos*, a2). This expression was intended in a straight historical sense, as meaning the early way of formulating the question in the development of Greek philosophy. There is no reason for attributing any derogatory overtone to it, since Aristotle highly respected the thought of Parmenides, in whose words the objection here is quoted. Just as little is there question of giving it a purely philosophical sense, as though the difficulty lay in an approach to the problem in terms of the PreSocratic *archai*. What

4 On the designation "focal reference," see G. E. L. Owen, "Logic and Metaphysics in Some Earlier Works of Aristotle," in *Aristotle and Plato in the Mid Fourth Century*, ed. Ingemar Düring and G. E. L. Owen (Göteborg: Studia Graeca et Latina Gotoborgensia, XI 1960), 163–190.

follows might suggest a query in that direction, for Aristotle at once throws the discussion into the alleged explanation in terms of being and not being, after the manner of the traditional opposites as the *archai* of the universe.[5] In point of fact, Aristotle (*Metaphysics*, 1.4.985b4–9) understands the doctrine of the atomists Leucippus and Democritus to mean that the basic elements of things are the full and the void in the sense of being and not being. But there is no hint in the present text itself that he was giving this significance to the Greek adverb for "in archaic fashion."

As the text stands, Aristotle merely mentions that his predecessors had to face the *aporia* posed by Parmenides. To them it seemed that all things would be one single thing, namely being itself, unless they met face to face the Eleatic's assertion that not beings never could be. They had to show that there is in fact not being. With this established, the plurality of beings will be explained by the composition of being with something else, something other than being (14.2.1089a5–6). It was in that way, through a single nature called "otherness" in combination with the nature of being, that the plurality had been accounted for in Plato's *Sophist*.[6]

It is against this notion of a single nature, opposite to the nature of being, that Aristotle directs his critique. He turns attention to the being that is seen in the sensible universe. This being is multisignificant. It may be substance. It may be any of the accidents in the list of the categories. No single nature (*phusis*, 1089a13), therefore, could be the cause of some things being substances, and others the various accidents. Various types of not being would be required to bring about this plurality. The alleged otherness could not be a single nature. It would have to correspond in each case to one of the various categories, so that there would have to be as many types of not being as there are categories of being. Nor does it help (as with Plato in the *Sophist*, 240C) if one tries to explain not being by falsity, calling falsity the nature (*phusis*, 14.2.1089a20) of not being. Not even in geometrical demonstrations are false measurements, as false, put into the reasoning processes, and things are not brought into being out of falsity, nor do they perish into it. Rather, from the not being that is the potentiality to each different category does each come into being (a26–31). This not being, then, becomes as multisignificant, as the categories.

5 Bonitz's *Index Aristotelicus* does not list any other occurrence of the adverb *archaikos*. In the context here the meaning of the term as "old fashioned" would be expected. At the same time, however, the Greek word *arche* carries overtones of ruling and governing. In treating of Parmenides at *Metaphysics* 1.3.984a27–b3l, Aristotle seems to have in mind the primitive historical approach to philosophy from a plurality of principles, along with the way this approach will ascribe efficient and final causality to a supreme principle for these comic processes. This is a framework that will allow for one ruler.

6 See Plato, *Sophist* 254A–258B. Not being appeared as "one kind of being, permeating all beings" (260B).

The one point brought out by all this arguing is that our philosophical procedure does not start from a single notion called being and another and opposite notion called not being. Not in that way are the principles or *archai* of our reasoning set up. Rather, we take the sensible world as it confronts us. In it, what we call being lies in a plurality of different natures as listed in the categories and as seen in their processes of becoming and perishing, with not being as the denial or privation of them. No nature that is not expressed in terms of being is ever encountered. But that being, as it is seen in all these instances, is not just one nature such as substance or quantity (14.2.1089b7). It is not predicated as a single nature that is identical in turn with each of its instances. None of these instances in the observable world is in fact identical with separate substance. Each instance is related to separate substance in focal meaning, insofar as each strives in its own way, and to the extent of its capacity, to imitate in its proper degree the permanence and stability of the immaterial forms. Inanimate things tend to retain possession of their matter, animate substances aim at perpetuity through the propagation of their species, humans seek their happiness in the exercise of their highest faculty upon its highest object. All tend in these various ways toward the perfection of the immobile separate substances. Through that relation all are beings, and being is predicated of each in turn even though none of them is identical with the nature of being. Each is identical with its own nature, whether this nature is substantial or accidental, and in the nature there is no real distinction between itself and its focal relation to the nature of immobile and separate form. Hence each is a being, for each is identical in turn with a nature that is so related. The identity is in this way supergeneric, not generic.

What Aristotle is emphasizing in this discussion in book Nu is that being is not a univocal object. As immediately known to us, being is an object that is present in different ways in the sensible universe. It is from that universe, and no other, that we get our notion of being (14.2.1090a20–b5). No matter how attractive the abstract objects may be to the soul, their basic origin has to be kept located in sensible things. Our original notion of being is spread throughout the categories. It is accordingly not univocal. Yet "nature does not seem to be a series of episodes, like a bad tragedy" (1090bl9–20). There is obviously order in it.

This order is discussed at considerable length in books Gamma and Zeta. The primary type of being in sensible things is substance. The other instances are beings through focal reference to this primary type, with mention both in Gamma (3.1005a35) and in Zeta (7.1032b2) of a primary instance within the category of substance itself. Book Epsilon in its last section comes to grips very concisely with this problem. Natural philosophy, it notes, "is theoretical about the kind of being that is able to undergo motion, and only about formal beingness that for the most part is not separate" (6.1.1025b26–28). Philosophy of nature, this means, is about one kind of being, namely about material being. It is about being with a superadded characterization and restriction. Accordingly in the description given at the opening of book Gamma (1.1003a23–26), the specifying object of natural philosophy would not rank as being just qua being. Rather, its object is being qua mobile.

This object will of course include the formal element in sensible things, since for Aristotle form is everywhere the cause of being. But it will be only about form that is for the most part not separate. The meaning of this assertion is clear enough from the *De Anima* (1.1.403a27–b16). Mind is the part of the soul by which the soul knows and thinks (3.4.429al0–12), and one factor in mind is separate (3.5.430al7–23). Otherwise, though, the forms of material things are not separate from matter. As cause of being for both matter and composite, the form may rightly be called the *ousia* of the thing, when the Greek word *ousia* is understood according to its formation from the participle *ousa*. It is the beingness of the thing, and in the present text may be translated this way.[7] The sequence of the thought (*Metaphysics*, 6.1.1025b26–28) is that natural philosophy is about changeable being, and about the intrinsic and non-separate cause of that being, a cause which though in itself unchangeable confers being upon matter and composite. That meaning is hardly expressed by the usual translation "substance," but it is carried by the term "beingness" in the signification of the perfection that makes something a being. The actual and relatively stable element in the changeable thing is thereby indicated. No matter what the translation, however, the element meant is the formal cause that was introduced in the first book of the *Metaphysics* (3.983a27–28) as *t¯e n ousian kai to ti ¯e n einai.* This cause was reached in the *Physics* (1.7.19la3–12) by reasoning on the analogy of artificial forms like those of statue and bed in relation to the bronze or wood out of which they were made. It is what enables a thing to be defined, in giving the thing the required permanence and stability for a subject of scientific study.[8]

At any rate, the topic of definition is immediately pursued in the text. The reason given is that without understanding of the way *to ti ēn einai*, or the thing's definition, is taken, the inquiry is vacuous. Book Gamma (4.1006a24–25) had shown that something definite was required in order to have a demonstration.

7 The notion of "beingness" brings out in this way the role of form as cause of being to the matter and the composite thing. Accordingly it is the primary instance of being in the composite, parallel to the way separate substance is the primary instance of being in the whole universe.

8 See Albert Schwegler, *Die Metaphysik des Aristoteles* (Frankfurt: Minerva), IV, 369-379. On the possessive dative in the Greek phrase, see also Robert Zaslavsky, "Note on Translating an Aristotelian Dative and to *ti en einai*," *The New Scholasticism*, 58 (1984), 256-261. Zaslavsky explains this dative as a "locative dative, of time" (259). For references to other recent discussions on the structure of this Aristotelian phrase, see Wolfgang Bernard, *Receptivität und Spontaneität der Wahrnehmung bei Aristoteles* (Baden Baden: Verlag Valentin Koerner, 1988), 15, nn. 20–21.

This requirement is now thrown back upon the formal cause. There is no doubt that the Greek expression *to ti ēn einai* signifies a form in the thing, whether substantial or accidental. But how the Greek expression comes to signify formal cause is not at all clear. Its grammatical ancestry is unknown, and efforts to explain its meaning on grammatical grounds have not been able to reach agreement. The phrase is interrogative in form, and meant to parallel the question about what a thing is. But the answer to the question about the thing's whatness can give either the matter or the form or the composite of both. The statue may be bronze, or Hercules, or the sculptured material. Only the form, however, can be given as answer to the other and parallel question. The form is what makes the thing be itself. It makes it be the kind of a thing it is. In the sensible universe it makes the thing require individuation through matter within its own species, and enables the thing to be known in universal fashion by the human mind. The matter may keep changing, as in the phenomena of nutrition, but the thing will remain the same even though all the matter has been replaced again and again. The size may change as in growth, but the individual remains the same. Similarly change in other accidents does not affect the thing's basic identity. The form is what keeps it the same thing, and allows it to be defined in the way required for scientific demonstration.

With this role of the form in mind, one may ask how the wording of Greek expression *to ti ēn einai* brings out the notion, and how the meaning is to be conveyed in English. Every developed language should be capable of expressing what has been said in another tongue, even though the way of doing so may vary considerably. The meaning in this case is the essential factor for a thing's identity. It is the factor that remains the same, and causes the thing to remain the same thing, no matter what other changes take place in it. As long as that factor remains, the thing itself remains what it is. What the thing essentially is, or what its essential being consists in, is the meaning to be conveyed. The essential being of the thing, in contrast to the changing of its matter or size or other accidents, is what has to be expressed. The matter may be replaced, the composite may grow or shrink, but the form keeps the thing the same identical being. In Greek the possessive dative was used to indicate the thing that possessed the form. In this way it expressed what is being for blood, or is being for a human person. The permanence and stability that goes with the notion of "being" was thereby read into the phrasing. But even where the possessor of the form was not mentioned, the difference between the permanence given by the form and the changeableness allowed in matter and the composite was conveyed by the use of the imperfect tense of the verb "to be" in the Greek. In the phrase the imperfect tense seems to have denoted timeless being, quite as Aristotle could argue that motion and time could never come into being or perish because they always exist – *aei gar ēn*.[9] The

9 *Metaphysics*, 12.6.1071b7. The argument is meant to prove eternal duration for the primary movers. Motion that took place in the past, even though without beginning,

fact that they always existed and always will exist is a conclusion drawn from their type of being.

However, instances of the use of the imperfect of the Greek verb "to be" in the sense of timeless being are too few and too uncertain in their application to make a convincing case in this regard. The sense of the Aristotelian *to ti ēn einai* has to be taken from the way it is used to signify the form as the element of permanence and stability in the sensible thing. While either form, matter, or composite may be given in answer to the question about what a thing is, only form can answer the parallel question about what its essential being is, namely what it has to have irreplaceably in order to be what it is. "Essential" seems to be the word in English to express this notion correctly. With that understanding the phrase may be rendered in English as the thing's essential being, or what the thing's being essentially is. When the possessor is named, it may be phrased as what is essentially being for that thing. In this sense "essence" provides a suitable translation, with the proviso that the medieval contrast of essence with existence be left out of consideration. In that medieval context "essence" could refer to matter and to composite as well as to form, since all three lie on the essence side of the essence existence couplet. On the other hand, "essence" and "essential," in their derivation from the Latin infinitive "to be," remain within the vocabulary of being. They do not introduce any other notion such as "always" or "permanently" or "irreplaceably" – concepts that are not expressed in the Greek verb. Accordingly these terms allow the translation to remain strictly within the content of the verb "to be." This would seem highly desirable from the viewpoint of a literal translation that keeps "being" as the noun in the phrase.

The concern of book Epsilon with this problem is that an understanding of what the thing's essential being is, enables the philosopher to locate it under the appropriate theoretical science. Of things defined as substances, some are taken with their matter, others without the matter (6.1.1025b30–34). An instance of mathematical abstraction and concrete presence is used to illustrate the issue. Concavity is a mathematical abstraction taken just in itself. Snubness is the concavity of a nose. Defined just alone, concavity does not contain in its notion the matter or subject in which it is found in the real world. Snubness, however, does contain the subject in its very notion. Aristotle presses home the point with a number of examples from the animate and inanimate worlds (6.1.1026al–3). Even soul insofar as it actuates a body has to include the subject or matter in its definition. These considerations show how things are discussed and defined in the philosophy of nature. The matter has to be included in their notion, and with that essential presence of matter in their substantial nature they are marked as mobile

could hardly be regarded, just in itself, as the ground for demonstrating their endless duration for the future. Accordingly the imperfect sense seems to function here in lieu of a missing gnomic aorist. It envisages as holding for all time something that occurred in the past.

or changeable things. Their matter can lose its present form and take on another form. They are beings, but changeable ones.

With what is Aristotle mainly concerned in making these observations? He is looking for the principles and causes of being insofar as it is being. Being had turned out to mean stability and permanence in the full sense required by the first principle of demonstration in book Gamma. Stability and permanence were seen in the substance that underlies the changing attributes of sensible things in book Alpha (3.983b8–16). From this viewpoint the substance of sensible things could be called being qua being in book Kappa (3.106la8–10): ". . . each of them is called 'being' in view of the fact that it is an affection of being qua being, or a habit of it, or a disposition, or a motion, or something else of this sort." Likewise being, as it is seen in the categories of substance and accidents together, can be called "being itself qua being" in book Epsilon (4.1028a3–4, Apostle translations). It is here contrasted with being through accidental connection, which lacks the intrinsic stability insinuated by being, and with being as true, which implies knowledge of it by the human mind. The stability or permanence has to come from being itself, in order to be considered as characterizing being, insofar as it is being. Finally, being qua being can mean an absolutely unchangeable separate substance as the specifying object of a science that is superior to the philosophy of nature (*Metaphysics*, 6.1.1026a29–32; 11.7.1064b6–14).

Does this mean, then, that the expression "being qua being" is itself multisignificant in graded senses? Does the addition of "qua being" fail to provide escape from the original multisignificance of the notion? The posing of the question in this way would seem to reveal a covert expectation that "being," when understood simply as being, would present a univocal concept that could be related in various ways to its inferiors. In ascending the Porphyrian tree one would come to the highest pair as corporeal and incorporeal substances. "Corporeal" and "incorporeal" serve there as differentiae added to the concept of substance. But there is no genus higher than substance, no genus that could be differentiated into substance and accidents. Being is common to all the categories, and being contains its own differentiae. There is no way in which the concept of being could be smoothed out in a manner that would allow superadded differentiae to be impressed upon it. It has to be predicated of everything in its own rich though gnarled and involved character. It cannot be equated with the ordinary universal in which the same specific or generic object such as tree or living thing is seen in the same way in all its instances. It cannot be "unpacked" into univocals that are related to one another in different ways. It has to be taken always in its own intrinsic complexity.

What, then, is the character of this supergeneric object for Aristotle as it is predicated of all things whatsoever, in universal fashion? Today we are easily tempted to say that a being is anything that exists. That way of thinking has its solid background in medieval metaphysics. Finite things are not their own being. They receive their being from something else, and originally through creation by a divine cause. Their being is given them by the reception of existence. Accordingly a being is conceived as something that exists. But, as already noted, this is not an Aristotelian setting. For Aristotle being and thing are really identical, and any conceptual distinction that may be made between them is irrelevant for metaphysics. The world always existed, for him, and will continue to exist forever. Existence is no problem. Efficient causes are regarded as initiating motion, but not as bestowing existence. All things are thoroughly identical with their being. Consequently an actuation coming from outside cannot be invoked as explanation of their being, as being is conceived by Aristotle. Rather, the stability and fixity that ground for him the basic demonstrative norm, the principle of contradiction, is the context in which being is assessed and described.

In regard to the sensible world, the stability and permanence of things is explained by the category of substance. The substance of a tree remains the same, as its accidents keep changing in the long process of growth from seed to full stature. Likewise in every sensible thing the substance remains identical throughout all its accidental changes. That, then, is what makes the tree a being in our most primitive acquaintance with it. It presents it as something basically stable and enduring, something that can be regarded as remaining so in contrast to radical indeterminacy. There is no hesitation in calling it a being, when it is considered from the viewpoint of its substance. As noted earlier, some malaise might be felt in giving its color, its size, its location, its proximity to and distance from other trees the designation of "beings." Yet for Aristotle all these accidents are *onta.* Each is a being. Today no qualms need arise in saying that each accident exists, quite as in the medieval framework. But that explanation cannot be used in a context where what a thing is coincides with "that it is." Instead, the Stagirite maintains that the accidents as well as the changes and privations and negations are beings because of the order they have to substance.[10] The substance, whether of an animate or inanimate thing, is what remains stable. Only in the way they are related to that basic feature are the other objects beings. It is the substance that is white, large, located in place and time, and related to other things. Through the substance the other features have the stability and the consistency that allow them to possess the character of being. On account of this role played by substance, each sensible thing is one ordered whole, despite the multiplicity of its accidental being. It is not an episodic collection of phenomena after the manner of a bad tragedy, but a solid, stable being that is capable of variation while remaining basically the same. The accidents are beings, but are beings because of their order to substance. They are what a substance accidentally is. All this is involved in the consideration that being is not a univocal notion. It can be asserted of accidents without having it exactly identical with the role it plays in substance. Yet both sub-

10 Apostle's translation at *Metaphysics*, 4.2.1003b10, expresses this clearly by the emphasis on the "is": ". . . we even say that nonbeing is nonbeing."

stance and accidents are beings as Aristotle conceives them. The predication is very different from the way in which plants and animals are said to be living things. The generic notion of life is univocal in the material world. It is not through being a plant that an animal is sentient, or vice versa. But it is through the substance in which it inheres that an accident is a being. The notion of being, in consequence, is not a basic univocal notion that is able to be differentiated by other univocal notions such as corporeal or incorporeal, quantitative or qualitative. Those added characteristics would need to have already the firm and stable character of being in order to do the differentiating.

That is, in fact, exactly what is meant in saying that being contains all its differentiae. By intrinsically containing these differentiae the concept of being is radically barred from univocity. It is multisignificant from the start. Being as first known by the human mind is accordingly a multisignificant object, whether or not the multisignificance is formulated.

To speak of being qua being, along with "being as taken simply," does not imply that there are differentiae lying outside its meaning. Rather, "qua being" reinforces the intrinsic multisignificant character of the object. Being qua being is graded in primary and secondary instances, and being as taken simply is not a generic notion. The "qua being" serves to emphasize the stability that the notion imparts to lower instances, as with substance in regard to accidents and immobile substance in regard to mobile things. This seems perfectly normal when Aristotle's conception of being as the permanent and the stable is kept in mind. To be reasoned about and discussed and communicated in language, things must remain so. That was Aristotle's explanation of the principle of contradiction. It was seen in every object of thought and speech, with final appeal (*Metaphysics*, 4.5.1010a33–35; cf. 8.1012b30–31) to the absolutely immobile prime movent. In this way being meant stability in contrast to becoming. But its instances were graded. Permanence and stability were present in their fullness in separate substance only. Relative permanence belonged to sensible substance vis-à-vis its accidents, and change and privations and even negations took on their definite meaning from the goal intended or from the object excluded or denied, so that even the object "not being" had enough stability to serve as an object of thought and discussion (4.2.1003b6–10). In calling separate substance being, or in saying that not being is not being, the one and the same multisignificant predicate is used. The accidents are because the substance is, each of them accidentally, the privations such as blindness and negations such as not being, are in fact because the positive object to which they refer has definite and stable meaning.

This polyvalence of the notion "being" gives rise to some startling reflections. The permanence and stability that the accidents enjoy are the permanence and stability of the sensible substance. The definiteness of privations and negations is that of the positive features they exclude. The notion they express first and foremost when they are regarded as being is the being that is seen in sensible substance. That is why we experience so much discomfort in saying that a size is a being, or that a color is a being, or that a relation such as quality is a being. It is a substance that is all these things. Yet for Aristotle they are all *onta*. Each is a different nature, and their coinciding in being does not in any way make them the same nature. Still more pointed is this consideration when it is applied to change or to privations and negations. The notion of change, as in alteration, growth, locomotion, or generation and perishing, seems rather that of "becoming" as opposed to that of "being" in Greek philosophical tradition. The notion of privation, as in blindness, seems rather the not being of something such as sight. "Nothing" seems the downright denial of being. None of them can coincide in nature with "being." Yet they all are, in one way or another, for we can think about them and talk about them. But in none of them can the object's own nature coincide with the nature of being.

In the Aristotelian context this situation cannot be met with the claim that all these objects exist in some way, at least in human cognition. As has already been noted, there is in Aristotle no real distinction between a thing and its existence, and for metaphysics a conceptual distinction is not helpful. What, then, does "being" mean for him? In book Gamma it was carefully explained as stability and permanence. Things stayed so and so, in such a way that they remained the same objects while they were being thought about and reasoned about, and while knowledge about them was being communicated to others. A thing was accordingly a being if it had the stability required for an object of intellection. With that it was something.

But this stability was graded. It was seen originally in sensible substances. These substances, such as stones, trees, and animals, had their stability and relative permanence as they changed in their accidents. The accidents had a relative permanence and stability, but a stability that could not last any longer than the substances themselves. Changing had as such no stability, though in the different categories it had definiteness and specification from the object that was its goal. Privations and negations were in turn specified by some one of those definite objects they excluded. The gradation was very apparent, and very striking. The fullness of permanence and stability, however, was found nowhere in the sensible world. As a whole, that world endured eternally; but nothing within itself could account for this permanence. The source had to be looked for outside sensible things. Greek mythology, with the permanence it attributed to the divine, was at hand to offer a reason. From the beginning of the *Metaphysics*, as has been seen, this was hovering over Aristotle's mind as a way to the required solution of the problem.

Looking then at the science of metaphysics as a whole, in the way a theoretical science may be held before one's view for study in its entirety, one may readily see how Aristotle is regarding the notion of being qua being as grounded ultimately on substance that has no matter. At this stage of the parallel treatment of the topic in book Kappa (7.1064a34–36), the projected demonstration of separate and immobile substance is explicitly announced. In point of fact that type of substance is shown in book Lambda (6–7.1071b3–1072bl4) to be the principle upon which the heavens and the world of nature depend. It exercises this causality in absolutely necessary fashion, so that the effect cannot be in any way other than it is. At least two such principles are required, one to account for the uniformity of the cosmic processes, the other for the regulated variety within them (6.1072a9–18). But the exact number is to be determined on the basis of the irreducible motions observed in the heavens by the astronomers (8.1073a14–1074bl4).

The pure actuality of separate substance is in this way the absolutely stable and permanent nature that is meant by being in its full sense. It is the nature that is predicated whenever anything is called a being. But the predication is far from univocal in regard to its various instances. Separate substances are being because that is their own nature, quite as Plato, Socrates, and Parmenides are human. A material substance, on the other hand, has a perishable nature. Its nature is not the nature of being. Yet it imitates the nature of the separate substances insofar as it is able. Inanimate substances retain their form as best they can, animate substances strive for immortality through the propagation of their species. That imitation of the nature of separate substance is what is meant when they are called beings. To say that they are beings, therefore, does not mean that they are separate substances. Rather, it means that though perishable they are realizing in their own degree the continued duration that is signified by being qua being. Each relatively stable accident has its own degree of permanence, dependent upon the permanence of the substance of which it is a modification. Changes, privations, and negations have their being through the fixity of the things to which they refer. Obviously, being has a different meaning in all these instances, even though it is referring in one way or another to separate substances in all the other grades.

Nevertheless the same notion is carried through all these various instances, and is expressed by the one word "being." But it is not taken univocally. Its content is the stable and permanent nature of separate substance. Yet like a camera that automatically adjusts itself to the varying degrees of light, it adapts itself spontaneously to the ways in which being is encountered in the different things. The things that everybody immediately sees and touches are at once recognized as beings. The reason for Aristotle here is that every one of these things has enough fixity and stability in one way or another to serve as an object of thought and conversation. But fixity and stability as such belong to a nature that has no potentiality whatever for change. Yet fixity and stability can be found in varying degrees in things that are not immaterial substances. To the degree and in the way they possess the fixity, therefore, they are beings.

Aristotle's procedure here, to anyone not too well acquainted with his work, may seem like an ad-hoc invention. Yet upon more careful scrutiny it reflects faithfully the way things appeared to him. He was alert to the difficulties raised by Parmenides in regard to a monotone expression of being. He was sensitive to Plato's position in the *Parmenides* about the requirement of stable forms for reasoning and discourse. He himself could see stable natures known universally, in a plurality of sensible things. That was sufficient to allow things to be regarded as beings, in the meaning necessary for thought and communication. But obviously they did not all have that stability in the same way. They had it in graded fashion. Yet they were all objects of thought, and from the viewpoint of that fixity in meaning they all came under the notion of being. The notion was a single one, yet it was multisignificant. To predicate it on a plurality of instances did not mean that all these instances had the same nature, as in the case of univocal predication. To say that substances and qualities and sizes and relations were beings, did not imply that all these objects had the same kind of being. It did not at all mean that they were all separate substances, even though separate substance was the instance in which being was found as a nature. That was the way things were, as Aristotle saw them, and his conception of focal meaning merely reflected that situation.

Aristotle had no hesitation in seeing a like situation in other predicates. "Healthy" was intrinsic to the disposition of a bodily organism, "medical" to a practitioner's art. All other instances were healthy or medical through relation to those primary instances. To say that cooked food was healthy did not mean that it had a living organic disposition, nor did the claim that a cure was medical identify it with the art in the mind of a human person. Though the word was the same and the notion was in this way the same, the things themselves were in each case of different natures. Correspondingly, the fact that a tree was a being and that a color was a being did not mean that the two had the same concept that readily adjusted itself each time to the particular reality it faced. Reality had fixed status in that way, and that was the way it was known by the human mind. Here the Aristotelian thinking is entirely straightforward. It is not erecting any artificial ad hoc framework in order to account for the difficulties inherent in the notion of being.

The claim that a thing and its being are really the same, and that its beingness and whatness are grasped by the same act of intellection, does not run counter to this conception of multisignificance. A thing is a being because it has enough fixity and stability in one way or another to enable it to confront the intellect. No differentia is added to what it is in order to allow it to appear as a being. The added observation that the making of a conceptual distinction between thing and being is less advantageous for metaphysics follows from the awareness of the temptation to keep ascending by route of ever widening genera that are divided by specific differentiae. On arriving at the supergeneric notion of being, no differentiae outside it are found. It itself has to effect all its own differentiations. The fixity inherent in material objects is their being. But the notion of stability as a nature is found only in the separate forms. Other things present that notion through the different ways in which they are related to supersensible substance. The nature expressed when other things are regarded as beings is accordingly the nature of separate substance, whether or not the individual human thinker realizes this when she or he is calling them beings. No added differentia is seen in the thing. Rather, the thing's own nature is seen as relatively something fixed. In this way it is implicitly grasped as related in one way or another to separate substance. Metaphysics makes this explicit by showing how the nature of being is the nature of separate substance, quite as the healthiness in a cooked vegetable is the healthiness of the one who eats it and not a disposition of the cooked vegetable itself. To say that the cooked vegetable is healthy means that it is the cause of health in a living body. Correspondingly in Aristotle to say that a material thing is a being means that it has a consistency and a permanence that are derived from dependence upon separate substance as the goal to which it is ordered. That may seem like making a conceptual distinction between its own nature and its relation to another nature. But that relation is identical with the nature itself, and is not something added by way of a differentia. Lack of attention to a conceptual distinction of that kind is in consequence an advantage in the approach to metaphysics, since it sidesteps the temptation to look upon being as differentiated by outside characteristics after the fashion of a genus. That seems to be the Stagirite's viewpoint here.

This general background of Aristotle's approach to the problem of being allows him to see being as a predicate of everything whatever, and yet to remain a nature that is found as a nature in the separate substances only. The nature of separate substance can in this way specify the scientific study of all things under their aspect of being, without at all meaning that every being is a separate and immobile substance. In its own nature being is separate substance, but it is not predicated of anything else univocally. It is predicated of other things by relation to that primary instance. To say that an accident or a privation *is* a being is not to mean that it is a separate substance. Nor does it mean that being has to be known first in its own nature before it can be predicated of anything else. Rather, the being that is first known in sensible objects is what provides the means for reasoning to the separate substances. In fact, if separate being were the immediate object of the human intellect after the fashion of the ontologists, no metaphysics would be possible. The knower would be identical with the object known and as a separate substance would not be able to extend the knowledge to anything else. Immediate knowledge of separate substance is definitely excluded by the Aristotelian conception of the science of being qua being. Metaphysics has to take its origin from sensible things.

* * * * * * * * * *

Against that deep Aristotelian background the text of the concluding section of Epsilon's first chapter may now be approached. The philosophy of nature deals with things that are not separate from matter. Having in their nature matter, which is the principle of change from one form to another, these things are essentially mobile. Natural philosophy may accordingly be regarded as a theoretical science that treats of things that are both material and changeable. Mathematics, also a theoretical science, deals at least in some of its branches with objects that are taken as immobile and separate from sensible matter (*Metaphysics*, 6.1.1025b34–1026a10). No explanation of this mathematical immobility and separation is given here, but other places in Aristotle show how he can say it is evident. Mathematics takes quantitative objects, such as points, lines, surfaces, geometrical solids, and discrete numbers in abstraction from the sensible qualities of the substances in which they are inherent, and treats of them in this way as though they were separate and immobile objects.[11]

So far Aristotle seems to experience little trouble with his Platonically trained audience. He could take for granted that they acquiesced in mathematical objects of that kind. But with regard to things higher than the mathematical order, his approach is more cautious: "Now if there is something eternal and immobile and separate, knowledge about it evidently pertains to theoretical science, yet not indeed to natural science (for natural science is about certain mobile things) nor to mathematics, but to a science prior to both" (6.1.1026a10–13). Aristotle is clear in asserting that the object of this higher science is meant to be outside the cognitive activity of the human knower, for it is projected as something eternal that is already there to be contemplated. It will be the object of a theoretical science, therefore, just as is the case with the philosophy of nature and with mathematics. The notion of "eternal" recalls the introduction of the science in book Alpha (2.982b28–983a10) as a science of the divine, in the context of mythology and religious belief. To this is added the philosophical descriptions of immobile and separate. The object of the science is placed above the fleeting world of mortals and above the notion of something that has to be taken together with its matter. Accordingly it is an object that is divine, incorporeal, and unchangeable.

The text in Epsilon then goes on to say that "all the causes have to be eternal, but these most of all; for they are causes of the observable instances of things divine" (6.1026al6–18). Knowledge of cause had been equated with knowledge of the universal in the passage of book Alpha (1.981al5–30). The ordinary universal was a stable and permanent object in all its instances. Knowledge of it was in consequence the awareness of an object that transcended time. To that extent the object was eternal. Highest of all in the scale of causality, however, were the causes that kept the heavenly bodies in eternal motion. For that reason they were eternal in the highest degree. Transcendence of time, the hallmark of the divine in contrast to the mortal, was in this way placed in the general context of universality. The implication would be that as scientific knowledge is knowledge in terms

11 See Hippocrates G. Apostle, *Aristotle's Philosophy of Mathematics*, (Chicago: University of Chicago Press, 1952), 1–17; 131–134.

of the universal, knowledge about the divine causes would be the most universal knowledge of all. That conclusion is presumed to follow, as the text proceeds to show that if the divine is to be found anywhere it is to be seen in the nature of separate and immobile substance, and that the most honored type of philosophy should be about the most honored genus of things. Even the wording suggests here that a contrast is felt between an object that is a particular genus of being, and the notion of a science that has the highest type of universality.

This latter point, however, is reserved for treatment in an *aporia*. The conclusion immediately drawn is that there are three kinds of theoretical philosophy, namely mathematical, natural, and theological. The designation "theological" follows obviously enough from the way the object of the science has just been equated with the divine.[12] It was insinuated pointedly enough in Aristotle's remarks in the opening chapters of book Alpha. But now it is explained philosophically in terms of separate and immobile substance. However, only here and in the parallel section of book Kappa is the science explicitly called "theological." It is not named "theology." In Aristotle, the term *theologia* (*Meteorologica*, 2.1.353a35) does occur, but in the meaning of the Greek mythologies. Similarly "theologians" (*Metaphysics*, 3.4.1000a9; 12.4.1071b27; 10.1075b26; 14.4.109la34) is used for the mythologists. Explicit testimonials on the reasons why the designation "theological" did not endure are lacking. Aristotle's specific designation in the present passage was "the primary philosophy," because it was specified by the primary instance of being. The title that became established in Peripatetic tradition was "metaphysics," a designation that has been traced back to as early as the third century B.C., but which is not found in Aristotle's own writings. It remains to this day the commonly accepted title for the science.[13]

In the wording of book Epsilon (1.1026a23) the *aporia* is introduced with the causal connective *gar*. The reason implied seems to be the difficulty involved in regarding the divine both as the highest type of being and at the same time as the most universal object of all. This objection would arise spontaneously when the object of the science was envisaged as residing in a specific nature (*phusei*, a20) and as constituting a definite genus (*genos*, a2l). In that regard the insistence on the character of the object as divine and most exalted called for justification. The insistence was necessary because somebody could raise the objection that this explanation did not show clearly whether the science in question is universal in

12 On the theological aspect of preceding Greek philosophy, see Werner W. Jaeger, *The Theology of the Early Greek Philosophers* (Oxford: Clarendon Press, 1947).

13 On the third century B.C. origin of this title, see Hans Reiner, "Die Entstehung und ursprüngliche Bedeutung des Namens Metaphysik," *Zeitschrift für philosophische Forschung*, VIII (1954), 235, and "Die Entstehung der Lehre vom bibliothekarischen Ursprung des Namens Metaphysik," *Ibid.*, IX (1955), 77–99. The hypothesis that the title is editorial dates only from Johann G. Buhley in a paper published in 1788. But there is not enough evidence to assign the coining of the term to any particular Peripatetic of the third century B.C., though Reiner suggests Eudemus of Rhodes.

its sweep or whether it is "about a particular genus and one particular nature" (a24–25). The alternatives were stated by Aristotle himself as sharply and as concisely as they were by Natorp and Jaeger in the modern era. The solution was based upon the primary status just accorded the science that dealt with separate and immobile substance. Its object thereby was the highest type of being, the type that specified the science of being qua being in book Gamma (2.1003bl6–17) and was the object upon which the other instances depended and through which they were called beings. Likewise in book Alpha elatton (1.993b24–31) the other instances had being and truth through causal dependence upon the eternal principles that had being in its supreme degree. So in describing the science as the "primary philosophy" in this present text of book Epsilon, Aristotle is locating its universality in the primary status of its object, separate substance. He thereby gives the answer to the suggested question about why he had insisted so strongly upon the divine character of its specifying object, the character that assured its primacy and thereby its universal coverage.

In the parallel passage in book Kappa (7.1064b6), however, the connecting particle is *de* giving the adversative sense of "but" or "now." That means it is understood as an objection to what has just been said, instead of the positive reason why the preceding statement had been made. If Kappa is taken as a later compendium of the contents of books Beta, Gamma, and Epsilon, made after those books had been established in their present order, it is not hard to see that in the interval a familiarity with the main philosophical problem here involved may have taken attention away from the sequence in which the thought had originally developed, and focused attention on the doctrinal issue only. Then the *aporia* would be understood as voicing a possible objection to the doctrine itself, instead of giving the reason for Aristotle's insistence on the function of the divine in explaining the object of metaphysics. The textual tradition seems firm for both passages, with no sufficient reason for rejecting either. If the situation has to be explained by the hypothesis of a very early emendation, the more difficult of the two readings would be that of Epsilon. In consequence it would have the preference for being retained. The more customary role of an *aporia* as an objection against a preceding doctrine, rather than as giving the cause for a statement that had just been made, would have occasioned the change. Yet the richer meaning of Epsilon's reading in showing the development of Aristotle's thought upon the issue would be an added incentive to allow its reading to stand as it is.

In any case, the philosophical doctrine itself is clear. After a parenthetical remark that even in the mathematical sciences there cannot be the same type of treatment in particular branches and in a science covering mathematical objects universally, book Epsilon (1.1026a25–27) proceeds to explain how the case is different with the primary philosophy. The difference between the two kinds of treatment in mathematics is given as a reason why one might expect a parallel distinction on other levels of scientific knowledge. A mathematical model, the inference seems to be, cannot be adopted here. A universal mathematics does not offer any primary nature that would be the cause of the quantitative aspects in all other things. If then there is no other substance besides those constituted by nature, that is, those composed of matter and form, the philosophy of nature will be primary science. No reason is given in the text for this assertion. Implicit seems to be the consideration that the philosophy of nature treats of sensible things from the viewpoint of their substantial principles, matter and form, and that substance is primary in regard to all the accidents, including quantity by which the mathematical sciences are specified. Quantitative principles cannot give a science a higher ranking than do substantial ones, despite the way in which matter as a substantial principle leaves the sensible thing a mobile being. But if there is immobile substance, the philosophy just listed (6.1.1026a23) as the most desirable of the theoretical sciences will be prior to natural philosophy and will be primary philosophy. It will also be universal by reason of this primary status, and will thereby have the task of dealing theoretically with being qua being, both with its nature and with the attributes that belong to it, qua being. The presentation of the doctrine in book Kappa follows the same line of thought, expressly calling the separate and immobile substance a nature (*phusis*, 7.1064b11), and saying that the science dealing with it is prior to natural philosophy and universal in virtue of that priority (b13–14).

There need not be the least doubt that in these passages the supergeneric universality of being rests upon the priority of separate substance in regard to all other instances of being. When anything whatever is called a being, the notion predicated of it will thereby be the nature of separate substance. But the secondary instance is not thereby identified even generically with the nature of separate substance, as already noted. The predication of being involves only the relation the thing has to that primary nature. Every nature, insofar as it can be thought about and spoken about, exhibits the stability and consistency that give it its relation to separate substance. The relation is not something superadded as an accident over and above the thing's own nature. That would leave only a union of two univocal notions. Rather, a sensible nature just in itself has the stability to make it what it is, and thereby to exhibit in itself the feature that is present as a nature in separate substance only. In this way the concept of being, when taken simply, is not a univocal concept, but is multisignificant according to the various degrees and manners in which it is realized in things. But it remains the one concept, and refers to one and the same nature just as "healthy" and "medical" are single notions referring in each case to an identical nature. In corresponding fashion the being of the separate substances is the nature referred to in every predication of being. That is what is meant by Aristotle's stand that the science specified by separate substance is the science that treats universally of all beings.

Quite obviously, this involves two different patterns for universality in Aristotle. We are naturally tempted to ask why he did not state plainly that this was the case. The Greek commentators accepted the situation as one in which a primary instance could be called universal on account of the causal influence it exercised upon all the others. Pseudo–Alexander explicitly contrasted the two types of universality, one by being predicated of many things, the other by dependence upon a common source. He suggested that people are accustomed to call the latter type universal, and that Aristotle was just following that custom.[14] It is hard to find any basis for this conjecture. The term "universal" was new with Aristotle. There is no evidence that a tradition of its use for denominating things from a common cause had existed. There is no entry for the term in book Delta of the *Metaphysics*, though the notion is treated as one of the ways in which a "whole" can be had (26.1023b29–32). In book Delta Aristotle was concerned with philosophical terms already in common circulation rather than with any of his own coinage. The lack of a deliberate confrontation of the two kinds of universality with each other, therefore, need not be too surprising.

Universality by way of reference to a primary nature, in fact, fitted neatly enough under book Delta's conception of universality in general. Each of the instances was severally "being" or "healthy" or "medical." Further, quite as the predication of "man" in the case of Socrates and Plato did not identify the one individual with the other, so predication through reference to a primary instance did not identity any of the secondary instances with the primary instance, which was the nature in question. The instances, including the primary one, were that nature only severally, one by one in turn. So "healthy" predicated of exercise or of nutritious food, did not make the nature of either be the nature of the quality in the living organism. Correspondingly, when "being" was predicated through reference to the nature of separate substance, it did not make any of its secondary instances a separate substance. "Being" pertained to all its instances only severally, one by one. The difference was in the type of concept respectively involved in the two ways of being universal. Where the notion was univocal, as in "tree" or "dog," the same plant or animal nature was found uniformly in all the instances. But where the notion adapted itself spontaneously to different natures on account of their reference to another and primary nature, the nature of each remained what it was. The notion itself was multisignificant in bearing. That was the way things were in reality, as Aristotle saw them. He was not deducing this explanation *a priori* from some primitively known idea of being. For him the things themselves were that way and had inherently that order of primary and secondary instances. In that way they were known by the human mind.

In that multisignificant way, then, being is a nature. It is repeatedly called by

14 See Alexander of Aphrodisias, *In Aristotelis Metaphysica Commentaria*, ed. Michael Hayduck (Berlin: Reimer, 1891), I^2, 1.661.36–39. The Aristotelian *katholou* applied to all the instances in a group. There does not seem to be anything to indicate that it was applied first to the generic universality, and only later to the supergeneric type.

Aristotle a nature (*phusis*) that is identical with separate substance. Yet because of the multisignificance it does not identify the natures of its secondary instances with the primary instance when it is predicated of them. It allows the secondary instances to be understood as beings because of the reference their own natures have to the nature of the primary instance. It is a reference that their natures have inherently, and that is implicitly known when they are first encountered by the human mind as stable objects for thought and discussion. But explicit acquaintance with the reason why they are beings comes about only after prolonged metaphysical study and reasoning.

These rather intricate considerations have been necessary in order to cope with the difficulties that still arise in regard to Aristotle's way of locating the specifying object of metaphysics. His explanation still gives the impression to some readers that his doctrine does not allow metaphysics to begin with the being first known in sensible substance. A careful understanding of being as a multisignificant object is therefore required in order to see how the study of its secondary instances can lead to knowledge of its primary instance. From the start that object is genuinely being, and does not demand prior knowledge of separate substance in order to be known as being. All it requires is sufficient stability to function as an object of intellectual consideration. The way is thereby open to reasoning to the first cause of the stability. Immediate knowledge of being in its own nature as in separate substance would be a suicidal conception of metaphysics for Aristotle, since its own intrinsic perfection would exclude knowledge of any other instance of being.[15] The multisignificance of the notion of being allows the primary instance to specify the science that deals with it, and at the same time enables the science to have its starting point in secondary instances. The alleged confusion here arises from attempts at projecting the being of separate substance and the being of sensible substance after the fashion of univocal notions realized in the same way in all their instances, instead of as a single multisignificant object of consideration. The foregoing observations are necessary for meeting the charges that separate substance as the nature of being would make every instance of it a separate substance, and would not allow metaphysics to begin its reasoning from sensible things. Understood correctly, however, Aristotle is fully consistent in maintaining that the science of a particular nature, separate substance, is universally the science of being qua being. Definitely "separate substance" is not thereby predicated of secondary instances when they are called beings.

The way the multisignificance of the notion of being functions may be more clearly seen if our original knowledge of it is kept in mind. Our intellect first grasps being in sensible things. Each thing in the sensible world presents itself with a fixity of meaning that makes it known as a being. But it does not present

15 See *Metaphysics*, 12.9.1074b18–35, for the reasons why an Aristotelian separate substance cannot know anything outside itself.

itself at all as a separate substance. The two notions, accordingly, are not exactly the same. The original notion adapts itself easily enough to accidents, changes, privations, negations, and finally in metaphysics to separate substances. The notion is simple, yet adaptable. That inherent adaptability is what distinguishes a multisignificant notion from the univocal type of concepts. The concepts of the natures of the various instances of being are univocal. Even the notion of "separate substance" is formed as a univocal concept. The univocal concepts such as "tree" or "horse" arise from our seeing an identical nature in a number of different instances. We do not see immediately any instances whatever of separate substances. We do not have the means of immediately grasping a universal in their regard. We take our notion of substance, seen univocally in sensible substances as a universal, and apply it to supersensible things through negation of the differentia "sensible." How the separate substances are differentiated from each other escapes our knowledge. But "separate substance" is a nature (*phusin tina mian*, 6.1.1026a25) and is characterized by Aristotle as a genus (a24–25). "Being," on the other hand, is supergeneric and multisignificant. The predication of the one concept, in consequence, is not the predication of the other. A sensible substance or accident is a being, but it is not a separate form. The two notions are different – the one multisignificant and other univocal – in our conception of separate form through our denial of the differentia "sensible" in the generic notion of substance.[16]

From these considerations one may also see why Aristotle can say that a thing and its being are really identical, and that it is more advantageous in metaphysical treatment not to make even a conceptual distinction between them. A thing's being is the inherent fixity of its nature, no different from the nature itself; and known by the same act of intellection (6.1.1025bl7–18) in the original grasp of the thing by the human mind. The nature of being itself can then be shown through metaphysical reasoning to be located in separate substance only. Distinguished in this way from being that is identical with sensible things, it is a univocal notion of something different from the natures of those things. It is no longer regarded as the multisignificant object universally common to all things sensible as well as separate. The use of distinct univocal concepts for the natures of substance and accidents and for the natures of sensible and supersensible things hinders the intellect's grasp of being as a multisignificant object found primarily in separate substance as a nature, yet in lesser degrees in all other things. The required inclusion of them all in the one multisignificant concept of being is therefore furthered by not insisting upon a conceptual distinction between being and thing in sensible objects. The "nature of being" always means separate sub-

16 A survey and critical discussion of the evidence concerning Aristotle's alleged changes in his treatment of words with focal meaning and with analogy may be found in Walter Leszl, *Logic and Metaphysics in Aristotle* (Padua: Editrice Antenore 1970), 329–372.

stance, and we conceive "substance" as a category. "Being" means, in contrast, either separate substance as the primary instance, or else as a secondary instance any other object that by reason of its fixity has a relation of one kind or another to that primary instance. If one wishes to call that contrast a conceptual distinction, there is no intrinsic ground for objecting. But it conjures up the model of two distinct univocal notions, such as in the case of "body" and "animate." In Aristotle it gave occasion for facing the *aporia* that a science specified by a particular nature could not be the universal science of being qua being. Today it still makes critics see an impossibility in the Aristotelian stand that metaphysics in treating universally of all beings is the science of separate substance. In a word, conceptual distinction between being and thing in Aristotle should not be insisted upon unless his notion of multisignificance has first been carefully explained. Apart from that explanation, it is more advantageous in metaphysics not to speak of a conceptual distinction between a thing and its being.

All this, of course, arises from the Greek conception of being as the stable and permanent in contrast to becoming and changing. There the notion of being is that of having existence, the situation is different. A being is that which exists. In the Judeo Christian and Islamic perspectives, the existence of finite things had to be received from something else, and ultimately from a first efficient cause. In this way existence was different from the nature of any finite thing. Existence was a nature in the first efficient cause alone. It was outside the nature of any finite thing, and when received by the thing it remained distinct from it. For Aquinas the distinction was real. The existence of things was known through judgment, while their natures were known through conceptualization. The result was that existence, even as subsistent in God, could not specify a human science. Existence was not known in the manner of a nature, even though it was a nature in its primary instance. In saying that metaphysics was the science of common being, or of being qua being, one was not saying that it had God as its specifying object. The specifying object had to include all else.[17]

Yet in spite of this vast difference between the two conceptions of metaphysics, Aristotelian principles and methods find a surprisingly exact application in Aquinas. Both start their metaphysical reasoning from sensible things known through cognitional identity with the knower and grasped in cognitional priority as things existent in themselves. Both reason in terms of actuality and potentiality to being as a subsistent nature, that is, to pure actuality. But for Aquinas pure actuality is existence subsistent in itself and unlimited by any finite form. It is unique and omnipotent, a creator, knowing and provident in regard to every detail

17 See Prologue to St. Thomas Aquinas, *Commentary on the Metaphysics of Aristotle*, trans. John P. Rowan (Chicago: Henry Regnery, 1961; South Bend, Ind.: Dumb Ox Books). I, 2. On the application to it of the Heideggerian designation *ontotheologisch*, see Hermann Weidemann, *Metaphysik und Sprache* (Munich: Alber, 1975), 38–39, 176–169.

in creatures, and capable of all the love and care revealed in the sacred Scriptures. For Aristotle, in contrast, pure actuality is finite form, open to plurality, closed in itself in its cognition, incapable of creation or providence or interest in anything outside itself. The potentiality that it excludes by being purely actual is matter, while for Aquinas the potentiality excluded is that of any finite nature or essence whatever.

Yet despite these shattering contrasts, the Aristotelian metaphysics can serve in admirable fashion the philosophical understanding of the revealed truths as undertaken by the medieval thinkers. When the Aristotelian procedure is transposed into an existential key, the steps follow in the same order but produce a radically different experience. They lead to pure actuality in each case, but actuality of a very different kind. In the one case the actuality is form, in the other case it is existence. The same score is being read, but the notes have a different resonance. Aristotle's highest conception of being qua actual, namely separate substance, would still be something potential for Aquinas. It would still be in potentiality to its existence. Aristotle's glowing and enthusiastic description of the life of separate substance in Book Lambda can well be carried over into the thought of Aquinas, but its quiet exultation would be transformed into the existential rapture of beholding subsistent existence.

If you ask what accounts for the profound difference between these two ways of metaphysical procedure in parallel steps from the same external sensible things as starting points, the answer is to be found in book Epsilon's first chapter. For Aristotle, what a thing is and that it is are known by the same type of intellection, while for Aquinas the one is known through conceptualization, the other through judgment. For Aristotle, the composition found in sensible things is the composition of form with matter, either on the substantial or the accidental level. For Aquinas it is also – and in the context of metaphysics, principally – the composition of existence with thing. Thirdly, for Aristotle the nature of being is seen in separate form. For Aquinas the nature of being is located in subsistent existence, unique and infinite.

Aristotle's stand on these three items is what locks his metaphysical procedure into the course it takes in his treatises. It is the keystone that holds the rest of the structure in place and gives it its logical sequence and consistency. It makes the procedure distinctively Aristotelian, in contrast to the Neoplatonic and Scholastic uses of this philosophy in the development of their own characteristic doctrines. A close understanding of it enables the reader to appreciate the depth and versatility of the Stagirite's thought, and at the same time to see how Aristotelian metaphysics can be always used for inspiration and guidance in one's own personal thinking. It brings one into direct contact with reality, and allows reality itself to beckon one on to new thought and to original philosophy. The two bases of the arch will remain sensible things and divine being. Yet the keystone that holds the different parts of the reasoning together will vary with one's historical approach, in full accord with post modern hermeneutical norms. But our debt to Arisotle will be unmistakeable, as it is with Plotinus and St. Thomas. Acquaintance with the tenets of the first chapter of book Epsilon will explain the reason why.

This painstaking and undoubtedly wearisome discussion of Aristotle's overall conception of universality has been necessary for a correct understanding of the closing paragraph of Epsilon's first chapter. What is at stake is Aristotle's projection of the primary philosophy as truly a science. Modern commentators have been exasperated at the way in that paragraph the primary instance of being is regarded as both universal and particular. The primary instance is located in a particular nature of a definite kind, namely separate substance. Yet that particular and definite nature is made the universal nature of being qua being. Hence many able writers dismiss this closing paragraph of Epsilon's first chapter as expressing a glaring contradiction, while others see in it an amalgam of clashing opinions successively adapted by Aristotle in different chronological periods of his development.

The impasse arises, one may readily see, from the radically different views of universality that are found respectively in Aristotle and in modern linguistic analysis. The differences require careful and incisive explanation at the approach to the relevant chapter in book Epsilon. In modern logical analysis a universal applies in strictly equal fashion to each of its instances. It does not admit graded understanding for its various occurrences. For Aristotle, on the contrary, a notion that is truly universal may apply to its instances loosely and for the most part, as it does in the practical sciences. Further, and most importantly in the present context, the universal object may for Aristotle be found in its own nature solely in the primary instance, while it is truly shared by all the other instances in secondary fashion and in graded meaning. This profound difference in the acceptance of universality has made the foregoing detailed study imperative for understanding Epsilon's conception of the primary philosophy as truly a science and as the highest of the sciences.

Part Two (Book Zeta): Microscopic Investigation

Z I (English Translation)

1028a10 Being is predicated in a number of senses, as we determined earlier in
our treatise on multiple significations; for it means, on the one hand,
"*what* is" or a "this," and on the other hand quantity, or quality, or any
one of the rest of things predicated in that way. But while being is pred-
icated in this variety of senses, it is clear that among them "*what* is,"
a15 which means *ousia*, / is primary. For when we say what kind of thing
this thing is, we say that it is either good or bad, but not that it is three
cubits long or that it is a person. But when we say *what* it is, we do not
say white or warm or three cubits long, but a person or god. The other
predicates are said to be because some are quantifying characteristics
of what is in this latter way, others are its qualities, others its affections,
a20 others something else of like / sort. For that reason one might even
bring up a difficulty about whether wa1king or being healthy or sitting
is each of them a being or not a being, and likewise in the case of any
one of the other predicates of similar type; for none of them is either
self-subsistent or able to be separated from the *ousia*, but rather, if any-
a25 thing, what is walking and what is sitting and what / is healthy belong
among beings. These latter, rather, are seen to have being for the rea-
son that there in something, their definite substrate (this is the *ousia* or
singular thing) that is seen within that kind of predicate; for "good"
and "sitting" are not predicated without it. It is clear, then, that through
a30 / this predicate each also of those others *is*, so that what primarily *is*,
and not just is in some way but absolutely *is*, will have to be *ousia*.

"Primary," indeed, is predicated in a number of senses.
Nevertheless *ousia* is altogether primary, in notion and in knowledge
and in times for no one of the other predicates is separate, but it alone
a35 is; and in notion this / one is primary (for necessarily the notion of
ousia is present within the notion of each); and we think that we then
know each thing best when we understand *what* a person or *what* fire
is, rather than its quantity or its quality or its whereabouts, for even of
1028b1 these latter we know each one when / we understand *what* quantity is
or *what* quality is. And indeed the problem under inquiry of old as well
as now and always, and always facing difficulty – the problem what

being is – is this, what *ousia* is (for some say that this [being] is one,
others that it is more than one, with some saying / that the things are b5
limited, others unlimited). Consequently for us also the greatest and primary and so to say the only task is to investigate what being in this sense is.

1 For the excision of this parenthesis, see note in Jaeger's text.

2 Cf. *Metaphysics* 4.2.1004a6–9.

Chapter 5

Ousia

The topic of book Zeta is referred to elsewhere in the Aristotelian Metaphysics as *ousia*.[1] Following upon the macrocosmic overview of the range and nature of being that was given in books Gamma and Epsilon, book Zeta sets its lens on the substance of sensible things, the humble things from which the whole metaphysical inquiry started. The being that was immediately encountered in these sensible objects, substantial and accidental, led to the positing of supersensible substance and to a science that dealt with it. On Aristotle's premises of the real identity of the thing with its being, and of the eternity of the cosmic processes, this way to separate substance as the specifying object of the universal science of being qua being followed in strictly logical sequence. The jump to separate substance, though, was made here prior to any careful investigation of the internal constitution of sensible substance from the viewpoint of its being. The jump, apparently, could be made without hindrance at this stage.

The result, however, is none too satisfactory for visualizing mentally the way the being of separate substance can function as the being that is predicated universally of all other instances of things that are. The nature of being was the nature of the separate substances. There was no intrinsic distinction between the two objects. Yet "being" was predicated of all the secondary instances, while "separate substance" was predicated of none of them. None of them was a separate substance, though all of them were beings. "Separate substance," moreover, was used like a univocal concept, while "being" was multisignificant.[2] If being and thing were as identical with each other as Aristotle claims they are, how could the nature of separate substance be predicated only of supersensible beings, while their being was predicated in varying ways of all other things?

Aristotle had used the examples of "healthy" and "medical" to show how in

1 See *Metaphysics*, 9.1.1045b27–32. The topic was sketched rapidly in the second chapter of book Gamma, but the reference here seems to bear on the more extensive treatment given it throughout book Zeta.

2 On "focal reference" as the most convenient phrase for designating this multisignificance, see G. E. L. Owen's paper cited supra, ch. 4, n. 18.

fact the nature predicated could be found only in a primary instance, while the natures of the secondary instances were different natures. The predication was made solely on the basis of the various relations the secondary instances had to the nature of the primary instance. That was the way the things were in reality, and that was the way the predication was in fact made. The case seemed as simple as that.

There is, nevertheless, an annoying difference between the illustrations of "healthy" and "medical" on the one hand, and on the other hand the situation they are asked to explain in regard to "being." The way in which the secondary instances of "healthy" are related to the healthy disposition of a bodily organism are readily apparent. You can see right away that nutritious food causes it, that exercise preserves it, that color is a sign of it. Similarly the way the secondary instances of "medical" function in the practice of medical art can easily be seen. But how the secondary instances of being are related to the separate substances is not at all so evident. When "being" is understood in the ancient Greek philosophical manner of remaining so and so, the reference to separate substance is by no means apparent. One can see how the stability of the universe as a whole is caused by the way it is held together by separate substance as the final cause of all cosmic motion. But how that is brought into the predication when one says that a tree or a stone is a being, is difficult to grasp. The ordinary person, in making that predication, does not have separate substance in mind in the way one is thinking of human health when making the assertion that cooked spinach is healthy. In the two Aristotelian illustrations you know what the primary instance is, before you relate the secondary instances to it. But in the Aristotelian explanation of beings the primary instance – separate substance – need not at all be known by people who have no hesitation in saying that plants and animals and humans are beings.[3] It is difficult to see how a stick or a stone or a size or a quality or a relation is so and so because of some reference it has to separate substance.

Real difficulty, then, is encountered in the effort to see how the secondary instances of being are related to separate substance in such a way that when you are calling them beings you are making the predication in virtue of their reference to that primary instance. How, one may ask, does the multisignificant notion of being adapt itself to the ordinary things of the sensible universe when in its own nature it signifies the being of separate substance? How is there any inherent reference of sensible things to separate substance in our everyday predication of

3 "Being" is described by the OED. 2nd ed., s.v., 4A, as "the widest term applicable to all objects of sense or thought, material or immaterial." This would mean that it is understood as anything that can be perceived, imagined, or thought of. Liddell and Scott, *Greek English Lexicon*, s.v. *onta*, phrases the meaning as "the things which actually exist," as though the Greeks in fact conceived beings in reference to existence. But for Aristotle "that a thing is" was identical with "what it is."

being in regard to the things around us, and how does it function in allowing us to say that a tree is a being or that a stone is a being?

Those are the questions we might ask when we turn our attention to the way sensible substance, known immediately in our intellectual cognition, functions in regard to the color and size and relations to which it gives being. An understanding of this role may be of help to us in probing the manner in which secondary instances of being are brought into reference to their absolutely primary instance. At least Aristotle explicitly states early in book Zeta that we have to examine "whether there is any separate substance besides the sensible ones, and why it is and how it is, or whether there is none, having first sketched in outline what substance is" (2.1028b30–32). Sensible substances are regarded as obvious for that outline. Upon their composition, accordingly, the philosophical lens is focused in microscopic scrutiny.

Referring back to Delta, book Zeta commences with the assertion that being is multisignificant. The reason is that sometimes being means what a thing is, in the sense of a "this" (*tode ti*). The meaning of "what" in this sentence is restricted by the explicative *kai* in the Greek to the first of the Aristotelian categories, namely *ousia*. The reason, quite obviously, is that this opening chapter of Zeta will go on to show that one must also know what each of the other categories is (1.1028bl–2). Later (4.1030al7–27) the notion of "what a thing is" will be shown to apply primarily to the first category, and in secondary fashion to the other categories and even to not being, quite as the predication of being had been explained in book Gamma (2.1003b5–10). Zeta (1.1028a13–31) goes on to emphasize this gradated order for being. Under the accidents such as color and size, it explains, lies something that is bounded off (*orismenon*, a27), there in itself, and separate from any sustaining subject. Quite as one comes to the end of one's property on reaching the fence that bounds it off, the passage seems to imply, so the sensible thing's substance is something bounded off and definite. In this basic sense of being, what the thing is is a tree, a horse, a human person. It is an individual thing, in the full meaning of that expression. That is what is usually intended when one asserts that something sensible is a being.

This way of leading to substance may at first hearing sound suspiciously like Locke's caricature of the sensible world supported by a great elephant, the elephant by a broad backed tortoise, and the tortoise by something one knows not what.[4] Aristotle is speaking here as though one first knows the color, size, shape, and other such characteristics of a sensible thing, and then looks for something else underneath them all and supporting them, something that one does not immediately see or feel but merely infers. This mysterious something would then be

4 John Locke, *An Essay Concerning Human Understanding*, 2.23.2, ed. Peter H. Nidditch (Oxford: Clarendon Press, 1975), 295–296.

postulated as requiring nothing else to support it. That is the way the situation would appear to anyone viewing the situation in this passage through Lockean eyes. Yet a bit of close attention to the Aristotelian text is sufficient to dispel that misunderstanding. The text explicitly states that the substance "manifests itself" (1.1028a28) within the notion of the accident that is predicated. You could not be aware of the accident without thereby being immediately aware of the substance in which it inheres. You could not know the accident "white" without knowing immediately a thing that was white. The very notion of an accident would be impossible without including the notion of a substance in which it inhered.[5] The notion of just "seated" contains the notion of someone who is sitting down. An accident could not be thought of or spoken about apart from the substance that sustains it.[6]

All this is philosophically poles apart from the manner in which substance and accident have been usually understood in modern philosophy from the time of Locke on. Yet for understanding Aristotle's account of *ousia* the difference between the two radically different approaches is crucial. For Locke what is known directly and immediately will be the primary actualities, such as size and shape and hardness. In his approach, as in the general Cartesian context, the immediate object of human cognition is placed in human ideas. From one's own ideas one has to reason to the nature and existence of sensible things. There is no immediate cognitive grasp of a sensible thing in itself. For Aristotle, on the con-

5 Aristotle (*Metaphysics*, 7.1.1028a35–36) emphasizes this priority of substance to accident in saying that the notion (*logos*) of substance has to be contained within the notion of an accident.

6 On the difficulties here, see W. D. Ross, *Aristotle's Metaphysics* (Oxford: Oxford University Press, 1948), II. 160–161. The difficulties become greater when approached in terms of whether or not a strict definition in today's sense is demanded, namely "whether an actual definition or whether a simple reference to (the) substance would suffice" – *Notes on Book Zeta of Aristotle's Metaphysics*, by Myles Burnyeat and others (Oxford: Sub faculty of Philosophy, 1979), 5–6. If the Greek term *logos* is understood here merely in the sense of notion or concept, this difficulty need not arise. The Cartesian requirement of clear and distinct ideas for a definition is not Aristotelian. The notion of an accident cannot be made "clear and distinct" in the way the Cartesian starting points for philosophy are envisaged. An Aristotelian "accident" confuses the two aspects in the one notion, namely the aspect of the modification with the aspect of the thing modified. The two aspects are distinguished by philosophical analysis and then expressed in distinction from each other. But as originally grasped they are fused together. For Aristotle that is the way perceptible things are, and our concepts have to conform to them. The Lockean procedure, on the other hand, tries to understand the qualities as existent apart from an underlying substance, thereby turning each accident into an Aristotelian substance that exists in its own self.

trary, the knower becomes and is in the actuality of the cognition the thing known. It is the sensible thing itself, a substance modified by accidents, that is directly and immediately known. The accidents also are known immediately and directly, but as in the substance.

In this direct and immediate cognition, moreover, a gradation in being is at once apparent to the knower. The person who is seated or who is six feet tall, the cooked fish that is white and warm, and the living animal that is healthy, all are seen to have being in a greater or higher degree than the kind of being that is recognized for those accidents. We much more readily acknowledge that each of those substances is a being. In comparison, an effort has to be made in order to say that position or height or color or warmth or health are beings (1.1028a13–7). That is the way the multisignificant notion of being appears to the knower in the thing itself, in the cognitional identity of knower with thing known. The difference of rank in being is directly and immediately seen in the external thing. Of the two grades in being, that of the substance is clearly seen to be the higher. In relation to the being of the accidents, it is at once recognized as obviously the primary grade of being in the sensible thing, and as being that is meant in independent fashion and not in some lesser way. It is not being that is had in virtue of some stronger type of being, in the way an accident has to require something else of which it is a modification. Substance, rather, has being of itself (*kath' auto*, 1028a23), insofar as it does not have to contain within itself the notion of any other kind of being in order to be what it is. From this viewpoint it may be described in English as self-contained, or in Latin as *per se*. An accident, on the contrary, has to allow the notion of substance to be contained in its own notion. It is not something that is complete just in itself.

Against the background of Aristotle's general conception of being as something stable in contrast to becoming and change, the priority of substance to accidents can be readily understood. A sensible thing has to be a metal, a plant, or an animal, before it can be considered as having the kind of accidents appropriate to it. A tree has the accidental features of a tree, a lion has the accidental qualities of a lion. The so and so of the accidents depends upon the so and so of the substance. From this viewpoint the nature of the substance has precedence. Likewise the nature of the metal, the tree, or the lion remains stable throughout the accidental changes in color, shape, or size. From this angle as well the substance has a stronger type of being, and may be regarded as prior because more permanent. Finally, our understanding of things consists in knowing what they are. But what they are is conceived, in our method of knowing, as contrasted with the way they are or how large they are or how many they are or where or when they are. Yet from the standpoint of our knowledge of them, all these accidents have to be represented as though they were substances. We think of them and speak of them in that way, when we go on to call them accidents through use of a noun, or refer to them as a color, a size, a location. From the viewpoint of human knowledge, the notion of an accident has to be formed in terms of the basic knowledge of substance (a36–b2). In this way also does the priority rest with substance. Aristotle expresses the situation succinctly by stating that "in all the ways substance has primacy – in notion and in knowledge and in time."[7]

How do these considerations help toward the general understanding of primacy in the case of being? Certainly the norm of sustaining accidents as a subject is not demanded. Sensible substances do not inhere in accidental fashion in separate substance, in the way a universal application of this norm would imply. They are not modifications of immobile substance. Nor does the notion of separate substance appear immediately and directly in the nature of a sensible substance, as the notion of substance is seen right away in a sensible accident. Color or size cannot be grasped apart from the awareness that each is the color or size of something. But a lead may be found in the reflection that an accident cannot be so and so without presupposing a substance that is so and so. Canine accidents cannot be found apart from canine nature, or human accidents apart from human nature. The dog or the person must be there to give them their canine or human character. Generically color or size may be present in other specifically different substances, but their specific character and combination depends upon the substantial nature they modify. Each accident has its own inherent nature, different from that of the substance, but it is so and so because of the nature of that substance. Since being is understood for Aristotle in terms of so and so, this relation of the secondary instances to the primary instance in sensible things opens an avenue for explanation in regard to the relation of sensible things to separate substance. Could each sensible thing be so and so if separate substance did not guarantee stability and permanence? Since in Aristotle sensible things do not depend upon separate substance for their existence, and their being is explained in terms of so and so, one may expect that their relation to the primary instance of being is to be found in the latter area. At least this seems a possible way of understanding the primacy of separate substance in regard to all other things, and of explaining its universality in the predication of being.

The third and last way in which Aristotle claims primacy in being for substance in this passage, is that questions about anything else have to be formulated in terms of substance. We cannot think about anything, or ask about anything, without representing the thing as though it had substantial status. Yet we can speak of sensible substances without requiring them to be separate from matter. Thus anything of which we think or speak has to be represented in a sensible image. But that does not mean we are thinking that it has matter in its own constitution. Nevertheless, if our way of representing separate substance is so manifestly deficient when it tries to picture something immaterial, need we be sur-

7 *Metaphysics*, 7.1.1028a32–33. Comparison with other Aristotelian passages in which similar distinctions are made may be found in Ross, II. 161.

prised that the notion of *ousia* has to be widened and strengthened by a much more profound conception of its primary instance? If so, the door is open for seeking the primary instance of substance in a type of being that is immobile and separate.

As it is, the first chapter of Zeta closes with the well-known assertion that the perennial question about what being is can be brought back to the question of what *ousia* is. The reason that had been given was the threefold priority of sensible substance to accidents, in the ways that had just been sketched. To Greek ears of the time the term *ousia* would conjure up the notion of material possessions, the things that were one's property. But the morphology of the word would suggest also the notion of beingness, on account of its abstractive formation from the participle *ousa*, the feminine singular for the participle "being." It was that which imparted being to the sensible thing, parallel to the way whiteness made a thing white. As in the last of the three ways of priority just listed, it is giving the answer in terms of a what, the way an answer to any question has ultimately to be understood. Since the study of being as taken simply is the study of its primary instance, the study of being in a sensible thing will be the study of the primary instance there, namely of its substance. Book Kappa (3.106la8–10) could refer to this sensible substance as being qua being, in relation to its accidental characteristics. The substance in which the accidents inhere is what abides permanently throughout all the changes from zygote to old age in humans, and throughout the various metamorphoses in frogs and butterflies. The contrast is between the permanent and the changeable. What is there as permanent, and accordingly as being, is the substance. The permanent substantial being is what enables the accidents to have their own being. In relation to them the being of the substance is to be regarded as being qua being.

Here the meaning is clear enough. But what single word is there that will express this two-sided notion in idiomatic English, or at least will not positively exclude either side of it? The substance of the sensible thing is something definite and particular, while the function of imparting being to the accidents seems to be something abstract and unsubstantial. How can these two apparently opposed notions be brought together and expressed by one and the same term?

A similar situation with Aristotle has already been encountered in book Epsilon. There, being was regarded as a universal predicate that could be asserted of all beings. From this viewpoint it was not a particular thing. Yet even in this same context it was simultaneously regarded as the nature of a particular type of being, namely of separate substance. The problem that was faced in the days of Natorp and Jaeger was precisely that these two notions of universal and particular being seemed to be incompatible with each other. From the standpoint of those interpreters Aristotle was accordingly involved in an open contradiction when he combined the two facets in the one specifying object of the primary philosophy.

The same problem seems present in regard to *ousia*, even though in Greek the one term denoted both beingness and personal property.

The difficulties are more acute when this problem of the primacy of *ousia* is faced in English translation. When Aristotle asserts that in relation to the accidents the sensible *ousia* is primary, the English rendition can hardly be "beingness." One cannot say that a stone or a tree or an animal is a beingness. One says that it is a substance, in each case. But thereby the notion that the substance is what endows it with being is not made explicit. "Substance" has first to be explained as the cause of being, if the message is to get across. Its application to accidents may become difficult to understand, as when "stillness" is said in book Eta (2.1043a22–24) to be the *ousia* of calm weather, or when in *De Anima* (2.1.412bl2–13) the accidental form of an axe is looked upon as its *ousia*, or when in the *Nicomachean Ethics* (2.6.1107a6–7) the *ousia* of a virtue is said to consist in a mean. In none of these cases does *ousia* refer to the sensible substance that underlies the accidents. The result is that *ousia* requires translation sometimes by "substance" and sometimes by "beingness," if the exact bearing of the Greek is to be carried over into the English.

These difficulties of translation need to be kept in mind as the second chapter of book Zeta surveys the various possibilities for locating *ousia*. The location of it in sensible substance would suggest spontaneously to the Greek hearer the connection with being, and even insinuate that the substance is what accounts for the thing's being, as would the term "beingness" in English. The text proceeds to show that *ousia* is most manifestly found in plants and animals and in natural bodies such as water and earth, and in the heavenly bodies. All these come under the traditional notion of substance in the Aristotelian categories, as contrasted with accidents. This substance, as so and so, makes possible the being of the accidents. If it were not for an underlying substance that was *so*, these could not be what they are. A color could not be a color unless it were the color of a physical body. This kind is easy enough to grasp, and fully justifies Aristotle's description of it as the "most manifest" (1028b8) occurrence of *ousia*. One readily sees that it renders some other kind of being possible. It is not identical with the secondary kind of being, for the substance is not an accident. But as the primary beingness in the sensible thing it is the type of beingness that grounds all the secondary instances. This, then, is the *ousia* known to everybody. Other types suggested in philosophy are the Platonic Ideas, the mathematical principles of the Pythagoreans, and Aristotle's separate substances (b13–3l).

Unfortunately, there is no single word in English that would carry gracefully these varying senses of the Greek term *ousia*. One may urge that any language can express in its own way what another language says. But this need not always be by a single corresponding word or by the same type of phrasing. Where one language can express a notion with a single word, another may require a plurality of words to express exactly the same thought. Or it may have to force the meaning of the word in a way that no native speaker would think of doing. Yet this is the situation one faces in regard to the rendition of the Greek term *ousia* in English. Obviously in the present context *ousia* has to signify "beingness," in accord with the morphology of expressing the nature of being. It has to carry the force of the characteristic that makes a thing be. Likewise it has to signify, simultaneously, the thing that has the beingness, such as a stone or a tree, or a human person or a god. That was the way *ousia* was introduced in this opening chapter of book Zeta (1028a27).

In the Greek idiom, however, no special difficulty seems to have been felt in allowing the one term *ousia* to stand simultaneously for both senses. *Ousia* in ordinary parlance meant one's personal property, and in the formation of the word the appropriate relation to being came to the fore. The Greek word was conspicuously open to the twofold meaning. It carried easily the double signification of beingness and the subject that has the beingness. In English the term "substance" performs in a corresponding way within its own signification. It can mean any chemical substance and in philosophy anything that exists in itself. It can likewise mean the basic characteristic that makes anything what it is, in standing for the "essential nature" or "essence" of a thing. That is why "substance" had so much success as a translation of the Aristotelian *ousia*. It lends itself readily to signifying both the thing that basically exists and the characteristic that basically makes the thing something. But it does not express the relation to being. Though the best of all the translations, it has proven unsuitable and misleading in Aristotelian metaphysics. The term "beingness" has to replace it when relevant questions are asked in the investigation of being qua being. Otherwise the main point is missed.

The term "entity" in English can be used for the concrete thing as well as for the abstract characteristic. It can accordingly function as a translating word for any of the instances of *ousia* in Aristotle. But it is a dull word, and does not carry any of the vitality and relevance associated with one's own personal property, as does *ousia* in Greek or "substance" in English. The notion of one's very own possession, implicit in the English "substance" or the Greek *ousia*, plays a role that should not be overlooked in the problem of a translating term in the present case. Moreover, although "entity" can serve severally for any one of the instances of the Aristotelian *ousia*, it does not adapt itself readily to expressing a simultaneous union between two of the senses. Yet that is what is required by the twofold function of *ousia* in the problem under consideration. It has to convey simultaneously the notion of abstract beingness and the notion of the concrete thing that possesses this characteristic.

An instance of that twofold way of signifying has already been noted in regard to the problem of being in book Epsilon. There, "being" had to signify simultaneously the notion of being that applied to all instances of being, and the notion of separate substance, a particular type of being. The two notions were combined in the notion of being qua being, the specifying object of the primary philosophy. In a roughly corresponding way, the term *ousia* has to signify simultaneously the notion of beingness and the notion of the subject that has the beingness. These notions can be looked at separately in reflection upon them, and distinguished satisfactorily from each other. But the one word *ousia* has to convey them both in the way they are combined in the thing itself.

Quite obviously a philosophy based ultimately upon ideas or concepts is not able to function in this way. The idea or concept of a separate substance is not the idea or concept of the universal predicate "being." The one is definitely particular, the other is general. But in the Aristotelian approach the immediate and direct object of human cognition is the external sensible thing in itself. In sensible things the individual and the universal aspects can be recognized and distinguished. Their distinction from each other and their combination in the one sensible thing can be seen and investigated. The same real thing contains them both and allows them to be distinguished in human reflection upon them. Ideas, on the other hand, are in the Cartesian tradition the clear and distinct starting points of philosophical reasoning. They cannot allow for the Aristotelian conception of multiple signification. They signify clearly what they are. They do not confuse different notions into one, in the way different aspects are confused in the one real sensible thing. Aristotle's metaphysics may well be asked how this approach is justified, and the answer has to be carefully probed. But from the start its difference from the approaches of both modern and postmodern philosophies has to be kept in mind if the sequence in his philosophical reasoning is to be appreciated.

In correspondence to this situation of things and concepts, the words conveying them should respect the differences in the concepts along with the unity in the thing. Accordingly when *ousia* signifies the individual thing under its aspect of beingness, as when it means a human person or a god in the present context, that combined notion of subject and characterization needs to be recognized. In English there does not seem to be any one weasel word that could adapt itself to the varying differences and yet leave the content intact. In explanation and discussion other terms may be used to bring out the exact meaning on each occasion, even showing for instance that *ousia* refers to an accident when it stands for the structure of a threshold or the sharpness of an axe, and calls for translation as "essence." But in a rendition of the Aristotelian text itself, the one way of conserving the unity of its meaning throughout all its variations, seems to be the retention of the original Greek term *ousia*. At least the use of the term *ousia* allows one to keep aware of the consistency of Aristotle in seeing the singular thing as the primary *ousia* in a logical context, the form of the sensible thing as the primary ousia in a physical context, and the supersensible forms as the primary *ousiai* (*Metaphysics*, 12.8.1074b9) in a metaphysical context. Likewise it allows one to see how Aristotle was able to call accidents *ousiai* on the ground that they in their own way give being to further characteristics that follow immediately upon them. It is in these ways that the opening chapter of *Metaphysics* Zeta has introduced in a wide-ranging manner the difficult topic of *ousia*. The second chapter of Zeta has glanced at the ways in which *ousia* has been located in sensible things, and in mathematical objects by the Pythagoreans, and in Forms as well as mathematicals in Platonic thought.

Against that backdrop book Zeta proceeds in its third chapter to examine what *ousia* is. At least four notions of it have been proposed. These are listed as: 1) The thing's *to ti ēn einai*; 2) the universal; 3) the genus, and 4) the substrate (1028b33–36). This chapter immediately shows what happens when the fourth, the substrate, is made the guiding line. Inquiry of this type would lead to the primary substrate as the principal kind of *ousia*. The substrate underlying the accidents in sensible things is a composite of matter and form. Within it the matter is the substrate for the form. This matter would be the ultimate substrate in the thing, and in consequence the primary *ousia* for anyone pursuing that line of argument to the end. But this ultimate matter has no determining characteristics whatever, either substantial or accidental. It totally lacks the hallmark of *ousia*, that is, of something separate in the sense of a "this" (3.1029a7–28).

What does that mean? With "being" understood in the meaning of so and so, the ultimate matter, which is not so in any way at all when considered just in itself, obviously cannot function as the primary instance of being. Alone by itself it has no knowable characteristics. Reached by the mind only through analogous reasoning in the *Physics* (1.7.19la7–12) from the observable changes of bronze and wood into statue and bed, it is grasped in a way that shows how it functions without contributing any definite characteristic to the thing. This suffices to show that the absolutely undetermined matter lacks the role of endowing the sensible thing with being. It cannot impart to anything else what it in no way has in itself. It cannot have the role of beingness in regard to anything whatever. The ultimate explanation of *ousia* cannot be given in terms of matter. *Ousia*, as has been seen, carries with it the characteristic of having a meaning separately just in itself, the meaning of something definite. Any attempt to explain it ultimately in terms of substrate cannot hope to be successful.

These considerations point out clearly enough the direction to be taken for the understanding of *ousia*. The search is not along the path of quantity, in the way Zeno (Fr. B 1–2, DK) had explained the being of things. Rather, quantity presup-

8 On the interpretation of Aristotle's assertion (*Metaphysics*, 7.3.1029a20–21) that matter just in itself is neither substance or quantity nor any other of the characterizations by which being is determined or defined, see Jacques Brunschwig, "La forme, prédicat de la matière?" in *Etudes sur la Métaphysique d'Aristote*, ed. Pierre Aubenque (Paris: Vrin, 1979), 131–166. The point is that matter just of itself does not confer any characteristic at all that could make a thing so. A thing is something material because its form requires inherence in a substrate that allows it to be spread out in parts outside parts and multiplied in individuals that have the same specific character.

poses an absolutely undetermined material element in its substrate in order to allow for change in size without change in form.[8] Nor, as Plato (*Sophist*, 247C) satirized, need a being be something that may be squeezed by hand. With sensible things as the starting point for the reasoning, their being will have to be sought either in their form or in a composite of matter and form. The formal element is absolutely required to account for a thing's being, when being is understood in terms of the so.

The possibility of finding the ultimate explanation in the composite of matter and form is set aside quite summarily (3.1029a30–32). The reason given is that the composite is something that follows upon the matter and the form, and in this sense is something subsequent to its components.

It is recognized as something clear, for it is known immediately in sensible things as the *ousia* that gives the tree or the animal its stability and permanence under the accidental changes. Though it has been shown all along to be *ousia*, it cannot be the primary kind of *ousia*, within the thing.[9]

From all that has been noted so far, one might expect to hear that form will be the most readily grasped of all three kinds of *ousia*. Instead, a warning is sounded that it is going to prove most difficult. It will occasion the greatest *aporia*. Yet it will have to be the factor that provides intelligibility for both the composite and the absolutely undetermined matter. It may be expected to have a deep background in the Platonic doctrine of the Ideas for which "forms" served regularly as an alternate term in the dialogues. Yet profound difference from the Platonic form is to be expected, for Aristotle will treat the Platonic form rather as

9 These considerations are sufficient to show that in a context in which the basic topic of discussion is the overall Aristotelian notion of *ousia* in its multisignificance, the use of the original Greek term seems imperative even in an English translation of the Aristotelian text. In other contexts, where the various types of *ousia*, are investigated separately, their idiomatic English designations, such as substance, being, beingness, essence, and existent and existence, will find their appropriate place. Bibliographies on *ousia* in Aristotle may be found in Frank A. Lewis, *Substance and Predication in Aristotle* (Cambridge: Cambridge University Press, 1991), 349–356; Michael J. Loux, *Primary Ousia*: *Essay in Aristotle's Metaphysics Z and H* (Ithaca, N.Y.: Cornell University Press, 1991), 275–281; and Mary Louise Gill, *Aristotle on Substance* (Princeton: Princeton University Press), 255–260. The basic equivalence in meaning of *ousia* with "being qua being" allows Aristotle (*Metaphysics*, 11.106la8–10) to refer to sensible substance as "being qua being" in relation to the sensible accidents. The substance in which those accidents inhere is what abides permanently throughout all changes from zygote to old age in humans, and throughout the various metamorphoses in frogs and butterflies. Hence in quite parallel fashion the universally predicable characteristic "being" can locate its primary instance in a definite kind of being, namely in separate substance, while in the sphere of sensible being a definite category – namely substance – may be regarded as the primary instance that makes "being" predicable of all sensible accidents.

a mistaken conception of the universal rather than of the form present in a sensible body. With this in mind, one can see the appropriateness of the passage that concludes the third chapter of book Zeta, or begins the fourth chapter (1029b3–12). The passage emphasizes the place of sensible things as the starting point for the metaphysical reasoning, even though these things are much less knowable in themselves than the things to which they will lead. In a word, knowledge about the Aristotelian form does not come through intuition of the form in itself or from recollection of the vision of it in a previous existence, but from cold hard reasoning about the constitution of sensible things.

Chapter 6

"Essential Being" (*to ti ēn einai*)

In examining the form of sensible things under its aspect of *ousia*, the fourth chapter of book Zeta (1029b12–14) proposes first to treat of it from the viewpoint of a concept (*logikōs*). What exactly does this mean? In the summary overview of the different ways in which *ousia* has been understood, as outlined in the preceding chapter, the form was referred to as *eidos* (1029a29) and *morphē* (a31). These are the terms used regularly to signify it in the *Physics*. There cannot be the least doubt that the form reached by the procedure of natural philosophy in the first book of that work (1.7.191a7–12), and regarded in the second book as the nature in a higher sense than the matter (2.1.193b6–7), is identical with what was introduced into the *Metaphysics* (1.3.983a27–28) as *to ti ēn einai*.[1] But the latter phraseology is not physical in origin or character. The precise history of its development cannot be traced. What this chapter (Z 4) undertakes is a discussion of form when its concept is so phrased. An agreement on the grammatical structure of the phrase, however, is necessary for any philosophical attempt to examine its meaning. Although this topic is still highly controversial, the analysis given in close detail in Schwegler seems by far the most acceptable.[2] In it the *einai* is a predicate infinitive: the imperfect *ēn* implies being that is not conditioned by time and that exercises a causal priority; the *ti* is interrogative, and the article makes the phrase signify the answer to that interrogation. This grammatical understanding of the Greek expression will at least help toward appreciating the force of Aristotle's arguments in regard to its philosophical meaning. The dative that often goes with it is possessive, referring to the thing that has the form. Perhaps the nearest English equivalent, as already noted (supra, chapter 4), is the "essence" or "essential being" (*einai*) of the thing. Since the term "being" (*einai*) is the predicate in the Greek expression, its retention is preferable in the English equivalent.[3]

1 Cf. supra, ch. 4, n. 8. This factual identity of *to ti ēn einai* with the thing's form provides the basis in reality against which the conceptually framed formula can be checked.

2 See supra, ch. 4, nn. 8 and 9.

3 With the infinitive in the Greek phrase accepted as a predicate noun, the English translation should be expected to render that obviously basic constituent in the phrase

In our passage of the *Metaphysics* (7.4.1029bl4–16), Aristotle asserts that the essential being of each thing is what the thing is said to be just in virtue of itself.

by "being" as a noun. The kind of being, namely the characterizing formal element instead of the indefinite material element or the accidental features, is thereby given as the answer to the question originally asked. The answer states the kind of being that makes the thing what it is essentially. From this viewpoint the notion "essential" is required in the English translation. The word "essential," in its ordinary use in English, refers to what is always required for something to be what it is. "Essential" signifies an indispensable aspect for retaining identity throughout all singular instances or accidental modifications, for example as a stone, a tree, a person. The matter or the composite may be different in each occurrence, but the formal characteristic in question remains the same. In the original Greek wording of the phrase, the permanence was signified by the imperfect tense in the verb. The notion "essence" conveys this permanence in an English translation. Hence "essence" has been the most popular rendition for the whole Aristotelian expression.

Some misgivings immediately arise, however, in regard to the capacity of the word "essence" to carry the basic force of the Greek wording. As Ernst Tugendhat, *TI KATA TINOS* (Freiburg/Munich: Verlag Karl Alber, 1958) tellingly notes, "being," as expressed by the infinitive in the Greek formulation, is "das Grundwort des Ausdrucks" (17). Tugendhat had stressed a twofold aspect of being for Aristotle – "eine Zwiefältigkeit des Seins selbst" (5), insofar as for Aristotle "being" always had the structure of an "Etwas von Etwas" (5–6). This structure is "das Ursprungsfeld der Grundbegriffe der aristotelischen Metaphysik" (6). Aristotle himself states that our understanding of something according to its "essential being" is true knowledge – *tou ti esti kata to ti ēn einai* – in contrast to acquaintance with it according to a haphazard aspect. Knowledge of what a thing is at a given moment can be in terms of the thing's matter or of its accidents, but knowledge of what the thing essentially is has to be in terms of its abiding form. This essential "being" of that thing is what the Aristotelian phrase means. What a thing is can be grasped in various ways. But the grasp of it in terms of its form is the grasp of it in terms of its "essential being." That is what the Aristotelian structure of being requires. "Essential being," and not just "essence," is needed for the import of the original Greek phrasing.

Distasteful as neologisms may be, they are sometimes necessary for expressing in English with required conciseness the meaning of something that had been said in a different language. Here the original Greek phrase asked what the being is that has to be present in a thing for the thing to stay what it is, regardless of the particular circumstances. The answer is the thing's formal component or formal nature. Exactly the kind of being that is brought about by the form is in question, and the form is identical with that being. In accord with the Aristotelian structure that has just been noted, this type of being will be "something of something," namely the abiding permanence of something throughout all the instances and accidental phases. Basically the problem is a problem of being. "Being," then, has to appear as the basic feature in the translation. "Essential being" respects this requirement. Its phrasing avoids any implied contrast of the thing's essence with the thing's existence, as the term "essence," when used alone, might easily suggest today.

As an illustration, he contrasts what you are in virtue of yourself with what you are in virtue of your acquired musical art. You could be the person you are without having cultivated the art of music. Your own "essential being," therefore, is not the being that is essential for a musician. This means that only what is contained within the concept of yourself just as yourself can belong to your essential being. No matter how much you like to say that your music is part of you in real life, it does not enter into the concept of what you are just in virtue of yourself. Likewise somebody can be a musician without being you.

The topic, then, is being approached strictly in terms of concepts.[4] The concept of yourself precisely as a human being does not contain the concept of musician. That is obviously enough the point that Aristotle is driving home. But the issue is not entirely simple. Elsewhere (*Posterior Analytics*, 1.4.73a34–b24, and *Metaphysics*, 5.18.1022a24–36) the notion "in virtue of itself" is shown to be multisignificant. In neither place are the various meanings of the phrase drawn up with any direct bearing upon the present passage of book Zeta. But they form a background against which the issues at stake in this discussion may be assessed. A study of that background is all the more necessary because the text itself is uncertain in important details of the explanation that immediately follows in Zeta (4.1029bl6–22). The wording of the text has to be reconstructed on the basis of the variants accepted, and these will be chosen in accord with what one thinks the meaning of the passage should be.

To illustrate the first sense of the notion of "in virtue of itself," the example of line in a triangle and point in a line was given in the *Posterior Analytics* (1.4.73a35). The reason is that the *ousia* of triangle and line has these as consti-

Remaining within the contours of the English language, therefore, one may express the puzzling Aristotelian notion as "what is essentially 'being' for the thing," or more idiomatically "what is the thing's essential being." One can thereby keep pursuing one's thought in authentically English grooves, without having to translate mentally back into Greek, on each occasion, the disturbing Aristotelian phrase. Smoother flow of one's thought is thereby assured. Here the use of a neologism seems amply justified.

4 One may compare *logikōs* here at Zeta 4.1029b13 with its use at 1030a25. In the latter place it is meant to explain how the concept "not-being" is formed on the basis of the object conceived positively as "being." The Greek commentator Asclepius, *In Aristotelis Metaphysicorum libros A–Z Commentaria*, 383.13–20; cf. 386.26–27, thinks that the term at 1029b13 may be understood in two ways. It may be taken, he claims, to mean "not rigorously exact," because the text here fails to distinguish being of substance from being of accidents. But, Asclepius continues, the term may also be understood here to mean the establishing of the material thing's form from the starting point of the thing's definition, even though the form is prior to this definition. This would mean that the definition is worked out on the basis of the thing's form, and when made on the metaphysical level it should provide insight into the functioning of form as the cause of the thing's being.

tutional parts. This means that they enter into the formal notion of triangle and of line, since *ousia* in a context like the present signifies formal in contrast to material cause. Where it is impossible for the form not to inhere in a subject, such as with straight and curved in a line or odd and even in some number, the predication is *per se*, but in a second sense. This inherence is explained in detail (b16–24). But, throughout, the contrast between form and matter is dominant.

The same background of these two different ways of *per se* is sketched also in book Delta of the *Metaphysics* (18.1022a14–34), with still sharper penetration into the ways in which the subject can be regarded as pertaining *per se* to the thing in question. After stating (a14–25) that "something in virtue of which" is multisignificant, in the sense of the form (*eidos*) or the *ousia*, and the sense of the proximate substrate (*hupokeimonon)*, matter (*hulē*), the text goes on to say that as a result the notion of "in virtue of itself" has corresponding senses. The signification is the "essential being" of each thing, in the way that Callias in virtue of himself is Callias and the "essential being" of Callias (a25–27). The corresponding sense of "in virtue of which" had been the way a person is good in virtue of goodness itself (a15–16), namely in virtue of the form or *ousia* involved. Goodness is very general. Callias is very particular, but can be regarded from the viewpoint of the generic feature in his definition, and in his way is *per se* an animal, the genus being the material element in the definition. Likewise a surface is white *per se* as being in virtue of itself the proximate subject for color, and a person lives *per se* since one's soul is the proximate subject of living (a27–32). This would seem to mean that a man could be *per se* any of the features implied by the genera under which he is ranged, when he is taken reduplicatively with the generic grade. Taken reduplicatively as an animal, a man would be sentient *per se*. This would hold on the ground that he has many such causes in these grades. According to the norm just laid down (a19–20) about the correspondence of the "in virtue of which" with the causes, he would be *per se* what these grades imply. In spite of this, however, a man is definitely a man in virtue of himself (a34–35), and moreover what pertains solely to one thing and in virtue of that sole possession of it, belongs to it *per se*, with the result that anything that has been separated from a subject is *per se* (a35–36).

The listing of these ways of belonging to something *per se* is fully in accordance with the character of *Metaphysics* Delta. That treatise is a collection of the various ways in which multisignificant notions are expressed. Corresponding to a different viewpoint at the moment, then, a *per se* classification may be given the same thing in more than one way. For instance, animal is predicated *per se* of a human being insofar as it is part of the definition, and also comes under *per se* insofar as an animal is a substance in contrast to an accident. Similarly a notion is predicated *per se* if it constitutes or pertains to the thing's formal nature, and likewise if it belongs to a thing solely and in virtue of that exclusive possession. These classifications in book Delta and in the *Posterior Analytics* were not drawn up in the order that might be desired for their application to Zeta 4. But throughout, the main division of meanings in virtue of the thing's form, and meanings in virtue of its substrate or subject or matter, is observed. Meanings in the latter sense are what Aristotle wishes to set aside in his explanation of the thing's "essential being," as a careful study of the text in Zeta 4 will show. This objective needs to be kept constantly in mind when reading that difficult chapter.

Returning to book Zeta, then, one finds that here Aristotle intends to limit the *per se* to a purposely restricted area in the use of the phrase. He wants it taken in a sense that excludes both the subject required for inherence and the genera that function as intelligible matter. This need not be surprising, since he had just dismissed the route of matter as the way for understanding *ousia*. He is now introducing the route of form. Yet one of his senses of *per se* predication included the genera, and another sense allowed the subject in which something necessarily inhered.[5] The inquiry, in consequence, needed to be kept focused on an explanation apart from the route of matter. But Aristotle is not intent here on explaining the background in detail. Rather, the text gives the impression of reporting in condensed fashion a lively debate in which possibilities and alternatives were suggested one after the other and dealt with just enough to allow passing on to the next point. No attempt at a rounded-out discussion of each for its own sake is apparent. The reader today has to keep this general character of the text in mind, in order to avoid missing the woods for the individual trees.

The first sense of *per se* predication to be excluded (4.1029b16–18) is the one that allows the required subject of inherence to come under the notion, as in the case of white and surface. The color white presupposes a surface on which it is found. Nevertheless one sees that the "essential being" of a surface is not the "essential being" of the quality white. The two belong to different categories, for the surface as extension pertains to the category of quantity. Even though the quality white supposes in virtue of its own notion a surface upon which it is extended, that surface does not signify a part of the color in the way a line is part of the notion of a triangle, or as points belong to the notion of line. Though a *per se* requirement, it does not enter into the formal notion of white. This second type in the list of *per se* predications is accordingly set aside in a search that has already gone beyond the attempt to explain *ousia* in terms of substrate. Here, where *ousia* in the sense of form is under scrutiny, surface and white have to be left to what the notion of each formally expresses just in itself. The direction is from the standpoint of form, not from that of matter.

However, another suggestion remains to be considered (b18–19). Could not *ousia* in its meaning of formal cause be the "essential being" of the one composite of both white and surface, namely the "essential being" of a white surface? This notion is difficult to express in English. Perhaps "whitesurfaceness" would

5 Aristotle, *Metaphysics*, 5.18.1022a25–32.

be the closest we could come to it. Here the notion of surface is formalized in the "essential being" of the composite of surface and white. The suggestion, however, is rejected. The reason for rejecting it is stated succinctly – *hoti prosestin auto*. This terse statement is difficult to translate unless one knows exactly what the referent of *auto* is. Since from the viewpoint of literary form book Zeta is a school *logos*, Aristotle could be pointing to a written sentence or diagram that would have pinpointed the antecedent that was meant. This antecedent, however, could hardly have been the main subject of the preceding sentence, namely the type of *per se* predication that is in question there. In that sentence Aristotle had stated that the type of predication at issue is not the kind in which an indispensable substrate is predicated *per se*. The reason for this denial was that the "essential being" of the color white is not the "essential being" of a surface. The denial is now extended to the question of the "essential being" for the combination of the two, namely to the "essential being" of a white surface. The following chapter in book Zeta (5.1030b14–1031a14) explains how the combinations in which the components belong in different categories can themselves, as combinations, have their own distinctive "essential being." In that discussion the *auto* (spelled out at 1030b32–34) is the substrate, namely the nose as the *per se* substrate of snubness. Snubness is a curvature of the nose, with the result that wherever it occurs it includes the concept of nose. Inevitably "nose" has to be added in its description. Similarly at 1031a5 the substrate "animal" is what occurs twice.

In this context, then, the *auto* that has to be added or repeated will be the substrate of the color white, namely the surface.[6] As a substrate, it is not assimilable into the formal notion of whiteness. It has to remain outside the kind of perseity that Aristotle is requiring for a thing's "essential being." The text then (4.1029bl9–21) generalizes this consideration, in asserting that the concept or definition of each thing's "essential being" states what the thing is without including the thing itself in the formulation. In the parallel example of "snub nose" the concept of nose is already contained expressly as the *per se* substrate of snubness, and is repeated in the mention of "nose." In both cases a parallel conclusion is drawn. If a snub nose and a concave nose are the same, "snub" and "concave" should be the same (5.1030b28–29). Likewise, if the "essential being" of a white surface is the "essential being" of a smooth surface, then the "essential being" of white and smooth is one and the same (4.1029b21–22). Repetition of the substrate, though, makes them differ.

The starting point for the discussion of this issue in Zeta 4 had been that the repetition of the same substrate, the surface, precluded the "essential being" of a white surface from functioning in the *per se* manner required for *ousia* in the

6 See Pseudo-Alexander, *In Aristotelis Metaphysica Commentaria*, 468.29; cf, Asclepius, *In Aristotelis Metaphysicorum libros A–Z Commentaria*, 383.31–384.3. See also Ross and Apostle translations.

sense of form. The perseity of an indispensable substrate did not suffice, for the "essential being" of surface is not the "essential being" of white. That assertion is made positively, as though one has merely to look at the two notions to see that they are not the same. The statement about the snub nose is made in an *aporia* (5.1030b28), and is worded in a way that leaves it open to discussion through analysis of the notion "snub." But in regard to "whitesurfaceness" the assertion is precise. It repeats the notion of a surface. Whiteness is as necessarily the color of a surface as snubness is the concavity of a nose. It includes the notion of "surface" through the second kind of perseity, that of the indispensable substrate. But "surface" is also mentioned expressly. It is a surface according to the first type of perseity, quite as Callias is *per se* Callias. There is in fact the double occurrence of the substrate.

What is the unavoidable consequence of this double occurrence? It keeps the formal notion of white from melding into a union with the formal notion of surface. "Whiteness" and "surfaceness" do not coalesce in "white surface." Although the surface is white, it is not whiteness. The result would not be a unitary formal notion "whitesurfaceness," but rather a new coupling of the composite "white surface" with the notion of its own "surfaceness." The reasoning why the indispensable substrate as matter does not enter into the kind of perseity required by *ousia* as form, is carried over into the argument that the formal union of the two cannot provide the "essential being" here. The indispensable substrate is not only present but is also repeated. In this way the sequence of thought flows smoothly, as it moves from the one suggested possibility to the next.

But how does this instantiate the general observation that the concept of each thing's essential being is the concept that makes manifest what the thing is, without expressly including in the formulation that subject itself? The obvious reason might be that to include the subject itself would restrict the extension of the definition to that one instance only. But the sole reason Aristotle himself gives here (1029b21–22) lies in the consequence that if the "essential being" of a white surface is the "essential being" of a smooth surface, then the "essential being" of white and of smooth are one and the same. Here smooth, a notion other than white and surface is introduced into the discussion. Aristotle notes elsewhere that for Democritus white coincides with smooth.[7] That would make those two notions identical. The one would be absorbed into the other. But as notions they are for Aristotle evidently different. So a person may be white, yet is not thereby whiteness (1030a1–2). The notions are not the same.

How, then, may one justify the conclusion that the "essential being" of white would meld with the "essential being" of smooth if the substrate surface did not occur twice in the formulation of the problem? "The surface is white" and "the surface is smooth" are compatible assertions. But thereby the substrate is repeat-

7 Aristotle, *De Sensu*, 4.442bl0–12. See Democritus, Fr. A 135, DK, II, 120.16.

ed, and the type of perseity required by *ousia* as form is precluded. Whatever belongs to anything in virtue of its own self in the first type of perseity must coincide with the very notion. It cannot function as a genus or as a substrate. In a word, a form taken just in itself expresses its whole meaning. Only by reason of substrate or genera can it be united with other forms.

This consideration shows decisively why the "essential being" of a white surface cannot be the basic *ousia* in anything. It likewise makes plain how the double use of the same substrate gives the reason why. The form is the unifying principle and to bring about unification it itself must be unitary. It coalesces with whatever enters its own notion. It can undergo differentiation only by reason of genus or substrate. That is why Aristotle can go on with the general statement that the "essential being" of a thing expresses what the thing is without mention of the thing itself. The intelligible content of the thing is prescinded from the thing that possesses it and is presented in this precision as the concept or logos of the thing's "essential being." The topic of precisive and non-precisive abstraction was elaborated in the middle ages by Thomas Aquinas.[8] A notion such as "animal" when abstracted non-precisively is straightway predicated of its subject, quite as for Aristotle a person may be white. But when the notion is abstracted precisively as "animality," it is not able to be predicated that way, any more than "whiteness" for Aristotle could allow the predication that the surface is whiteness.

There is of course a great difference between Aristotle and Aquinas in their respective views on the ultimately unifying principle of things. For Aquinas it is existence, which in creatures is other than essence. For Aristotle, as seen in his discussion in book Epsilon, existence and essence are identical. But on the tenet that the essence of a thing, namely what the thing is, can be considered both in the thing and also as just in itself apart from the thing, there is agreement. You can express what the object is in both those ways, namely as animal and as white, and as animality and whiteness. When you conceive something as an animal or as white, you are including in your concept the subject that possesses the characteristic. When you conceive the characteristic as animality or whiteness, you are prescinding from the subject in which it was seen. This procedure is possible for both Aristotle and Aquinas because cognition for them bears directly upon something external to the cognitive act. The same thing can accordingly be conceived in different ways without detriment to its identity. The question is not about reasoning from one concept to the other or to the thing itself, but rather of judging the concepts by the directly known things.[9]

8 See Aquinas, *On Being and Essence*, 2.6–13, trans. Armand Maurer, 2nd ed. (Toronto: Pontifical Institute of Mediaeval Studies, 1968), 38–44.

9 A discussion of the difficulties that arise when this Aristotelian issue is approached from modern viewpoints may be found in Myles Burnyeat *et al. Notes on Zeta* (Oxford: Sub-faculty of Philosophy, 1979), 17–25. With Aristotle, the thing itself is known directly while awareness of the concept is concomitant. Whether this concep-

Hence Aristotle is able to make the general assertion that the "essential being" of anything is what the thing is when the thing itself is not expressed in the notion. There is no question here of prying the essence loose from the thing and setting the two up as separate objects in contrast with each other. Rather, it is a question of looking at the thing itself and noting how the essence functions in that thing. The point at issue is that if the "essential being" of a white surface were the "essential being" of a smooth surface, then whiteness and smoothness would be one and the same notion (1029b21–22). The repetition of the substrate "surface" in these notions prevents the consequence from coming into effect, and thereby excludes the type of perseity required for *ousia* in its sense of formal cause. The point made is that whatever enters into the form as cause coalesces with it in strict unity. Any differentiations will have to be explained through matter in which it inheres or the genus to which it belongs.

In this way the form is the source of intelligibility in the thing. Matter just of itself has no intelligibility. Matter is understood as the receptacle of the form and the principle of its extension through quantitative dimensions. It does not add any intelligibility to what the thing is. All that is intelligible is unified in the causal function of form. Octave Hamelin concluded his study of Aristotle's philosophy very aptly with the words, '"The form explains all the rest and is self-sufficient in itself."[10] In Aristotle there is no way of going any further for the source of the thing's being. In Aquinas on the contrary every finite form is still in potentiality to its existence, and from that viewpoint calls for further explanation. But in Aristotle the quest stops there, with the form. The result will be that everything, here and elsewhere in Aristotle, will have to be traced back to form for its ultimate explanation. Unity and being, in anything, have to be accounted for by form. Form will have to be one in itself, and will impart its unity to whatever it actuates.

But this situation brings up the multisignificance of being and unity in Aristotle. Both substantial and accidental unions have their being and their unity. How can all be explained through form? Obviously only the first category, that of substance, can allow complete perseity. Since all the other categories are accidents, a substrate is required for the accidental form. Accordingly an investigation of the multisignificance of being and unity from this viewpoint is undertaken in the present text (1030a17–b13). The account given in book Gamma (2.1003a33–b12) is repeated in detail, with special application to the problem that

tual awareness is framed as "an actual definition" or by way of "a simple reference" (Burnyeat, 5) does not affect the grasp of the same thing through different concepts of it. In either case the one and the same thing is being studied in the different conceptual representations. (At 1029b2 the one referent, *auto*, is the thing that is being defined.)

10 "La forme explique tout le reste et se suffit à elle-même." Octave Hamelin, *Le système d'Aristote* (Paris: Alcan, 1920), 405.

comes to the fore in the present chapter of Zeta, namely the problem of formal unity. The text shows how both being and unity always belong basically to a thing's substance, and secondly to its accidents through *pros hen* reference. How may this be best explained today? A human person, one may suggest, is basically a being and a unitary substance because of one human form, the soul. Yet the same person's features and brain and heart and other organs are also human, but in a way that follows upon the basic form. Each of these organs has its own accidental form, yet they all share in the characteristic of "human" that proceeds from the basic form of the person. But each of those accidental forms adds something over and above the human form. Each makes the distinct organ what the organ is in its own particular nature, a brain or a heart or a liver. Each of those accidental forms is a principle, an origin, in its own right. Each of the accidental forms is exercising its own formal causality and is bringing about the accidental unity that each organ has. but always under the ever-present embrace of a human person's substantial form. The same holds for all the human person's actions. They are all human actions, because of the unitary substantial form in the agent from which they proceed.

This will mean that an accidental as well as a substantial form makes something what it is, each in its own way, throughout the order of substance and accidents. The basic substantial form requires added accidental forms to give the thing its color, its extension, its activities. Each of these accidental forms is in this way a new principle, a new beginning, but in a gradated way. The gradation in unity as well as in being runs throughout. Aristotle finds that things are that way in fact, but adds that one has to consider not only the way they are but also how they are to be expressed in concept and speech (4.1030a27–32). By drawing upon this ordered ranking in unity and being, one is able to see how each form, whether substantial or accidental, has a whatness of its own and is able to make its own original contribution to what the thing is as a whole, but always in the proper gradation.

In consequence, one may in the Aristotelian framework readily speak of the "essential being" exercised by an accidental form. Each form is in its own order a unit of whatness. "Whitesurfaceness" could well stand for the form of the accidental combination of white and surface. That would express what it is, and thereby would allow it the status of "essential being." "White surface" is a correct notion of an accidental combination. The notion can be prescinded from the instance in which it is found, just as whiteness itself was prescinded from the subject in which it inhered. The double presence of the substrate surface in its components prevents it from having the perseity required by the first type in the list of *per se* predications. But it does not interfere with its status of an intelligible unit that exercises its own type of formal causality in the accidental composite. It is in this way an added type of "essential being," over and above the "essential being" of the underlying substance and that of each of the two accidental components.

What does all this add up to in regard to the functioning of "essential being" in the accidental composites? There will be a number of different kinds of "essential being" in the one composite thing. Each will be a formal cause that brings new intelligibility into what the thing is. But always there will be the graded order,

> and "essential being" [*to ti ēn einai*] will likewise belong primarily and absolutely to the substance, and in subsequent order to the other components, just as does whatness [*to ti esti*,] not "essential being" absolutely, but the "essential being" of quality or quantity.[11]

This statement is very plain. 'Wherever there is a substance or an accident, including an accidental combination, there will be a distinct "essential being" at work. It functions as the formal cause, either substantial or accidental, of anything that can be described as whatness in the thing, either in the substantial or in the accidental order. Each is a unit of intelligibility that can be prescinded in itself apart from the thing of which it is exercising its formal causality, and in this way can represent what the thing is substantially or accidentally, without thereby mentioning the thing itself in the concept. Each form, accordingly, is a distinct unit of intelligibility in the thing. Each suffices for its own explanation through manifesting its own intelligible content, and each plays its part in the ultimate explanation of the whole composite. In this way form explains all the rest and is self-sufficient in its own right.

Through these considerations the force of the expression "essential being," or in the Greek wording "that which was (timelessly) being for the thing" makes itself felt. Each such unity of intelligible content plays its part in accounting for what the thing is, both substantially and accidentally. Each form functions as a distinct unity, and imparts appropriate unity to the thing. A unit in itself, and functioning as a unity, it impresses all its meaning upon the thing of which it is a form. Hence Aristotle could insist that if the "essential being" of the white surface is the "essential being" of a smooth surface, the "essential being" of white and smooth will be one and the same (1029b21–22). White and smooth would coalesce into the one notion. The term "essential" in the phrase makes the kind of being that is in question here belong to the very nature of the thing, so much so that without it the thing would not at all be what it is. But the notion has to go further, according to Aristotle's description of the way it would make whiteness and smoothness coalesce. Not only the presence but also the fullness of the form is essential here.

11 *Metaphysics*, 7.4.1030a29–32. My translation, to bring out the gradated order of being.

The term "essential" covers everything in it. Anything not essential in this way has to be left to matter or genus for explanation. The full meaning of what it embraces has to be imparted to its subject. The strict formal unity of an essence is required, in making the thing a being. "Essential" in this context belongs under the first-named type in the list of *per se* predications, namely what belongs to the form in virtue of itself only. That is the requirement for the "essential being" of anything, whether substance or accident.[12]

In reading this section of book Zeta, one has to keep constantly in mind that Aristotle has introduced (3.1028b34–1029a7) the topic of "essential being" as that of form in contrast to matter, equating it with the terms used in the *Physics* to describe the formal cause of corporeal things. There is not the least doubt that here in the *Metaphysics* he is understanding the "essential being" as the thing's form. Since the matter is of itself unintelligible, all the intelligibility in the thing comes from the form. Even when there is question of conceptually prescinding the form from its subject, the whole intelligible content of the thing lies in this "essential being." In consequence, its definition is the definition of the thing (5.1031a11–14). Both formulations express what the thing in question is.

Form, accordingly, provides the thing's intelligibility. Understanding of it in all its amplitude and extent will be the goal envisaged in the opening sentence of the *Metaphysics*, namely that by their very nature all people desire to know. For this, not only acquaintance with the form of the thing's substance is required, but also knowledge of the thing's accidental forms. In that way the objects of the different sciences are set up, as outlined in the first chapter of book Epsilon. Not only the primary philosophy but likewise all the other sciences will have their distinct starting points, guaranteeing to each science its independence. The notion of "essential being" thereby holds for every form, whether substantial or accidental, even though the forms are not all on the same level. There is the gradation in being and unity that enables the one basic or substantial form to bring all the other forms into the unity of a single whole, while allowing each of the others to be a distinct starting point for knowledge of that one and the same thing.

This procedure in Aristotle is made possible by the direct cognition of the thing itself, a thing external to the cognitive act by which it is attained. Aristotle is not proceeding through the concepts to reach the thing. Rather, the thing itself is the starting point, with the concepts known only concomitantly and *in obliquo*. The concepts can later be brought under focus through reflection upon them, and can then be compared with the things to ascertain their corresponding truth. But for anyone who approaches Aristotle from a Cartesian background, this procedure will be incomprehensible and will be dismissed as naive realism. In that approach the content of each concept will stand as a term in its own right and will be con-

12 The list is that of *Metaphysics*, 5.18.1022a14–36, where the various kinds of *per se* predications are briefly discussed.

fined to its own distinct contours and placed on equal footing with all other terms. The Aristotelian gradation in being and unity will become unintelligible.

Throughout this discussion in Zeta 4 the Greek term *logos* has been used regularly to denote the notion or concept of the thing. The Greek term has a wide range. It can mean a word or a phrase or a definition, or a philosophical treatise, or a poem like the *Iliad*. Aristotle is careful to point out that in the present context the term does not necessarily mean a definition (7.1030a7–8). Each *logos* will in its own way give an account of the thing it is meant to express. In regard to the topic at issue in Zeta 4, the conclusion is that there will be a *logos* and definition of "white man," but in a different way from that of "white" and that of substance (1030a12–13). This means, evidently enough, that "white man" is an accidental compound of a person and a color. That formulation expresses what the object under consideration is. What it in this way is can in its intelligible content be prescinded from the instance in which it is found and thereby be understood as the "essential being" of a white man, just as has been seen in the case of the white surface. The notion "white" preserves its status as an intelligible principle in its own right for the understanding of the composite. It is not fused into the underlying substance. But the substance retains the primacy in being. The whiteness has being, not as something existent in itself, but only as a modification of the substrate in which it inheres. Explanation through focal reference safeguards the originality that is proper to each of the components as a principle of intelligibility, while leaving intact the primacy of the substance. The Aristotelian situation is far from being a case of allowing both components equal status as terms in a proposition. The discussion of the topic continues through the following chapter (Zeta 5), and ends by repeating the conclusion that the definition of a thing is the notion (*logos*) of its "essential being," and that "essential being" belongs either solely or primarily to substance. In this way the aporematic cast of much of the two chapters is respected, but the main point is driven home (1030b14–1031a14).

Finally, there is the question about the force of the Greek term *logikōs*, in the present discussion. At the beginning of the discussion (1029bl3), Aristotle stated his intention of saying some things about "essential being" from this particular standpoint. The contrast evoked by the term would be with *phusikōs*, and so with "from the science of nature," as at *De Generatione et Corruptione*, 1.2.316a13 (Oxford trans.). In the philosophy of nature, any form of a thing is conceived in the manner of the shape or figure that will make the wood in one case into a table, in another case into a chair. That is the model on which the notion is developed when used in that branch of philosophy. Now, in the primary philosophy, the explanation has to be given in terms of being. The concept will be of exactly the same object, but will be framed in metaphysical fashion. It will aim at making manifest the kind of being that the form involves. It will be meant therefore to express in strictly metaphysical language the way the form is always the basic type of being for the matter and the composite. In both substantial and accidental gradations, it is what makes each substance or accident be what it is, in the sense of something that is so and so, and thereby distinct from other things. It is what remains permanent, as the physical thing goes through its various changes and activities and undergoes the action of others upon it. While in the philosophy of nature the notion of form is developed on the basis of analogy with the shape or figure of corporeal things, in a metaphysical discussion the explanation will have to be given in terms of the kind of being the form exercises in the thing.

In the present context this sense of explanation through concepts is illustrated by the extreme example of "not-being." Even "not-being" has to be conceived through the positive concept of being. Book Gamma (2.1003b5–10) had already shown how the notion of being is in its various ways carried through the categories and extended into privations and negations. Now, in book Zeta the term *logikōs* (1030a25) is used to describe the manner in which the concept of "not-being" is elaborated. The positive notion of being is held before the mind and is represented as negated. Thereby one knows what not-being is. In this way one has the concept of it. One is expressing it *logikōs*. The notion of being is brought under the negation, quite as in the accidental categories the basic notion of being is taken with the appropriate categorical modification such as qualitative being instead of the absolute understanding of being. Accordingly something positive and definite always lies at the basis of the concept, and in terms of the modification or privation or negation of that basis the object under consideration is understood. To this extent one knows what the object is. In that way likewise one knows what the unknown is (1030a33–34).

Applied to the topic immediately at issue, namely the type of perseity required by a thing's "essential being" (1029b13–14), this explanation of the term *logikōs* will refer to the way the formal cause of a thing is to be conceived in a strictly metaphysical context. That cause has to be expressed in terms of being. As form is what makes the thing so and so, it basically accounts for whatever being the thing has in both the substantial and accidental orders. Each type of accidental being in the thing will require a distinctive "essential being," but always in accord with the proper gradation in being and unity. The last chapter of book Zeta (17.1041a6–b3l) will explain in detail how the form is the cause of being to all else in the thing. Here the concept comes to be framed strictly in terms of being, instead of on the analogy of the shape or figure given to a corporeal thing.

The term *logikōs*, then, is not a pejorative designation, as though it denoted a merely dialectical formation in contrast to a real definition. It is meant to express as concisely as possible the metaphysical role of forms, accidental as well as substantial, in the constitution of things. It denotes the way a thing is to be understood when the ultimate explanation in terms of being is sought. Its perseity is thoroughgoing in the first and highest sense of *per se*, namely that it expresses its full meaning in virtue just of what it is in itself. For this reason it is thoroughly a unit just in itself, so much so that whiteness and smoothness would be one and the same notion if the two were combined in the one "essential being."

All this is implied in the notion of *logikōs* as it is developed by Aristotle in the present section of book Zeta. He will have to keep reminding his hearers (e.g., 10.1035b32) that by "form" he means this "essential being" of the thing. In readily understood English vocabulary the notion may be carried in the term "essence." Insofar as "essence" is commonly understood to mean that which makes a thing be what it is in virtue of its own self. But today in this regard care has to be taken to remember that in Aristotle this term "essence" does not imply distinction from existence, and also that "essence" is applicable to accidents as well as to substances. In phrasing the notion as "essential being," however, one keeps basic in it the aspect of being, and in this way renders more understandable the application of the phrase to both accidental and substantial essences. At least, the phrasing in "essential being" helps one to remain as close as possible within the normal flow of English linguistic expression in the effort to follow Aristotle's thinking. The phrase could hardly, however, expect recognition as a standard formula. Even Aristotle's own expression of the notion never entered into normal acceptance in Greek speech, and to this day the respective force of the components in his concise original phrasing remains debatable.

Finally, one might note in this regard how the tenets of the present section in book Zeta permeate Aristotle's whole conception of human life and culture. These tenets make one sensitive to the inherent force that vibrates incessantly throughout his thinking. Aristotle began the *Metaphysics* by focusing on the profoundly innate desire in all people for knowledge. He then traced rapidly (1.980b27–982a1) the ways in which that knowledge is laboriously developed by the work of the various sciences. In the tenth book of the *Nicomachean Ethics* (7–9.1177a12–1180a28) he explained how the supreme goal of human endeavor, namely *eudaimonia*, consists primarily in the exercise of the highest human faculty, intelligence, upon its highest objects (1177a19–21). Secondarily, and through *pros hen* reference to this primary goal, *eudaimonia* is placed by him in correct political order and general economic prosperity, together with upbringing from earliest years in conduct according to right reason and in constant association with others in the gradated orders of friendship. The attitude was explicitly social. All this gave intense appreciation of and pleasure in the moral goodness and aesthetic beauty that both went under the same Greek designation, the *kalon*. Such was Aristotle's far-ranging outlook.[13]

This whole moral panorama came together in constituting human happiness, quite as the manifold kinds of being merged together in gradated order in the one

13 For the way Aristotle incorporates these considerations into the correct attitude of the ordinary morally good person, see *Nicomachean Ethics*, 1.8.1099a22–31.

universe in which all people live. The parallelism is profound and far-reaching. At the head there stands on the one hand separate substance through which all other things are beings, and on the other hand intellectual contemplation through which all else provides happiness, Both had aspects of the divine. Intimations of the separate substances had been handed down, though in very vague guise, in the religious traditions of the human race.[14] Similarly in the *Ethics* Aristotle indicates that something above the human level is required for the attainment of *eudaimonia*.[15] The very word *eudaimonia* seemed to imply supernatural intervention, namely the influence of a *daimon*.

Further, in the physical order, the successions of coming-to-be and perishing were eternal for Aristotle. They had always been taking place and would continue forever. The rise and fall of civilizations was similarly cyclic.[16] There would always be something new to contemplate. The innate desire to know would never lack a new object. The physical as well as the metaphysical framework in Aristotle corresponded exactly to the ethical requirements. The enjoyment of that contemplation throughout a complete lifetime on earth seems clearly enough to be what Aristotle understood by human *eudaimonia*. No question of any necessity for it, or enjoyment of it, after bodily death seems to enter into his consideration. It was something to be attained and enjoyed during the forty or so years of the human individual's mature life on earth. No future existence after death is required for its explanation. The *eudaimonia* would continue through successive generations of individuals as each person lived out his or her life at the level in the cyclic stage in which each had the fortune or misfortune to be born.

Does not book Zeta's notion of "essential being" as the source of intelligibility in things provide the background for this vision of *eudaimonia*? The primary instance of "essential being" coincides with the primary instance of being *qua* being. It is separate substance, which is pure form and actuality without any admixture whatever with matter or potentiality – *to de ti ēn einai ouk echei hulēn to prōton*.[17] Separate substance is intellection and intelligibility at the highest peak, and in its light all other things can be understood in their proper order. But all other substances and all accidents, even the loosest combinations, have their own "essential being." In every instance this "essential being" is the source of intelligibility for all that follows upon it in the thing. The number of new intelligible sources is in this way inexhaustible with the eternal sweep of time. There would always be new stimulation and new satisfaction for the perpetual human desire for knowledge, as the various sciences continue their development. This vision of Aristotle is remarkably coextensive with the outlook of persons today

14 *Nicomachean Ethics*, 12.8.1074bl0.

15 *Nicomachean Ethics*, 10.7.1177b26–34.

16 *Metaphysics*, 12.8.1074b10–13.

17 *Metaphysics*, 12.8.1074a35–36.

who would describe themselves as eagerly seeking knowledge primarily even though not exclusively for the sake of knowledge.

Such would be the indefinitely wide view of contemplation as envisaged for human *eudaimonia* in Aristotle. Even the humblest accident or the most transient occurrence is a new instance of "essential being," and thereby a source of intelligibility. The gradated order of being in the *Metaphysics* from the highest instance in separate substance to the most lowly in the corporeal accidents corresponds for him to the ever active human desire to know. It provides the ordered intelligibility always sought and loved by the human soul. With new intelligibility offered in every occurrence throughout the eternal succession of generations, there will always be new sources of intelligibility for the human mind to investigate and master through its dominating scrutiny. For Aristotle the knower becomes and is the thing known, in the actuality of the cognition. The actuality of thought is in this way its highest life.

All this follows cogently enough from the role exercised by "essential being" in the sensible things from which human cognition originates. In Aristotle's epistemological approach things external to one's cognition are already there to be directly known. They are not produced by the mind's activity. They are known as present to its gaze, with only concomitant awareness of the mind's cognition of them. The mind's goal is to understand them. That understanding is given through the grasp and probing of each thing's "essential being," which expresses what the thing is without limitation to the one instance before the mind's eye at the moment. Because the thing itself is not included in its definition, the way lies open to the universality that gives rise to the development of science. In this manner the "essential being" renders the thing intelligible, presenting the cause of what one immediately sees. In the language of the *Physics*, this "essential being" is the form of the thing as contrasted with the matter and the composite. As isolated in itself it is the principle of intelligibility and the cause of all the being that is in the thing.

These considerations will be pursued in the following chapters of book Zeta. For the present, one may stress the way they are meant to bear on the thing's intelligibility in terms of being. The intelligibility, however, is understood in terms of what the thing is, and not in terms of any existence over and above the whatness. As explained in book Epsilon, the two coincide for Aristotle. When approached against the background of Judeo-Christian tradition, this vision of the universe as something always there in itself, and of human destiny as consisting of eternal contemplation of it by eternally successive generations of individuals, will deeply jar with religious belief. Yet even here there is no exception to John Herman Randall's keen observation that Aristotle's ethical views are applicable "to any cultural heritage."[18] In this case Aquinas in medieval Christendom felt quite at

18 John Herman Randall, Jr., *Aristotle* (New York: Columbia University Press, 1960), 248.

home in applying Aristotle's view of contemplation as the supreme destiny of rational beings in a Christian milieu. With existence received ultimately from a Creator as the actuality of every form, the most basic principle of being in anything will be the thing's existence, and not its form. This will locate the highest intelligibility of the thing in its existence, and will make subsistent existence the object contemplated for all eternity in the beatific vision of God after bodily death. That is a very far cry from Aristotle, but it illustrates sharply the claim that Aristotle's conception of human destiny as inexhaustible contemplation is applicable and helpful even in a Christian culture.

For the moment, however, to understand Aristotle in his own setting, one has to keep in mind that he is locating in form the most basic principle of a thing's being, and is consistently following that lead in explaining the constitution and activity of all beings. This leads him to make intelligibility the great prize sought ultimately in all human endeavor. The form is what makes the thing intelligible, in contrast to the matter, which of itself is unintelligible. The supreme purpose of human effort, then, will consist in isolating that "essential being" of things and presenting it in each case for intellectual consideration. That will show what the thing is, and allow the thing to be understood in terms of the being that is basic to it, and in this way essential for it wherever and whenever it may be found. Through it the ultimate account of the thing is given. To repeat the wording of Octave Hamelin's conclusion, for Aristotle "form explains all the rest and is self-sufficient in itself."[19]

19 Supra, n. 10.

Chapter 7

"Essential Being" and Singular Thing

The fourth chapter of *Metaphysics* Zeta (1029b19–21) had maintained that each thing's "essential being" is what the thing itself is, even though the individual instance thereby defined is not explicitly included in the definition. The thing and its "essential being" in that way coincide, since each of them is what the thing is. Nevertheless on the physical level the form was an object really distinct from the matter it actuated, while the composite thing itself included both the matter and the form. The matter, however, taken just in itself added no intelligibility to the thing. Is the problem on the metaphysical plane parallel insofar as the subject of inherence, namely the thing that has being, adds nothing in the line of being that is not already contained in the form?

The reason given expressly in the text for the pursuance of this topic is its relevance to the study of beingness (*ousia*):[1] "For it is of some help in regard to the investigation of *ousia*, since each thing does not seem to be other than its own *ousia*, and the 'essential being' is said to be the *ousia* of each thing." In this passage Aristotle is glancing back at what was already stated in the fourth chapter of Zeta (1029b22–1030a32), namely that one way of defining *ousia* is to say that *ousia* is the "essential being" of a thing in the first and strongest sense of perse-

1 Aristotle, *Metaphysics* 7.6.1031a16–18. The text then compares accidental union with substantial union: "in the case of accidental predicates it might indeed seem to be different, for example a white person is different from the 'essential being' of a white person" (a19–21). Jaeger puts the immediately following lines (a2l–28) in parentheses. They outline in tentative fashion the problem of accidental identity versus substantial identity, quite in the fashion of a school *logos* – Myles Burnyeat, *et al. Notes on Book Zeta of Aristotle's Metaphysics* (Oxford, 1979), 35–36, notes that the final comment in this passage (1031a28) is not explained by Aristotle and can be interpreted in different ways. But the issue is undoubtedly important for Aristotle. It points in the direction of form, whether substantial or accidental, as the cause of being. Though distinct from the composite individual in either case, knowledge from the viewpoint of the form is knowledge of the whole thing and is applicable in universal fashion. Correct understanding of the identity of form with singular thing and yet of the real difference between the two is necessary for explaining the universal aspect of human knowledge.

ity. That would be *ousia* in the sense of the first of the Aristotelian categories. Within it, a person is of course identical with herself or himself. In a white person, also, there is indeed the one composite thing. But the identity of the two components is not so readily grasped. The two components, namely "white" and "person," belong to different categories. The unity is there, but it is accidental unity, not substantial unity, The two make up the one composite thing, but not by way of *per se* unity. Yet each in its own way expresses what the thing is. The same thing is something substantial and something white.

Here the framing of the question calls for discerning study. The contrast is obviously enough between the predication of a thing's substantial nature, as for example "Callias is a human person" and the predication of an accidental nature in the thing, for instance "Callias is pale." Callias would thus seem to be Callias and the "essential being" of Callias, so that the two predicates could be regarded as identical. But one could not argue on that model to the conclusion that Callias is the "essential being" of the accident "pale" because he happens to be pale. A human person is not the "essential being" of the color pale by the fact of being pale. So with regard to the person's substantial nature there is a genuine problem. Is the person identical with that substantial nature in a way that would make the human person and the "essential being" of the person one and the same object? Or is a differentiation to be made between them, and if so, how?

Such is the broad formulation of the problem. One can see easily enough that a substance is not whiteness because it happens to be white (4.1030al–2). So the text (6.103la22–25) merely mentions that way of talking without for the moment giving it special attention. The translation of *ousia* by "substance" in this text brings out the point in very clear fashion, for the substance remains the same under different changes in color. With the English reader the term "substance" will restrict the meaning quite definitely to the first of the Aristotelian categories. One would not easily say in English that the "substance" of an axe is its power to cut, or that sight is the "substance" of the eye, as Aristotle uses the term *ousia* in the *De Anima*, or as he can say that stillness is the *ousia* of calm weather.[2] The general translation of *ousia* in English, as already noted, has to be kept wide enough to cover Aristotle's multivalent meanings of the term. But in the present instance, the rendering of *ousia* by "substance" can easily throw the question back on the failure to recognize multisignificance in the notion. Failures of this kind were continually signalized by Aristotle in his discussions of philosophical topics. So today the restriction of "substance" to the first of the ten Aristotelian categories can easily occasion a question about a relevant difference between the problem of identity or difference of "essential being" in substances and that of the identity or difference of it in accidents. In designating the first of the Aristotelian categories as "substance," the Anglophone thinker readily sets it off as basic to all

2 See *De Anima*, 2.1.412bl9; *Metaphysics*, 8.2.1043a24.

else in the object under consideration. "Substance" is thereby projected as the foundation of every other aspect in the thing. No need arises and no possibility is given for digging deeper and then inquiring, what else there is in the "substance" that would function as its own "essential being." One has reached bedrock, and the inquiry is at a dead end. So represented, *ousia* as the first category rests in itself and should allow nothing else to make it what it is. It is thereby conceived as necessarily identical with its own "essential being." On the other hand, the accidental predicates will by their very nature need something else to explain them. If that something else is the subject in which they inhere as accidents, the accident's formal notion will be prevented from fusing with the formal notion of the substance, as Aristotle (4.1029b16–19) had already demonstrated.

The same technique that had been used for answering the question of "essential being" for the accidental combinations is continued here. The framework of focal reference for the predication of being had been recalled (1029b22–27) as the solution of the difficulty. In treating the question today, one would explain carefully that accidental combinations such as a white person do have their own type of being, and accordingly a type of "essential being" that explains the combining of the substance and accident into the one unit. But in a school *logos*, such as *Metaphysics* Zeta, that simple recalling (1029b2–8) of the differences among the kinds of composites in the categories was sufficient. Each would be seen to have its own type of "essential being."[3]

What was needed, then, was to place the problem in the framework of focal reference. The solution was thereby indicated. In that framework one sees readily that the "essential being" of a human person is not the "essential being" of the color white, for personhood and whiteness do not coincide. In the case at hand, however, the subject that is white does in fact coincide with the subject that is

3 The point emphasized here is that "there is knowledge of each thing when we know the 'essential being' (*Metaphysics*, 7.6.1031b6–7) of the thing." What for Plato had been something external to the immediately encountered thing, namely its Idea, must for Aristotle be within the thing itself. The thing's whatness must be identical with the thing itself, and at the same time other than the singular thing in order to allow universality. That is the overall issue of this whole chapter. In it the stakes are high. They involve the basic difference between Platonic and Aristotelian conceptions of human knowledge. For Aristotle, the task is to explain how what the thing is can be identical with the thing itself and yet extend to all the other singular instances of that thing. What the thing is cannot be a separate Idea, something apart from the instance in which it is currently found. In one way the thing has to be identical with what essentially is its being, and in another way has to be other than it. This holds proportionally for accidental combinations. Each of these combinations, regardless of how loose the combination may be, has its own proper form. On this topic, see *Metaphysics*, 8.1–3.1042a4–1043b2. The term "analogous" (1043a5) is used to describe the situation.

human. The one subject serves as the subject for both features. Hence the text can note parenthetically but forcefully in terse staccato styles:

> As to what is expressed by way of an accident, such as something musical or white – on account of the double signifying, it is not true to say that the "essential being" and the thing itself are the same (for both the accident and that to which it is accidental are white). In consequence there is the possibility that the "essential being" and the thing itself are the same, on the one hand, and on the other hand the possibility that they are not the same; for with the person and the white person they are not the same, but with the modifying feature (*pathos*) they are the same.[4]

This is closely packed reasoning, and has to be read in context. The type of composition is that of the traditional school *logos*. In it propositions and conclusions are assembled. They are drawn up in aporematic style for oral discussion. Here even at first reading one becomes aware that the style is not that of today's essay or monograph, in which the author draws his own conclusions in logical order from premises that are deemed acceptable to both writer and reader. Here, rather, different positions are succinctly stated, and then left to the discussants for

4 *Metaphysics*, 7.6.1031b22–28. For *pathos* in this wide sense of any modification at all, see 1030a14 and b31. Cf. Bonitz, *Index Aristotelicus*, 556a60–b44. Aristotle does not spell out in detail the reasons why a thing in the category of substance is not the same as its own essential being. He merely gives an example, allowing the doctrine to emerge from that example. In the case of a white person both the substance (the person) and the accident (whiteness) are white. Whiteness itself is white, and the substance here modified by it is white. This holds throughout all the categories of the accidents. On the other hand, while both the person and the white person are substances, neither personhood itself nor white personhood is a substance. Personhood does not live or breathe or struggle, nor does white personhood. Generalized, this means that an accident and its accidentality, namely its essential being, are the same, while a substance and the essential being of that substance, namely its substantiality, are not the same. Accordingly substantiality, the essential being of a substance, is not itself a substance. The use of "substantiality" and "personhood" as the grammatical subject in sentences does not at all transmogrify them into substances. So while accidentality remains accidental in character, substantiality does not become a substance. From that viewpoint, the viewpoint of predictability, a thing in the category of substance is not the same as the essential being of that substance, though from the viewpoint of knowability the two are in fact the same in expressing what the thing in question is, whether that thing be a substance or an accident. Basic in the whole problem is the consideration that for Aristotle being is not a still-more-underlying subject in which both substance and accidents would be regarding as inhering. Rather, the predication of being is always made through focal reference to a primary instance. This gives a thing in the category of substance its place as the ultimate subject for predication, and therefore as absolutely bedrock in this regard.

evaluation as well as for the directions that the procedure in regard to dealing with them is to take in the subsequent deliberation. In the present passage, the dominating notion is the double occurrence of the same subject in accidental combinations. This double occurrence had been abruptly advanced shortly before (4.1029bl9) as a basis for arguing. It is used as though it were a notion familiar to the hearers, and needed only a mention to bring it to their minds. It was the ground for the argument that the "essential being" of white and the "essential being" of surface could not fuse with each other. The repetition of the same notion, that of surface, prevented their melding. The surface remained only the subject of the whiteness. The surface and the color did not blend into the one notion. So in a surface that was both white and smooth, the whiteness and the smoothness did not become one and the same in notion, even though they both qualified the same subject. In that way they were one in subject of inherence, but did not become one in notion. If both had fused with the subject, they would have fused with each other. But the double occurrence of the subject, functioning differently in each of those two occurrences, prevented that fusion.

In the present passage (1031b3) the "double signifying" by the same subject in something musical or something white keeps the "essential being" of the color white or the musical proficiency from melding with the subject they qualify, or with each other. They do not become the same as the person or the white person, even though they are accidents of the one and the same subject. The same person may be white and musical, but the basic nature of the person, namely human personhood, is neither whiteness nor music; nor do whiteness and music coincide in notion. On the other hand, the quality white and the undergoing of that qualification by the person are one and the same in their "essential being." The accident does not need another accident to unite it with the subject in which it inheres. If it did, each accident would be what it is in itself but would require an accident over and above to join it to its subject.

That further accident would require another accident to bring about its own union with the subject. Thereby an infinite regress would be set up. The danger resulting from such a regress was something that was holding Aristotle's attention in this discussion.[5] Each new instance would in its notion present yet-another instance without ceasing, just as in standing between two mirrors facing each other one sees image after image of the same thing as far as the visibility extends. Rather, an accident, just by being an accident, is its own union with its subject. That pertains essentially to its own gradation in being. It is not a being that stands in its own right in the way a substance does. Through being white it is a qualification of a corporeal substance, and does not require or allow any further accident to bring about that modification or qualification. The "essential being" of the modification coincides accordingly with the modification itself. There is no

5 Cf. *Metaphysics*, 7.6.1031b28–1032a4.

"double occurrence" of a subject to prevent the fusion of the two. The subject is not functioning first as subject of white and then as subject of the union of that accident with the substance. Being white and being affected by the color white coincide in meaning. Hence Aristotle can say that for this modification of the subject the "essential being" of the accident and the accident itself are one and the same. There is no "double signifying" to keep the two from fusing. Through functioning as the subject of the color white, the human person is thereby functioning as the subject of the accidental union with the color.

The staccato manner in which these considerations are presented in the text of book Zeta indicates clearly enough that the method is not that of our philosophical articles or monographs today. The course of the reasoning is extremely difficult for us to follow. But if this discussion in book Zeta is regarded as the report of a school discussion, need there be anything surprising about its format? The present passage is introduced as though it were proceeding on the basis of a display (*kata tēn ekthesis*, 1031b21) before the eyes of the hearers. With each item being pointed out on the board as it came up – or at least the symbol standing for it – the hearers would have no trouble in seeing at once the exact object to which Aristotle was referring. Today we have to track it down painstakingly from the text. But this explains why we have such difficulty in following the discourse. We look to Aristotle for a straight answer to our questions whether accidental combinations have an "essential being" and definition, or not (4.1029b22–1030a18). Instead of a precise yes or no, we are merely told to look at the gradations in being. Being is not something with the same definite meaning all the time. It can mean substance or any of the accidents, or any of the looser combinations of them.[6] One has to expect a different sense of the notion when it is found in different categories. With these different senses displayed in a synopsis on a board in front of the hearers, a mere pointing to the sense intended would be sufficient. The hearers would know precisely what they were dealing with, and would be in a position to work out the solution for themselves. They would not have to grope for the particular item meant, as we do when reading the text today. The staccato style would be normal under the circumstances. There would be nothing either mysterious or careless about it.

In fact, the effort needed to probe out the meaning today has its advantages. It incites the present-day students to do their own thinking. The answers are not served up to them in cut-and-dried fashion. Their minds have to look at the external world, which for them as for Aristotle is the direct object of human cognition, and let it itself speak to them as it did to the ancient Greek thinker. They may not agree with Aristotle's conclusions, but they do learn from him how to do their

6 See *Metaphysics*, 8.2.1042b15–1043a26. In this context (1043a5) the notion of analogy is used to describe the relation between form and matter in the one case, and between substance and accident in the other.

own thinking. He will remain for them "the teacher of those who know," even though they are doing their own thinking on the basis of their accepted principles or starting points. They become trained to contrast their own methods and the methods of others with the procedure of Aristotle, and to benefit deeply by the comparison. They are made to feel at home in a pluralistic philosophical world, the philosophical world we have today. Aristotle is not doing their thinking for them, but the effort they must make to understand him habituates them to do their own original philosophical thinking in the face of texts that baffle them when read in any other philosophical framework, but which have profound meaning when finally read as following from Aristotle's own starting points. That is the vibrant force of Trendelenburg's oft-quoted dictum *Aristoteles ex Aristotele*. The effort required today to read Aristotle as Aristotle can hardly help but train the student to evaluate all other philosophies in the light of their respective starting points, for it shows tellingly how these different starting points give rise in consistent fashion to the radically different conclusions drawn by the various thinkers.

The style appropriate for the reporting of a school *logos* has accordingly to be allowed its role in the interpretation of the present passages in book Zeta. One has to search painstakingly for the objects to which rapidly successive references allude. The "double signifying" (1031b23), which could be made unmistakably clear by a quick pointing to subject and qualities successively as displayed on the board, has to be traced back today to the text's earlier use (4.1029b19) of the double role played by one and the same subject for preventing the fusion of the "essential being" of white with the "essential being" of surface, and consequently barring it from melding with the "essential being" of smooth. Today the same reasoning can be seen, though laboriously, as functioning with consistency throughout the entire passage. It is not spelled out anew each time, but merely recalled in the fashion adapted to the report of a school *logos*.

In the aporematic setting of the passage, moreover, correct answers to the questions raised were not required. Different positions kept arising from the background, for instance a Platonic conception of the separation of a thing's idea from the perceptible thing itself (6.1031a29–31). These required answering only insofar as necessary in clearing a passage for Aristotle's own doctrine at the moment. The answer, in fact, need apply only to a particular point readily indicated in the display, but which today will rest upon our own analysis. For instance, Burnyeat's record of the London seminar on book Zeta notes that the answer, "this is not actually thought to be the case" (1031a28; Oxford trans.) could mean either "the reduction does work" or "the reduction does not work."[7] For the hearers at the school *logos*, the side intended for the comment could be definitely indicated by a quick pointing to the alternative meant to be excluded. In the aporematic procedure the various historically factual positions on the topic, or the possible posi-

7 See Burnyeat, *Notes* (supra, n. 1), 35.

tions, needed only to be mentioned and ruled out, and in this way leave the path clear for the progress of the main argument.

Likewise in this type of recording a school *logos*, there was no call for spelling out the definite answers that we would expect today in philosophic writing. We would like to know definitely, for instance, whether or not the loose combinations of accidents that are contrasted with substances in Zeta 4 have an "essential being" or genuine definition.[8] Instead, the panoramic focal vision of being, already given in book Gamma, is merely displayed before our eyes. We are left to our own effort for concluding that in the sense of substantial being the accidental combinations do not as such have new substantial being, but that in the sense of the being that is proper in its own grade to the loose combinations of accidents they do have their own appropriate "essential being" and definition. That fact enables them to be known for what they are, as the text will soon (6.1031b6–10) have occasion to mention. But for the moment no need is felt to spell out the answer that the accidental combinations have their proper essential being. The hearers are simply alerted to recall the graded character of the being that is spread throughout the categories, and to draw at once their own conclusion. Again it is a question of the advantage of Aristotle's method in training students to do their own thinking under the guidance of his general procedure.

At this stage, however, the crucial importance of the identity of a thing and its "essential being" comes to the fore. To know a thing is to know its "essential being" (1031b20–21). This is presented as a basic norm, and as holding for each thing in a way that allows no exceptions. The tenet will mean that a thing has to be thoroughly identical with its "essential being" in order to be known. But knowing is the core of Aristotle's conception of *eudaimonia*, that is, of human destiny. The *Metaphysics* opened with the assertion that all people by their very nature strive for knowing. The expansive vision of generation after generation of people yearning continually for further knowledge all through the rise and fall of successive civilizations would demand unlimited opportunity for knowing more and more things. Not only substances and their immediately apparent accidents, but also the actual and possible combinations of them no matter how loose, would fall under the scope of this insatiable desire. Likewise in the eternal flow of ages yet to come, there would always have to be the prospect of appeal to the natural craving for further knowledge. Everything would in its turn be knowable. From this viewpoint each individual thing would require identity with its own "essential being," regardless of its status as substance or accident or loose combination. In principle the Aristotelian framework allowed no limit to the number of knowable things.

That this consideration is uppermost in Aristotle's mind, in the present discussion, immediately comes to the fore. Positions opposed to Aristotle's own tenets had been coming up in aporematic fashion in the text. He now meets the

8 On the looser combinations, see supra, n. 6.

general Platonic view that what a thing is, namely the thing's nature or essence, is to be found in something prior to the thing itself and functioning as a separate Idea. What the thing is should therefore be investigated. In that higher and better occurrence of it. For Aristotle this would mean that the thing and its "essential being" would be separated from each other, with the result that there could not be any knowledge of the thing itself and that the "essential being" of anything could not have the status of a being (6.1031b3–4). What existed, then, could not be known, and what was known could not exist.

For us, these assertions bring in important epistemological considerations. Certainly we wish to know things that have being. Without doubt our innate desire for knowledge extends that far. What a thing is, is basically the thing's "essential being." It has to be present in thorough identity within the thing itself, for it is what the thing itself is. It cannot be separated from the thing. Yet it must in some way be different from the thing itself, or the position that they are different could hardly have arisen. What needs investigation is the reason why any question of separate status for them could have made its appearance.

The issue here is not the modern epistemological problem of relating concepts and ideas to external things. Only from the time of Descartes on is that approach to be found. Ancient Greek Skeptics, Atomists, Platonists, Neoplatonists, and so on, regarded things as directly known in themselves, various though their ways of explaining this immediate cognition were. None of them took the stand that what the mind immediately knows will be ideas or concepts, and that the mind then infers that there are objects apart from them that exist outside them and correspond to them. For Aristotle (*Metaphysics*, 12.9.1074b35–36), expressly, what is immediately and directly known in the concept is something other than the concept itself, with the concept known only concomitantly in the cognition of the other thing.[9] Only with Descartes and Malebranche did the attitude become entrenched that what the human mind knows immediately and directly are its own ideas. Nothing could be more present to the mind, this attitude claimed, than the mind itself and its content. Accordingly knowledge of things outside the mind had to be based upon the ideas that were in the mind. To know about the stars you did not make a journey around the heavens, but reasoned to conclusions about them from the ideas present in your mind. Our ideas or concepts are therefore the basis of our knowledge of what things are in themselves, and scientific or philosophic knowledge has to be based on clear and distinct ideas. Little place is left in truly philosophical procedure for concepts like that of the Aristotelian notion of being, which ranges in orderly fashion through varied but related senses. Rather, the Aristotelian procedure is based directly upon the things themselves. It finds them, as known directly in themselves, to have those

9 On this topic of cognition *in obliquo*, see John E. Smith, "Hartmann's New Ontology," *Review of Metaphysics*, 7 (1954), 583–601.

focal gradations. To the things themselves it looks for scrutiny of what they are, and not directly to the concepts.

The question here, then, is not whether the thing itself is the same as or different from the human concept of that thing. In this context "what the thing is" means what the thing is in itself. Both the thing itself and what the thing is are regarded as known directly in themselves. What is asked is whether the two are the same. The answer is that they have to be the same, if what has being is to be known, and what is known is to have being. The question is not at all whether internal concept corresponds to external thing.

What, then, is the exact concern of the present question? Does it not bear obviously enough upon things that are seen in the real world, things directly known by the human mind? The question is whether each of those things is identical with what the mind knows about it, or whether what is known about it is different from the individual thing itself. The reason of the question should be apparent from the whole course of the *Metaphysics*. The reason is the problem of universality. The *Metaphysics* in its opening chapter showed that human knowledge is characterized by universality and thereby differs from the type of cognition possessed by the lower animals. It is in fact developed by way of the universal. The definition is of the universal, and accordingly enables human knowledge to reach things far beyond those immediately known. What the thing is, then, ranges beyond the individual thing itself. The question, therefore, arises about how the individual thing and what it is are identical, and how they are different. They have to be identical if human knowledge is to be of real things. They have to be in some way other if the knowledge is to be universal. The sameness and the otherness are being regarded as aspects located in the things themselves. The question is not focused upon the difference between the concept that exists in the mind and the thing that exists in the outside world. It concentrates on a situation that is seen in the things themselves. It finds that to know each thing is to know its "essential being" (6.1031b6–7; cf. b20–21). In this way it is brought face to face with the crucial problem of how the grasp of the individual thing's "essential being" is the knowing of the individual thing itself. Hence the question is worded in terms of an identity and difference that are found present in the things themselves, and not between the things in themselves and the concepts of them that are formed by the human mind.

Reading back from this explicitly stated goal of the general inquiry, one is now in a position to judge the import of the various steps taken to reach the present stage of the discussion. The question is worded in terms of the identity of the individual thing with its "essential being," on the one hand, and on the other hand, of the difference that has to be recognized between the two. The continued repetition of the Greek term *hekaston* throughout the text (1031a16–b20) shows that the individual thing is meant. At the same time, an operative distinction between what the thing is as identified with the individual instance, and what its intelligible content is when extended to other individuals of the same kind, has to be acknowledged. The universality required for human knowledge, as outlined in the opening chapter of the *Metaphysics* in contradistinction to cognition in the lower animals, manifests the difference. *What* each thing is, is individual in that particular thing. In human knowledge, however, what that same thing is becomes universal and predicable of other individuals. Socrates is a person, but also other individuals are equally persons. Hence in a thing's definition, which expresses its "essential being," the particular thing thereby known cannot be mentioned (4.1029b19–21). Other persons are not Socrates, though they are persons.

The central issue here at stake, then, is how human knowledge of individual things can expand into the knowledge of the whole universe, in the way pursued by scientific and philosophical endeavor. It is about the way in which the soul can be all things, as in the wording of *De Anima* (3.8.431b21). It concerns the destiny and ultimate beatitude of people. Though things exist as individuals, they all have "essential being" that is identical with them, but which nevertheless differs from the individual in extending outside the individual limitations. In a word, the question bears incisively upon the meaning and purpose of human life. For Aristotle, this consideration amply justified the meticulous inquiry here into the difference between things themselves and their "essential being," a difference effectively present in the things themselves without detriment to the real identity of the two. For us today, it should prompt careful attention to the way in which individuality and universality, which *prima facie* seem to be mutually exclusive characteristics are nevertheless combined in the basic objects of human cognition. In those objects which are individual things, the ground for universality is directly seen. How that aspect of universality is known is a problem to be considered in the next chapter.[10]

But from the conception of the knowing intellect in *De Anima*, (3.4.429a22–24), one sees that it can add neither content nor structure to the things it grasps. For Aristotle there is no prior structure in the mind, by which things could be given their form. There is only the potentiality for receiving those forms and thereby becoming cognitionally what the objects themselves are. All the actuality in the object known has to come from the source outside the intellect. For Aristotle there is no prior structure in the mind by which the things known could be constructed for human cognition. All their features have to come from the things themselves. No a priori framework can be appealed to for their explanation. The explanation has to come from the side of the things. If one is following Aristotle's explanation of cognition, one cannot look for the ultimate ground of the universality in the activity of the human faculty. The ultimate account has to come from the nature of the thing itself. The structure of the intellection has to be explained by the structure of the thing known.

10 See infra, ch. 8, nn. 6–9.

It is against this Aristotelian background that the conclusion of chapter six in book Zeta is to be assessed. The conclusion runs: "How the 'essential being,' then, is the same and how it is not the same as each thing, has been stated."[11] The issue is worded in terms of simultaneous identity and difference. There is no tendency to exclude either side. On the one hand, there is the individual thing, whether the thing meant be a substance such as a person, or an accident such as an instance of the color white, or a loose combination of objects. On the other hand, there is likewise a condition in each of these things that allows it to be grouped under universal headings and accordingly makes possible the knowledge that is scientific and typically human. The conclusion of this chapter of book Zeta explicitly retains both these sides. Both sides have to be acknowledged. Taken together, they show how human knowledge grasps individual things and how the things we know in universal fashion have individual being in themselves. Neither side is to be jettisoned. Both are required in order to explain how human knowledge is of individual things yet extends far beyond the things that are immediately knowable.

What each individual thing is, then, has to be identical with that individual. Yet it has to be different from that one individual when it exists in other instances. The object "person" is identical with Socrates in Socrates himself, but in Callias it is other than Socrates and identical with Callias. How can this two-sided condition be explained? The issue at stake is the way the universal feature reaches out

11 *Metaphysics*, 7.6.1032a10–11. From the viewpoint of knowability, the viewpoint with which Aristotle is here concerned in contrast to the Platonic view of knowledge as something based upon forms separate from the individual things, this statement is undoubtedly clear. In every case to know a thing is to know its essential being. From that viewpoint the two are always the same. From the viewpoint of predicability, however, somewhat closer scrutiny is required. With things in the category of substance, Aristotle (1031b27) had just stated that the thing and its essential being are not the same. Here he is not saying anything to the contrary. He is stating that in things in which the predication is being made in the same category and not through an accidentally added category, the thing and its essential being are one and the same. Predicates that belong to a person as a person, in contrast to those that belong to the person as white, come under this observation. It holds wherever the predication is made within the same category. That is the force of the term "primary" at 1031b14 and 1032a5. It means that no further category is introduced for making the predication. The thing's essential being is the basis for universality, and therefore has to remain one and the same with the thing throughout the universal predication. That holds respectively for substances and accidents. But to ground universality in the category of substance, the essential being of that substance has to be different from that substance itself, for the substance itself is individual and just as such could not be the ground for universal predication. With accidents, on the contrary, the individualization comes from the substance in which the accident inheres. Accordingly from this side also an accident and that accident's essential being can be identical.

beyond the immediate instance. That feature holds necessarily and at all times. It finds expression in the Aristotelian formula worded *to ti ēn einai* – the "essential being" of the thing. The Greek imperfect conveys the timeless character of what the thing is, namely something that remains stable as it extends through all the individual instances. It likewise has the overtones of what is basic in the thing's nature, something that was there all the while and now has finally been reached in the procedure for understanding the thing. But despite this way in which it differs from the individual thing, to know it is to know what that individual thing is. To express it in a definition is accordingly to state what the individual is.

It is a question, therefore, of showing how the identically same object can be known both as something individual and something universal. One and the same intelligible object, namely what the thing is, is grasped in two different ways. In both ways it is known. This is the sense in which the sixth chapter of book Zeta reaches (1032a10–11) its ultimate conclusion that each thing and its "essential being" are from one viewpoint the same and from another not the same. No further explanation is offered. This is understandable in the procedure of a school *logos*, in which positions arising from various philosophical traditions are brought forward for discussion. In the context they require discussion only insofar as they might appear as roadblocks (*aporiai)* to the progress of Aristotle's own reasoning. Placed in that aporematic setting, they are not examined against their original backdrop and on the strength of their own intrinsic merits. They are merely checked to make sure that they present no hindrance to the cogency of Aristotle's thought as it follows from its own starting points. Here the position brought forward is from Platonic circles. It claims that what a thing basically is has to be separate from its individual instances. Aristotle for the moment does not discuss that position as it arises in its own historical setting. He merely shows that on his own understanding of things, the individual thing would not be known at all. This is sufficient to remove the roadblock. Nothing further is required in the aporematic procedure of the school *logos*.

A different situation, however, has to be faced today when the problem is placed against the Cartesian background in which the immediately known objects of the human mind are its own ideas. An *aporia* of this kind would send the present-day reader back to Aristotle's own notion of cognition. For Aristotle, what is directly known in any act of human cognition is something other than itself, for the knowing mind, because entirely potential in the cognitive order, does not add anything to what is directly known. The distinction in question here cannot lie between the idea in the mind and the individual thing in the real world. The basis for the distinction will have to lie in the thing itself, and not in the activity of the human intellect. The human intellect merely knows what it sees in the thing. It does not impose the structure on the thing itself. We today have to go to the detailed doctrine of the *Posterior Analytics* (2.19.99b15–100b3), in which the individual thing is shown to have the same intelligible content as the universal, while the soul (100a13–14) is of such a nature that it is acted upon by the intelligible object in this way. The purely potential nature of the knowing intellect requires that the actual structure of what it knows must come from the individual thing itself. Nothing can be added to the individual thing by being known. Basically the universality of what it is has to originate in the individual. Aristotle himself, however, had no occasion to face an *aporia* of this kind. When it is brought forward today, it calls for treatment as a roadblock to be removed on appeal to Aristotle's general stand on the nature of human cognition, which does not add anything positive to what it knows. Surely the aspect of universality is something positive in things. In the human mind it can be actualized separately as a universal in contrast to the singular, for the purposes of philosophical understanding in regard to the processes of judgment and reasoning. But like all other positive features, it has to come from the thing that is known. The feature of universality, as Aristotle understands it, has to be accounted for on the basis of the thing that is external to human cognitive activity. It is not something that accrues to it solely from the mind's activity, something that originates in the idea of the thing in contrast to the thing itself.

With this understanding of the situation, the steps pursued in chapter six of book Zeta fall into intelligible focus. The problem it faces is expressly formulated in terms of whether the "essential being" and the individual are the same or whether the one is not the other (6.1031a15–16). This formulation would suggest that the answer is going to exclude one of the two alternatives. But, as just seen, the conclusion of the chapter (1032a10–11) claims to have shown how the two are the same and how they are not the same as each other. On careful investigation they are found to be in one way identical with each other and in another way not identical. They are identical insofar as both mean what the thing is. The intelligible content is the same. But while the notion of that content, namely of what the thing is, stays limited to the individual instance in that first way of knowing it, in the second way it extends beyond the individual instance and is applicable to all other instances in which that notion may be found. In this way it grounds in a necessary manner the knowledge of instances outside the individual in which it was originally known, and makes possible the expansion of knowledge in accord with the deepest human yearnings. Knowledge of it in this latter way is knowledge of its "essential being." It is knowledge of what the thing is, but now in a way that reaches outside the individual instance in which it is encountered and provides for unlimited expansion to other instances in accord with the human desire to know. It provides the stable feature that runs through all those instances and makes scientific knowledge of them possible.

The topic is approached in the tentative fashion of a school *logos*. The hearers are presumed to accept the stand that each individual thing is not something other than its own substance (*ousia*) and that the "essential being" is meant to be the substance of each thing (1031a17–18). From the viewpoint of the Aristotelian schema of the categories, this would express the notion that substance, the first of the categories, is basic to all else in the thing. The thing's substance underlies them all, pervades them all, and gives them all an abiding and unifying characteristic. The nature of the human person spreads in this way through all the accidents, making all the organs and all the activities human in contrast to the corresponding accidents in other living things. Similarly with the hearers coming from Platonic circles, what the thing is could be located outside the individual thing in the region of the Ideas. It would remain fixed and permanent, grounding the necessary and unchanging features in the thing that made cogent reasoning possible and allowed human knowledge to be extended far beyond the limits of the individual thing confronting the mind. This separation of what the thing is from the thing itself is what Aristotle aims to contest. But for the moment it can be paired with the first of the Aristotelian categories in showing how the "essential being" of a thing may be regarded as its substance. It is the kind of being that makes a thing be what it is throughout a number of different instances and through accidental changes with the course of time. Socrates will remain Socrates and the person will remain a person, however one may care to explain in Platonic fashion the "essential being" of Socrates. The point is that one may readily admit the identity of "essential being" and individual instance when one is speaking of the thing's substance. In accord with the aporematic procedure of an Aristotelian school *logos* a possible roadblock has been removed, and the main reasoning of the treatise can proceed.

With regard to accidental categories, however, the removal of the roadblock is not so easy. A white person is something other than the "essential being" of a white person, as Aristotle had already shown (6.1031a19–24; cf. 4.1029b16–22). It could seem, then, in contrast to the case of substance, that in each individual instance of an accident the "essential being" may be other than the accident itself. Where the union of the features is just accidental, the unity required in the middle term for reasoning is not attained. The extremes do not come together in the middle term. That a person is white does not give that person all the features involved in whiteness, such as being a color or a quality. The person is white, but not whiteness. The main purpose at issue here, namely the validity of scientific knowledge, would not seem to be guaranteed by accidental unions.

This *aporia* to the acknowledgment of identity of "essential being" and individual instance in the case of accidents is met by a closer look at the way the extremes may come together in a middle term (1031a25–28). May they not coincide in accidental fashion, as for instance in the case of the "essential being" of white and the "essential being" of musical? The import of this example is not given further development. The person can be both white and musical simultaneously. In this way "white" and "musical" may be regarded as coinciding accidentally. May not the "essential being" of each of them be regarded as coinciding with each other in functioning as a middle term? A negative answer is suggested.

But whether the negation bears on the use of this example to illustrate the situation, or whether it is meant to rule out the possibility of an accidental union serving as a middle term, is not clear from the written report of the school *logos*. Certainly whiteness and personhood do not come together in the same middle term in the way that "animal" serves as a middle term in a syllogistic sequence. A horse is an animal and an animal is a living thing, therefore a horse is necessarily a living thing. But the possibility that the accidental combination might serve as a middle term is suggested. In that case would the "essential being" of the white person be identical with the individual instance? Such is the question as it may be phrased today. An affirmative answer may be suggested. Socrates is a white person, a white person is a living thing and the subject of accidents, therefore Socrates too has those predicates. Yet white personhood could not be substituted for white person as that middle term. The "essential being" and individual instance do not appear to be identical. "White" and "subject of accidents" could each serve in turn as the middle term. But the accidental combination of the two could not. Or could it?

Here Aristotle (1031b24–28) offers the explanation that the thing itself and the "essential being" of the thing are in this case the same and not the same. They coincide in constituting the same accidental composite, the white person. The accidental union of white and person is nothing other than this modification of the substance by the color. From that viewpoint the "essential being" of the accidental composite is exactly the same in notion as a modification of a substance by an accident, and as the undergoing of this modification by the substance. Accordingly, the higher genera in each of the respective categories, namely substance and quality, are predicable of the individual Socrates. They are each what Socrates is, to the extent of their signification. As a person, Socrates is something living, something sentient, and something rational, according to the ascent to the supreme genus, or category, under which these predicates fall. They are genera in the category of substance. As white, moreover, Socrates is visible and sensibly perceptible, in accord with the ascent in the category of quality. Both sets of predicates, in consequence, apply to the white person. They furnish, each in its own way, the ground for understanding in universal fashion what the other individual instances are. From that viewpoint they extend outside the individual white person in which they are originally seen.

If this were not the case, what an individual thing is would be completely confined to that individual itself. Nothing in it could help in knowing other things. Nothing in it could serve as a middle term in which the extremes would coincide. Knowledge of the individual Socrates as a person or as something white could not be extended outside Socrates himself. But the facts are that it can be, as is observable in the way the human mind extends its knowledge. It is not a question of deducing this from any a priori notion, but rather of observing what actually takes place in the reality of human reasoning. That is sufficient to remove a roadblock, where the procedure is aporematic. The objection here is that what a thing is has to be outside the individual instance, in the fashion of a Platonic Idea, if it is to ground the expansion of human knowledge.

This *aporia* is set aside by Aristotle (6.1031b14–18) in showing that the extension of what a thing is, namely its "essential being," to its presence in other individuals does not require separate Ideas. Rather, it will perhaps be better guaranteed without separate Ideas than with them. Because separate from the individual, as in the Platonic view, the Idea would obviously be something other than the individual thing. Further, the Idea would then not be predicable of the individual as something that the individual is, but only as something in which the individual shares. Surely this is the tone of an aporematic procedure, in which politeness to an objector in his presence rings through and through. It is not the language of a straight exposition of one's own positive tenets. To point out that here the "essential being" of the individual thing can remain identical with the thing while abstracting from the individuality, is sufficient to remove the roadblock. It does not explain positively what abstraction in this sense is. It merely shows that as a matter of fact in the human cognitive process no such separation of "essential being" from individual thing need be involved. The way is thereby left open for further consideration of identity yet difference, without hindrance from the reasons that prompted the Platonic appeal to separately existent Ideas.

As one faces the facts, then, Socrates is a person without being personhood. Others can be persons without being Socrates. The "essential being" of a person, namely what Socrates is, extends beyond him to other individuals. The universality of the predicate "person" is thereby established. It is what Socrates is, and accordingly identical with him. But it extends beyond him, and from that viewpoint is not the same as he is. That is what the situation is, as it confronts one in reality. This combined identity and difference holds similarly for all the higher predicates in the category of substance. Socrates is a sentient being, a living being, a corporeal being, a substance, as one ascends the category. He is each of these. But he is not animality, life, corporeity, or substantiality. In this way, as the facts confront us, he is respectively the same and not the same as his "essential being." The identity of himself with his "essential being," and at the same time the universality grounded in that "essential being" insofar as the "essential being" is identical with each of the other instances in turn, are both guaranteed.

This is not too difficult to see when one remains within the same category. But what takes place when two different categories are involved? The one individual Socrates is indeed a white person. But he is not white personhood. The repeated occurrence of himself as a person and as white prevents the two predicates from fusing with each other, as Aristotle (4.1029b14–22) had already insisted. In every accidental category, he had noted there (b23–25), a composite of substance and accident is to be found. Here both the person and the accidental predicate are white. But the same reasoning holds as in the case of person and personhood. Socrates is a white person, yet he is not white personhood. Individuals other than Socrates can be white persons. The "essential being" of a white person therefore grounds universality. Here also the individual instance and the "essential being" are the same and not the same, according to the respective viewpoints.

But how can the two predicates, each from a different category, coalesce in the one middle term? As a fact they do so. White persons are easily susceptible to sunburn, Socrates is a white person; therefore, Socrates is easily susceptible to sunburn. Knowledge of what a white person is grounds universal application to other instances. The universality of the knowledge does not follow from either of the two predicates taken separately, as it did in the case of the predication of superior genera within the same category. Within the same category it was easy enough to see how the individual thing could be each of the higher predicates. But here, in the accidental composite, the two supreme genera do not coalesce in any univocal notion of being. Substance and quality are not species of being. The relationship of the secondary instances of being to one another follows from the relation of each of them to the primary instance of being. The relationship remains *pros hen*. It never becomes *kath' hen*. Accordingly, the link that combines a quality or any other accident with a substance. In the way in which the composite of the two can act as a middle term in reasoning is not predicable of them in the way the categorical designations are. Both substance and accident are being, but not univocally. Hence Aristotle can say that because both the subject here affected and the accident affecting it are white, it is true to say that here "essential being" and thing are the same and not the same, for they are not the same in either the person or the white person, but they are the same in the case of the accidental modification.[12]

What does this mean? Modification of the substance by the accident, and the modifying by accident, are the same. This situation, already noted, is parallel to Aristotle's teaching in the *De Anima* (3.2.425b25–426a5) in regard to the efficient causality in sensation. The efficient causality and the undergoing of that efficient causality are one and the same. In the present context the modifying and the being modified are likewise one and the same. No new accident, which would generate an infinite regress, is required or allowed. There is no special difficulty here in seeing how the modifying and the being modified must coalesce. The difference of "essential being" from individual thing follows cogently from what Aristotle (1029b13–17) had already said about the way reception in a subject prevents the fusion of the accidents with substance or with one another in the case of a white surface or (b27) a white person. But the individual accident "white" is its own accidentality, since any accident is its own accidentality by not requiring or allow-

12 Text supra, n. 4.

ing anything else to unite it with the substance it modifies. It is its own "essential being" and accordingly grounds universal predication. It remains an accidental connection, for that is what it is. But that same kind of accidental connection is seen in other individual instances. The extremes in the reasoning that uses it as a middle term remain accidentally connected in every instance, and accordingly connected with each other in universal fashion. Individual instance and "essential being" are thereby the same as each other from the standpoint of the accidental modification. It is in that modification that the two are joined together and constituted as a unitary accidental predicate that applies universally to its other instances. In its case the extremes do coalesce in a middle term.

This procedure is sufficient for the aporematic side of a school *logos*. It removes the roadblock emerging from the claim that accidental connection cannot ground cogent reasoning. As a matter of fact that type of reasoning does take place. The above discussion merely explains how that type of reasoning is justified. One might well ask, however, why such intricate and difficult reasoning has any worthwhile purpose in the philosophy of Aristotle. Aristotle himself does not face that question explicitly. But the answer can be seen vividly enough in today's expansion of the sciences. The experimental and social sciences are dealing entirely with accidental combinations of the kind that has been studied in the above survey. Experimental and social scientists are not at all interested in going up and down the Aristotelian categories in which their topics are encountered. They are concerned only with composites of substance and accidents. They do not deal, for instance, with water just as a substance. Their starting points are its freezing and its boiling, its weight, its relations to things around it, and its role in human living. All these are composites of substance and accident, just as is the white person that Aristotle took as an example. The combinations can be strict as in the case of the chemical properties of water, or loose as in the case of a river or an ocean. The social sciences deal with accidental combinations of the latter type, such as societies and nations. For Aristotle himself, all moral and all productive philosophy dealt with combinations of substance with action and substance with production. Even in the theoretical order, natural philosophy bore upon combinations of substance and quantity, the mathematical sciences of astronomy, acoustics, mechanics, and the like dealt with combinations of substances with extension, and accordingly were concerned with composites of substance and accidents. The vastly overwhelming part of human scientific endeavor, in consequence, bears upon accidental composites, as Aristotle understood that phrase. To show *how* universality could be had in the study of these composites was in that regard an important task, and merited the intricate consideration given in book Zeta of the *Metaphysics*. In all the cases of reasoning in these sciences, the "essential being" had to be both identical with the accidental composite as an individual thing, and yet differ from that individual by allowing its intelligible content to extend to other instances. As in all other cases of reasoning, mention of the particular thing was not present in the definition that served as a middle term. In all the cases, the same thing is known in two different ways.

In concluding this chapter of book Zeta, Aristotle (1032a4–6) notes how in things that are primary and not predicated of anything else (cf. 1031b13–14), each thing and its "essential being" are one and the same. These things are the separate substances. Since they have no matter, they have no principle that would permit pluralization within the one species. Knowledge of what one individual is could not be extended in universal fashion to knowledge of anything else. Here self-knowledge does not allow knowledge of anything else. The knowledge of each separate substance is confined to itself. It is completely identical with the knower, and extends to nothing outside itself. This is the doctrine of book Lambda of the *Metaphysics* (12.9.1074b15–35). It accordingly bears out the implications of book Zeta in regard to the coalescence of individual and "essential being" in the primary substances. There is only one way in which these immaterial things can be known immediately, and in that way of knowing them no extension of the knowledge to other things is possible.

With regard to material things, however, there is a second way of knowing. Though the individual is known as identical with what it is in itself, it is also known in a way that allows its intelligible content minus the individuality to be predicated of other similar individuals. That is a fact of human thinking and discourse. It is not an abstract deduction. But an objection to it at once arises from the Platonic mentality. Knowledge of individual instances, in the genuine sense of knowledge, is for Aristotle the knowing of their "essential being." In Platonic language, this would mean knowing their Idea, which is separate from them. Aristotle wishes to remove this roadblock to the progress of his thought, by showing how the union of "essential being" and the individual is better guaranteed without Platonic Ideas than with them. The individual instances are different from the Ideas. To know the Ideas, then, need not mean knowing what the individuals are. The Idea could be wrapped in itself after the manner in which the Aristotelian primary beings, which are not predicated of anything else, are confined each to itself. The Aristotelian view can place both aspects in the individual thing itself, and yet maintain that what the thing is can be known in two different ways. What it is can be known as individual in each instance of it, and still at the same time can be seen in precisive abstraction from the individual as it manifests itself in the definition that does not expressly include its mention. The individual subject of the color white is white, in Aristotle's (1030a1; 1031b24–25) example. This is an instance of it. But the color itself, whiteness, also is white, regardless of the particular subject in which the individualization occurs.

Further, as Aristotle (6.1032a9–10) notes in concluding the chapter, it does not matter here whether one uses the starting points from which the objection was framed, or those from which one may successfully solve the problem. In either case, this observation would seem to mean, the fact of combined difference and sameness does not block the progress of the Aristotelian analysis. The combined difference and sameness is present in the Platonic explanation, for the Idea differs from the individual instance through its separation from it, but exhibits the same intelligible content in making possible the genuine knowledge of the singular thing. That brief way of treatment is understandable in the aporematic procedure belonging to a school *logos*. The one illustration given is the problem whether Socrates and the "essential being" of Socrates are the same. Here Socrates and Socratiety coincide.[13] Socrates is not predicable of anything else, quite as an Aristotelian separate substance is its own individuality. The problem arises only when the "essential being" pertains to a subject other than itself, as is the case in corporeal substances and accidental composites. In them, "essential being" differs from thing in a way that grounds universality in predication. Within each distinct category, there is no problem about the genera being predicated of the same subject, as a person remains the same subject under the generic predications of being, living being and corporeal being. In composites that unite substance and accident, as in a white person, each particular accident is its own accidentality. This avoids an infinite regress. By not bringing in a new subject for the accidentality, it also keeps the accidental composite firm and unchanging, and thereby allows it to serve as the same middle term throughout a whole reasoning process.

13 *Metaphysics*, 7.6.1032a8. Aristotle here remarks that it makes no difference in this case whether one is using one's own principles or those of the discussant, for the purpose at hand. This holds in the method of a school *logos*, where the purpose is to remove a roadblock. In the example of Socrates, Socrates himself remains a substance and as such cannot be the same as his own essential being. But the notion is universalized in the adjective "Socratic," e.g. in expressions such as Socratic method, Socratic discourses, Socratic character. In this way the distinction between Socrates and "Socratiety" has been paralleled with that between *homo* and *humanitate*. Cf ."Uno modo quo distinguitur et constituitur formaliter sicut homo humanitate et Socrates Socrateitate." Thomas Aquinas, *Quaestiones Disputatae de Potentia*, 8.3. Resp., ed. P. M. Pession, 9th ed. rev. (Turin's Marietti, 1953), 220b. This, however, is the only instance of "Socrateitas" found listed for Aquinas in Busa's *Index Thomisticus*, s.v. The one point of interest here is the way Socratiety can be paralleled with human personhood. Each of the two is thereby represented as something standing in its own right, though neither is to be regarded as a substance. But each does convey in adjectival fashion the meaning contained in the noun. In accord with one's viewpoint at the moment, then, one will regard a thing in the category of substance as the same or as not the same as its own essential being. From the viewpoint of knowability the two are the same. From the viewpoint of predication, however, they are not the same. The substance itself accounts for its own individuality, but its essential being enables it to be predicated of other individuals in universal fashion. From this viewpoint a thing in the category of substance is not the same as its own essential being, even in the case of Socratiety. Socratiety is not a substance, though Socrates is, and Socratiety can be seen in the activities and conduct of other persons.

That is the import of Aristotle's (6.1031b27–28) assertion that "essential being" and thing itself are not the same in the case of person or white person, but that they are the same in the case of the undergoing of the accidental modification.

Much of this material in the sixth chapter of book Zeta makes extremely difficult reading for today. The topics are not presented in the running expository style of a modern scholarly treatise. Much seems left to our choice, such as the answers to the questions whether accidental composites have an "essential being" of their own, or whether the extremes can coalesce in a middle term when the reasoning is about those composites. But that procedure is to be expected in a school *logos*. The answers to those questions, however, can be gathered readily from what the treatise positively establishes. The treatise recalls the gradation of being in the Aristotelian categories, which demands a different kind of being in a substance and in accidents, with the implication that the same kind of "essential being" is not to be looked for in an accidental composite as in a substance. Nor is the same kind of self-identity to be expected in an accidental composite as in something that belongs to just one category.

The positive information necessary for meeting the problems is accordingly given in this treatise and its method is stimulating and rewarding, even for today's demands. The effort required for understanding the Aristotelian text engenders careful thought about the difference between the abstract and the concrete, and about the role of the abstract in extending human knowledge beyond the individual things immediately perceived. But to be of genuine help today, the text has to be read painstakingly against the background of its own original style and composition. That is what is meant by the dictum *Aristoteles ex Aristotle*, at least in regard to the immediate problem at issue here.

Chapter 8

"Essential Being" and Form

As noted earlier,[1] Aristotle in introducing the four causes in book Alpha of the Metaphysics (3.983a26–32) uses the phrase *to ti ēn einai* in a context in which it is synonymous with the thing's form, that is, with the formal cause that had been studied in the *Physics*. Similarly in book Delta of the *Metaphysics*, the book in which the various senses of philosophical terms are discussed, the phrase is given the meaning of the shape or form of the thing. Shape and form are the designations used for it in the *Physics*. These designations are repeated in *Metaphysics* Delta (8.1017b21–26) even while the expression is being explained as the account given in the thing's definition. This is quite the way the thing's "essential being" is looked upon in the chapters of *Metaphysics* Zeta that have just been examined. Does this mean, then, that the "essential being," which provides the genuine knowledge of the thing, is synonymous with the thing's form?

There are numerous indications in the continuance of book Zeta that this is the case. At Zeta 7.1032a15–27 the discussion is placed in a strong background of natural philosophy. The physical form is what grounds universality. It does so by enabling like traits to be found in other individual instances. This is what the thing's essential being made possible in the preceding discussions. The background in natural philosophy is also stressed at Zeta 11.1037a14–16, where the philosophy of nature is expressly called a secondary type of philosophy in contrast to the primary philosophy, because it bears upon corporeal things. The form that grounds universality in corporeal beings is clearly what Aristotle has in mind when regarding form as another way of denoting "essential being."

In this perspective, the form is explicitly called *to ti ēn einai* and the primary *ousia* of each thing (7.1032b1–2). Aristotle at 10.1035b32 bluntly declares that by form he means the "essential being." At 7.1032b14–16, the form considered without the matter is the "essential being" of the thing, and knowledge that proceeds from the form is knowledge proceeding from that "essential being." Also at 11.1037a28–b4, form without matter is equated with "essential being." At 10.1035b16 and 11.1037al–2, form and "essential being" are used as equivalent

1 Supra, ch.6, n. 1.

notions, and at 13.1038b14–17 and 17.1041a19–b9 "essential being" serves as an alternative expression for *ousia* in the sense of form or formal cause.[2]

These considerations are amply sufficient to show that by "essential being" and by form Aristotle means exactly the same entity. The only difference in the two is that the one is phrased in terms of concepts while the other is taken from terms used in the philosophy of nature. There can be no doubt about the fact of the equivalence of the two expressions from the viewpoint of reference to the same object. But there are difficulties in seeing that basically the two mean that same thing. Form tends to be looked upon as something that can be separated from the matter in which it happens to be present at the moment, as for instance the form of a table disappears from the wood when the discarded table is chopped up to help with a bonfire. Moreover, the same matter takes on a new form when the wood is burned to ashes. On the other hand, the subject of the "essential being," namely the individual thing, seems from this viewpoint to be really inseparable from that "essential being." The difference between them lies in the way the human intellect knows the "essential being" in precisive abstraction from the individual. It is true that the same material thing provides the ground for being known in those two different ways. What an animal is can be expressed in the content of its definition. So known, it can be predicated in universal fashion of all individual animals. But also, what the animal is can be known in precisive abstraction as animality. So prescinded, it cannot be predicated of individual animals. No individual animal is animality itself. Taken in this way it is the "essential being" of the individual animals qua animals.

In this model of precisive abstraction, however, there is no question of any real subject such as matter that could be contrasted with form. The contrast is of form with the individual thing as a whole. The subject here is the entire individual. It includes both the matter and the form. Socrates, as distinguished from his Socrateity, includes both those constituents. The distinction between the individual as the subject and the "essential being" as characterizing it in the way animality makes something an animal, is not a distinction that would allow the subject to pass over into a new form in the fashion of physical matter. In the model of physical change, the same matter is represented as passing over to a new form through the destruction of one individual and the generation of another and new individual. But with the "essential being," quite differently, one has something that is really identical with the individual and distinct from it only in the prescinding cognition of the human mind, which in this case does not express the individuation. More bluntly, from the angle of the subject, matter is something that can

2 Even though at 1041b8 the explicit reference to "form" may be regarded as a later insertion (see Jaeger's text, ad loc.), it at least indicates that "form" was traditionally understood as *ousia* in this sense. Jaeger also excises, as a later addition, the sentence that repeats the equating of the formal cause with the thing's "essential being" in the assertion at 104la28.

change in form, while the individual is not a subject that can change in "essential being." How, then, can the two designations, namely form and "essential being," refer to the same object?

The difference between individual and "essential being" had already been carefully scrutinized in book Zeta (6.1031a15–1032a11). The individual and its "essential being" are in one way the same, for each expresses what the thing is. In another way they are not the same, for the one includes the thing's individuality while the other leaves it out. The distinction between them, accordingly, takes place in the human mind. What the material thing is, lends itself to being known in that twofold way. No distinction is thereby located in the thing itself. The distinction is only a mental one. On the other hand, the distinction between the matter and the form is present in the real thing, regardless of human consideration. The physical matter is something that goes on to exist under another form, when the previous form has gone out of existence. In the original illustrations in the *Physics* (1.7.189b30–191a12), observable objects such as stone or bronze or gold take on new shapes through the work of the artist.[3] Through analogy with these observable subjects in accidental changes, Aristotle reasons to an unobservable subject that remains the same in the generation of natural objects, as when earth, air, fire, and water (*Physics*, 1.6.189b4) are changed into each other. One of the constituents, the matter, remains in existence. The other constituent, the form of earth or air or fire or water, is no longer there. The distinction between the form and the matter, as presented in this model, seems to be something very real. How, then, can it allow the notion of form to be equated with that of "essential being"? At least, it gives rise to hesitations. It suggests a close look at the Aristotelian notion of matter, to determine how it involves any new reality in the individual thing.

For Aristotle, matter taken just as such is not something that can be an object of thought. In the present context he states decisively: "But matter is unknowable in itself."[4] Likewise, near the beginning of the present discussion, he had asserted that matter has none of the characteristics by which being is determined. Nevertheless it is the subject of which the substance is asserted.[5] Here one is encountering the notion of something that does not add to the intelligible content of a thing. The matter is indeed a constitutive part of the corporeal composite, yet it is not the source of any new intelligibility for it. The intelligibility, even in regard to the matter, has to come entirely from the thing's other constituent, that is, from the form.

3 For this illustration in the *Metaphysics*, see 7.3.1029a1–7.

4 *Metaphysics*, 7.10.1036a9, Oxford trans.

5 *Metaphysics*, 7.3.1029a20–24. On this text, see J. Brunschwig, "La forme, prédicat de la matière?" *Etudes sur la Métaphysique d'Aristote, Actes du VIe Symposium Aristotelicum* (Paris: Vrin, 1979), 131–166.

This will mean, then, that the matter and the composite itself are knowable only in virtue of the form. Aristotle expresses that tenet concisely in saying that what is to be expressed in concept or word is the form and the individual insofar as it has the form, but never the material constituent just as itself.[6] Only through its form is the matter or the composite thing knowable. This fits in neatly enough with Aristotle's repeated assertion that to know a thing is to know its "essential being." The notions of "essential being" and of form coincide in this function of grounding one's knowledge of the thing. Aristotle is clearly looking upon them as one and the same object. He can say with ease that soul and the "essential being" of soul are the same,[7] since the soul as the form of the living body requires nothing more basic for its being. It itself is what makes it a soul. If one could say "soulness" in English, it would have exactly the same meaning in the Aristotelian context as "soul." Aristotle's philosophy has no place for a disembodied soul that would continue to exist as an individual thing and thereby require a further "essential being" for grounding universality.

But how can the form be the source of meaning in something so opposite to it, the matter? This question calls for detailed consideration. In the model from which the distinction is taken, namely the change of material substances from one accidental form to another, the marble block is made into a statue. The marble, though here the material, is knowable as marble in virtue of its own form. But it is not thereby known as a statue. The form of Hermes cannot be seen in it by looking at it just as marble. That form has to come to it from another source, the mind of the artist. Knowledge of the visible object as a statue of Hermes, in consequence, does not come from the matter. But the form of a statue does require certain definite traits in the matter in which it is embodied. It requires a material that is solid, not liquid or vaporous, and that is able to be carved by a chisel or molded into a shape that it will retain. Those traits in it can be deduced from the notion of a statue. They are what make the marble or the bronze the appropriate material for statues. In this way the matter in question is determined by the form and is knowable through the form. The form is the source for knowledge of it as the material for a statue, even though the materials in this case already have their own forms as substances. In themselves they are not formless, though of themselves they do not have the form of a statue.

When the entirely formless matter in the category of substance is encountered, a somewhat different, though analogous, situation has to be faced. Here the

6 "For only the form, or the objects as having form, can be expressed in the concept; whereas the material element by itself cannot be expressed in the concept." *Metaphysics*, 7.10.1035a7–9, Richard Hope trans. Hope's translation seems to express with requisite clarity in English the meaning of the Greek text here. On Tugendhat's explanation of the twofold aspect of being, as Aristotle conceives being, namely "something of something," see supra, ch. 6, n. 3.

7 *Metaphysics*, 7.10.1036a1–2.

matter has no form of its own, in the way wood and bronze and marble have their own proper forms. The knowledge about the matter in this case has to come entirely from the form. To account for the observable phenomena, the basic matter in material substances has to be a constituent that allows the same form to be extended in three-dimensional space without any formal difference whatsoever. The same human form pervades all the parts and organs of the body. They are all human. More easily observable, the same form of iron or gold or water is found throughout all the parts of the various instances. Formally, the thing in question is the same throughout. The thing is extended in space without any formal change in the kind of thing it is. This extension requires a constituent that is entirely formless in itself. How, then, can it be known? It can be so known only because the form in this case is of such a nature that it could not exist without thereby actuating a matter that is entirely formless in itself. This is a demand in the very nature of the corporeal thing. It is a demand of the form, and becomes known to us only through the form. We cannot see it, we cannot feel it, we cannot even know it as something just in itself. We can know it only insofar as it is indicated by the corporeal form. We know the observable body immediately, we see it extended as the same in form throughout its different parts, and we reason to the presence in it of a constituent that by itself is entirely formless. That constituent, accordingly, is known only as a requirement of the corporeal form. In itself it is unknowable. If it had any knowable feature in itself, it would be making a formal addition and thereby changing the substance into something else.[8]

The same conclusion follows also from the change of one substance into another. Hydrogen and oxygen, for instance, are changed into water. The new substance has very different properties from the two elements out of which it was generated. Yet it has relations to those elements that remain constant. The spectra of the elements remain in it, and the weight is conserved. We know the products in each case as new and different things. A drop of water is not a bit of oxygen or of hydrogen. This is explained by saying that the form is changed but the matter remains. Aristotle did not have today's high-powered chemical examples. But in the change of living to non-living bodies, and vice versa, he had before his eyes examples that were just as trenchant. The corpse resembles the living person in features and weight, yet there is change from one substance into others. The substantial form, the most basic form in the thing according to Aristotle's natural philosophy, has changed. There is nothing more of formal nature in the substance that could remain. What remains, accordingly, is entirely formless. The same reasoning is applied to Aristotle's basic elements, earth, air, fire, and water. They were changed one into another with the same consequences as in the case of living and non-living bodies. In all those cases new things were generated. The same

8 This point may be illustrated by the way addition of a unit in the category of quantity changes the species of a number.

explanation was required. New forms were induced into a matter that in itself had to be entirely formless, and which was known only through the exigencies of the form.

What are those exigencies? A corporeal thing is an individual of a species. Other individuals specifically the same are differentiated from one another by their matter. They are existent in different matter. But even that requirement is an exigency of their form. The form is of such a nature that it requires individuation in matter. If it did not require matter to individuate it, it would be a separate substance and the only instance of its kind. It would not be a corporeal form. But in point of fact the sensible things in which our cognition takes its origin are all corporeal things – stones, metals, trees, animals, human persons. They are all individual things, as Aristotle assessed them. There were no Platonic Ideas. Their forms provided specific similarity, but also the demand for individual differentiation by matter. That demand originated in the form, not in the matter, for the matter had in itself no determinations of any kind. Though required for individual distinction as a condition, it had nothing in itself that could give rise to distinction. Of itself it was utterly featureless. The form of a material thing, however, of its very self required individuation in matter. It could not exist without that individuating constituent, or even be an object of thought apart from that requirement of matter. It was the principle of individuation as well as of specific similarity.[9]

The point of all this discussion is that the individuation of the corporeal thing and its material principle are known only through the form. The matter is known as the requirement for the extension of the specifically identical form through parts outside parts in space, and for its multiplication in a plurality of instances. What is known first of all is the composite individual thing, namely this piece of gold, this tree, this horse, or this person. The form as such is known only through the reasoning in Aristotelian philosophy of nature, and so by comparatively few persons today. The individual material things, on the contrary, are known by everybody. Yet despite this prima facie anomaly, each material thing is knowable only in virtue of its form. The form is what renders it knowable, even though the form is not isolated in ordinary discourse. To have a good digestion it is not at all necessary to understand its physiological process. In like manner it is not necessary to understand the philosophical niceties in knowing a material thing as such. Knowing things will go on regardless of our own epistemological views or our lack of them. Whether we are aware of it or not, from Aristotle's viewpoint we are knowing the individual things only insofar as each has its form.[10]

9 On the complex character of the problem of individuation in the Western philosophical tradition, see Jorge J. E. Gracia, *Individuality* (Albany: SUNY Press, 1988) and the papers in *Individuation in Scholasticism: The Later Middle Ages and the Counter Reformation*. 1150–1650, ed. Jorge J. E. Gracia (Albany: SUNY Press, 1994).

10 See text supra, n. 6.

This consideration facilitates our understanding of the way Aristotle identifies the thing's "essential being" with the thing's form. To know a thing, he has said repeatedly, is to know its "essential being." The thing itself is what is known, but that knowing takes place through the grasp of its "essential being." Yet the ordinary person knows things without any explicit philosophical knowledge of the notion of "essential being." But like it or not, from the Aristotelian viewpoint one is knowing the individual thing through knowing its "essential being." That is the only way the thing can be known, for the "essential being" is what the individual thing is basically and enduringly, in contrast to the fleeting cognition of it through sensation. All this parallels exactly enough the doctrine of the knowledge of a thing in virtue of its form. From both standpoints, the individual thing itself is what is known. But in every case, the thing is known in virtue of its formal principle.

From this viewpoint, then, the form and the "essential being" of a thing coincide. The one is the other. But in the way each of them is reached, there is difference. The form is isolated through the study of change and spatial extension in the philosophy of nature. The "essential being" is known by precisive abstraction of the intelligible content of the thing from the individual subject in which it is found. What is left out in the one case is the unknowable matter, and in the other case the knowable subject. The form is regarded as really distinct from the matter, and the "essential being" as conceptually distinct from the individual as a whole. But does the residue coincide in these two cases? What the form is distinguished from is the real matter. What the "essential being" leaves out is the individual.

Obviously they are not the same. But need that fact affect the object with which they are respectively contrasted? The contrast with form is on the level of natural philosophy, referred to in context as a secondary type of philosophy.[11] The distinction from "essential being" is on the level of the primary philosophy. Is it not possible, then, that form and "essential being" are in fact the same object, but regarded in their respective relations to two different types of subject? At least, this possibility calls for adequate consideration. The subject of form in the philosophy of nature is the real matter in which the form adheres. The subject of the "essential being," on the other hand, is the particular individual thing that is contrasted with that "essential being" in the metaphysical inquiry of book Zeta.

What does a close look at a comparative study of these two different types of subject show? When the subject of the form in the category of substance is assessed, it turns out to be utterly unknowable in itself. Because the point of departure for the study of the Aristotelian notion of matter is from the accidental changes of subjects such as bronze or marble into a statue of Hermes, the tendency is to imagine matter in the category of substance as an extremely fine type of

11 *Metaphysics*, 7.11.1037a14–16.

dust or powder that can be given shape or consistency by the form. But in itself the Aristotelian matter in the category of substance does not have enough actuality to be represented even in that way. That kind of representation arises from the analogy of its function with the functions of wood or marble in construction and art. The materials for art and construction already have a form of their own. But the matter in the category of substance has no form whatever, and, in accordance with the Aristotelian norm that a thing is known in virtue of its form, this matter is in itself utterly unknowable.

It is known only through the exigencies of corporeal form. Those exigencies are inevitably present in the very nature of this type of form, since a body has to have spatial extension through parts outside parts without any formal differentiation in itself on the substantial level. Likewise, bodies are multiplied in individual instances that may be specifically the same, in the way that all human persons belong to the same species. From both those viewpoints a substantial principle that adds no formal differentiation is required. As pure potentiality, this further substantial principle will lack even the minimum of actual characterization that would be required to make it knowable just in itself. It can be known only through its form.

Further, although Aristotle sees the origin of human knowledge in individual sensible things, he makes, in this context of book Zeta, a statement that may at one's first reading seem quite surprising. He asserts that these individual things from which human cognition begins "have little or nothing of being" (3.1029b9–10). His overall view here is of course that our cognition takes its origin in material things and proceeds from and through knowledge of them to the knowledge of separate substance. In separate substance the nature of being itself is finally reached by way of metaphysical procedure. In comparison with separate substance the individual material things from which the reasoning began can easily be regarded as having "little or nothing of being." But the fact that Aristotle could express himself in that way gives pause for thought. How could he look upon the individual sensible thing as having practically no being at all? In the present context of book Zeta, does it not indicate that here he is locating the being of an individual thing in the thing's intelligible content? In book Epsilon he had shown that what a thing is, and if it is, coincide. The problem here does not lie in any real distinction between essence and existence. Rather, it is between the individual thing itself and the intelligibility that the individual thing enjoys. In that perspective, the notion that the individual material things from which human cognition originates have little or no being makes good Aristotelian sense.

Against this background, the identity of physical form with "essential being" is not hard to see. Each of them contains the whole of the individual thing's intelligibility. In a philosophy in which the supreme goal of human life is intellectual contemplation, what basically counts is that intelligibility. Intelligibility is what all persons look to and strive for. In the individual thing the intelligibility proceeds from the form only. The individuality of the thing adds nothing to it. One's *eudaimonia* is not grounded in the number of individual instances with which one is acquainted, but rather in the intelligibility that is uniformly found in each of the instances. From that viewpoint the individuals as such may be regarded as adding little or nothing. What the thing is, is fully contained within its "essential being." Its "essential being" exhibits what it basically and necessarily is, namely its being when "being" is taken in the genuine Aristotelian sense of being in its contrast to becoming. There is no question of saying that the individuals do not exist, when it is stated in this context that they "have little or nothing of being." They do exist, and have for Aristotle the role of the starting points for all human knowledge. But the individuation is omitted, and has to be omitted when they are defined. The individuation does not pertain to what they are, even though it is required by what they are quite as matter is required by corporeal form in spite of the fact that the matter is unknowable in itself and adds nothing to the intelligible content of the thing.

All this leads up to the consideration that in the precisive abstraction by which the "essential being" of a thing is known, nothing that is in itself intelligible is left out, quite as the omission of the unknowable matter does not take anything away from the intelligibility given the thing by its form. "Animality" has all the intelligible content of "animal," even though it prescinds from the individuation and cannot be predicated of its instances. Dogs and cats are animals, but they are not animality. When one says that a cat or a dog has animality, one is regarding the individual instance as the subject that has the "essential being," parallel to the way matter is called the subject of the form. The parallelism is from the standpoint of a principle that confers intelligibility. But here the subject is different in each case. The subject of the physical form is the matter that, as such, is unknowable except through the form. The subject of the "essential being" is the whole individual constituted of both the matter and the form, and known directly and immediately in the way an individual dog or tree is grasped in human cognition, but which is left out of consideration when that knowledge is applied to other instances.

The difference between these two ways of functioning as the subject for the reception of a formal principle cannot help but make the subjects distinct from each other. The subject in the one case is the matter taken alone just by itself. In the other case, the subject is the composite of matter and form taken as a unit. The problem is that difference in subject might in this case impinge upon identity of form and "essential being" in the way these two notions refer to the same entity in the Aristotelian text. Their own content is the same. But does the difference in their respective subjects clash in any way with their reference in Aristotle to one and the same reality? The point of contention would be that a thing's matter as such does not contain any intelligibility whatever in the case of matter for corporeal substances in general, and in cases of matter for artificially produced things does not provide knowledge of the design that is to be worked into it. The subject for the "essential being," on the other hand, is the individual composite that contains within itself the form as one of its constituent parts. How, then, can it be equated with a subject that has no formal intelligibility at all? Yet if form and "essential being" are exactly the same object, how can this difference in their respective subjects be explained?

The contrast in the case of matter and form is clear-cut. The matter as such has nothing of the form. But in the contrast of the individual thing with its "essential being," the thing does contain the form as a constitutive part. This raises the question of how individuality can be regarded as not adding any intelligibility to the thing, parallel to the way matter adds none to it. If the thing's intelligibility is located in its "essential being," in accord with the dictum that we know each thing when we know its essential being (7.6.1031b6–7), the individuation has to be regarded as adding nothing to the intelligibility of the thing, at least nothing that adds to our understanding of it. That indeed is what Aristotle seems to imply in saying that the corporeal things from which our knowledge begins have little or nothing of being. Though the direct bearing of the comparison here is upon the fullness of being in the separate substances and the lesser grade of being in corporeal composites, the wording suggests that while from one viewpoint these corporeal substances do have a slight grade of being, from another viewpoint they do not have any being at all. Certainly the individual substances exist and are something. But does their individuality add any being to their formal element? Are they not knowable only in terms of their form, quite as their matter is known only in terms of their form? From that viewpoint the individuation would be adding nothing to their being and their intelligibility.

In a philosophy like that of Aristotle it is quite possible to think in this manner. When one knows that water is composed of two parts of hydrogen with one part of oxygen through making a particular experiment, that knowledge is not increased, even though it may be confirmed by acquaintance with further instances of the same experiment. The multiplication of the individual instances provides no further scientific knowledge of the chemical composition of water. The accumulation of tokens does not add anything to one's knowledge of the design they bear. From this viewpoint the individuals may be regarded as adding "little or nothing of being" to the notion itself. For Aristotle the exercise of intelligence in its highest degree throughout a complete lifetime was *eudaimonia*, the supreme goal of all human striving. It was increased little if any at all by the repetition of individual instances. These had been occurring from all eternity, and would go on occurring through future instances forever. The individual thing and the individual contemplator came and went, but the contemplation went on without cease. For us today, in the wake of highly developed personalist philosophies, and after centuries of Judeo-Christian preaching about the inestimable worth of the individual person, this Aristotelian outlook may well seem strange. But it does explain how Aristotle could regard "essential being" as the equivalent of form in spite of the different type of relation that they have to their respective subjects. Form is what actuates the unknowable matter and makes it into a knowable composite. The "essential being" expresses what the thing is even though it omits all mention of the subject that possesses it. Animality is the same notion regardless of the individual animal in which it occurs, quite parallel to the way matter does not add any intelligibility to what is given the thing by the form.

No objection, then, need arise to Aristotle's repeated references to form and "essential being" as denoting one and the same object. For him they are identical. The only difference between them lies in the two different philosophical levels on which they are respectively framed. The notion of the form as the actualizing principle of a body, as for instance the soul is the first actuality of a living body, is obviously given in terms taken from the philosophy of nature. Accordingly it may be referred to as a physical definition. This type of definition regards matter as the subject that receives the form, and that stands to the form in the relationship of potentiality to actuation. The definition of that same object as the thing's "essential being," on the other hand, is worked out in terms of concepts such as necessity and permanence and ultimate meaning for all else in the thing. That is what the imperfect tense of the verb in *to ti ēn einai* seems intended to express. It focuses on the being in the thing that is absolutely required for the thing to be what it is, as the chemical combination of two parts of hydrogen to one part of oxygen is absolutely necessary for something to be that specific substance. It is what abides throughout all the accidental changes of the substance, such as the boiling into steam or the freezing into ice. It is what is basically required to make any particular instance a drop of water. It is what necessarily and abidingly is the being of water throughout all its instances. Contradistinguished from what the water happens to be at a particular moment, the "essential being" is what the water eternally and necessarily is in order to be water. Any corporeal thing can be explained in terms of matter and form as its constituents. These are objects that can be imagined on the model of bronze and figure in a statue. It can also be explained in terms that can be conceived but not imagined, such as necessity and the abstraction from time and place.

In the one case, then, the definition is physical, in the sense the term "physical" has in the Aristotelian philosophy of nature. In the other case, the definition is given in terms of concepts, here metaphysical concepts. That seems obviously enough the sense intended here for the Greek *logikōs* in a recognized contrast with what is physical.[12] But the main consideration in the present context is that

12 See Bonitz, *Index Aristotelicus*, 432b7–8. Cf. the repetition at *Metaphysics*, 7.17.1041a28, see supra, n. 2.

the two definitions refer to exactly the same entity. The soul, for instance, can be described by Aristotle with equal ease as "essential being" or as form. Likewise with all corporeal things the form and the essential being are regarded as coinciding.[13] The primary "essential being," moreover, has no matter at all.[14] It is form only, and in it the "essential being" coincides completely with the thing. From whatever angle one cares to view the situation, one finds that form and "essential being" refer to exactly the same reality, though in physical and metaphysical terms respectively.

There remains, of course, some difficulty in viewing the soul as received into the individual body as form is received into matter. The difficulty is partly that we have an imaginative model for the reception of form into matter, but none for the reception of "essential being" into the individual. Also the Judeo-Christian tenet of the human soul's continuance in existence after bodily death may be playing its part. In Aristotle, however, there is no trace of a soul apart from a body. In general, with him the individual seems to function as a subject for "essential being" as readily as his unknowable matter functions as subject for form in the category of substance. Each corporeal being may be regarded as having its "essential being," in contrast to the separate forms that are their own "essential being." A horse, for instance, is not animality. Rather, each individual horse is regarded as having animality. Each is something that has the "essential being." Though the individual instances "have little or nothing of being," they are not negations or privations of being. They have a higher gradation than merely privation or negation, in relation to the primary instance of being. This gradation may appear as "little or nothing" in terms of "essential being," when it is assessed just in itself. Nevertheless the "essential being" makes the individual be, quite parallel to the function of form in making the entirely potential matter be something, that is, in making the matter be the composite thing. Quite as the matter, then, is something that has the form without being the form, so the individual horse or stone is something that has the "essential being." Thought out carefully, there does not seem to be any more difficulty in conceiving the individual as the subject of the "essential being" than in conceiving the entirely potential matter as a subject for receiving the form. Having "little or nothing of being," and having no actuality whatsoever, hardly differ at all from the viewpoint of the effort required for understanding their respective functions. One also sees thereby how the "essential being" of the thing is known in the definition merely by omitting the express mention of the individual. The individual, quite as the matter, is regarded as not adding anything knowable.

What any matter is, and what any individual is, is accordingly known in terms of form. The form of a tree or of a horse, is such that it requires entirely

13 See supra, n. 2.

14 *Metaphysics*, 12.8.1074a35–36.

formless matter in the category of substance, and types of formed matter in the accidental categories.[15] Because it is a corporeal form, it cannot have existence outside the mind unless it is actuating matter. Otherwise it would be an incorporeal or separate form. Likewise, in requiring matter in this way it is open to individuation in a multiplicity of instances. All these conditions are requirements of the form and are knowable through the form.

The parallelism of the two definitions, one in terms of physical constitution, the other in terms of metaphysical concepts, is in consequence clear enough. Both definitions bear on exactly the same object, though from different philosophical viewpoints. Both convey the notion of a principle that is definite, in contrast to the indefinite capacity of matter and the indefinite number of individual instances. That definite principle is what makes the thing intelligible. To understand it, accordingly, is to understand the individual thing. While there is no doubt whatever that for Aristotle the immediate objects of our cognition are all individual things, the principle in virtue of which these things are known is the form whenever the definition is given on the level of the philosophy of nature. It is the thing's "essential being" when the definition is couched in metaphysical terms. In both cases the object is exactly the same. In consequence, the knowledge of what the thing is according to the thing's "essential being," and the knowledge of the thing by reason of its form, express one and the same tenet. They are definitions of the same object, but are given on different philosophical planes.

In this regard, one might emphasize that there is no incongruity in phrasing a notion of the soul as the form of the living body and at the same time viewing the soul as the "essential being" of the living thing.[16] Quite possibly one's first reaction may be that here Aristotle is confusing the two orders, the physical and the metaphysical. Soul is a physical principle, according to his philosophy of nature. On the other hand, "essential being" is a complex of metaphysical concepts. Consequently it is hard to see how one and the same object may be expressed in these definitions even though their philosophical levels are different. How can the soul be a physical constituent of the body, really distinct from the matter in which it inheres, and still function as the "essential being" of that body when there is only a conceptual distinction between it and the living body it makes knowable? In a word, how can a physical constituent such as the soul be also a metaphysical principle for knowledge of the thing on the level of the primary philosophy?

The proper answer to that question lies deep in Aristotle's philosophy of human cognition. What is known immediately and directly, for him, is the thing

15 See *Metaphysics*, 9.7.1049a14–b2.

16 The consideration here descends even to the level of the individual instance, in which one may speak of Socrates and his "Socrateity." On the notion "Socrateity," see supra, ch. 7, n. 13.

external to knower and to the cognitional activity. Here as everywhere else human cognition originates in external things. The question, then, is not one of looking at clear and distinct ideas for the basis of philosophical discourse. The thing itself, whether known immediately as the living individual, or mediately through reasoning as in the case of the soul, is what one must scrutinize when one is seeking an answer to the present question. So scrutinized, the soul shows itself in the philosophy of nature to be the form of the living body, and in the primary philosophy to be the "essential being" of that same living thing. There is no conflict or confusion in the two approaches. But today an effort is required to overcome the Cartesian epistemology where one has been brought up in it. The tendency will be to look at ideas with their mental existence instead of at the thing in its own real existence outside the human mind.

In Aristotle, then, both form and "essential being" denote exactly the same entity. This entity is basically physical, but it has an important metaphysical aspect. Somewhat as the separate forms, existent in reality, are the being qua being that is the primary instance of being and makes possible the universal predication of being, so the physical form of corporeal things is what grounds universal predication in their regard. The real being of the corporeal form is what enables the corporeal thing to be known and understood. That consideration helps greatly for the interpretation of the Aristotelian formula *to ti ēn einai*. It shows why the mention of being should be retained in the translation of the phrase, for it indicates how the phrase bears on the basic and stable being of the corporeal thing, something which the translation "essence" seems to miss.

Because "essence" in modern thinking tends to be contrasted with existence, and because "essence" is difficult to equate with the actually existent form of the corporeal thing, it can give rise to confusion in the present context. Matter has to be included in the essence of a corporeal thing, yet matter has to be kept really distinct from the corporeal form. Accordingly "essence," despite its wide acceptance, is unsatisfactory as a translation of this tantalizing Aristotelian phrase.

Chapter 9

Form and Universal

The English word "universal" is of Latin origin. As a Latin adjective, *universalis* dates back to the first century A.D.[1] Etymologically, the term conveys the notion of things "turned toward" something one and thereby regarded as a distinct unit. The totality of the world's constituents is accordingly called the universe, because of the relation of the parts to one and the same whole. So in philosophy the term "universal" suggests the notion of individual instances turned toward something one, as for example all individual houses converge into identity as they meld one by one into the same specific notion of a house. In the sixth century A.D. the neuter of the Latin adjective was used as a noun (*universale*) by Boethius, and through him passed into the vocabulary of Western philosophical tradition.[2]

Aristotle's Greek term for this notion had likewise been based upon the concept of a whole (*holos*). The Greek *kata holon* was already in existence. But with Aristotle it becomes a single word, *katholou*. It was foreshadowed in Plato, both doctrinally and etymologically.[3] Aristotle had accordingly to take great care in dissociating his conception of one and the same nature in many different

1 ". . . quorum omnium similis est ratio, forma diversa, quia sententia universalis est vox." Quintilian, *Institutio oratoria*, 1.9.3.

2 "Sed quoniam substantia proferri non potest nisi aut universaliter aut particulariter intelligaturs nam cum dico homo, rem dixi universalem, idcirco quod nomen hoc de multis individuis praedicaturt cum vero dico Socrates vel Plato, rem dixi particularem. . . . Universale autem est quod aptum est de pluribus praedicari." Boethius, *In Categories Aristotelis*, 1: *PL*, 64, 169D–170B. In this way the process of thought seems to reflect the status of the original Aristotelian notion as adverbial in force, but with the neuter of the adjective coming into use as a noun standing for the subject that is defined. Cf. ". . . quod de universali praedicatur, praedicatur et de individuo." Boethius, *In Porphyrium dialogia Victorino translati*, *PL*, 64, 135A. The comparative *universalior* (137A) allows for degrees in the extent of the universality.

On the influence of Boethius on the medieval controversies regarding universality, see Etienne Gilson, *History of Christian Philosophy in the Middle Ages* (New York: Random House, 1955), 98–100.

3 See *Meno*, 77A; *Republic*, 3.392DE; *Timaeus*, 40A, 55E. For the etymology, see Hjalmar Frisk, *Griechisches etymologisches Wörterbuch*, II, s.v. *holos*.

instances as a universal from the conception of it as a Platonic Idea. The latter gave a separate existence to the nature shared by the individual instances. The Ideas had to be known through some vision of them in their separate state, a vision that could not be explained satisfactorily. The problem for Aristotle, in consequence, was to show how the individual sensible things, in which human cognition originates, can account for the universal cognition experienced in intellectual discourse.

Aristotle's approach to this problem in book Delta of the *Metaphysics* (26.1023b26–32) is in full accord with the etymology of the Greek term. The approach places the question within the inquiry about the meanings of "whole." The revised Oxford translation (2nd ed., 1928) conveys very precisely the type of "whole" that is meant by the universal "as being each severally one single thing" and "a whole in the sense that it contains many things by being predicated of each, and by all of them, e.g. man, horse, god, being predicated severally one single thing, because all are living things" (1023b28–32). The term "severally" brings out effectively the distributive sense of the Greek expression *hōs hekaston* that the instances are one by one, that is, each in its turn, the object signified by the universal. Each individual tree is a tree, each individual horse is a horse, and Socrates, Callias, and Plato are each a person, but in a way that does not include all or any of the other instances in the predication. To say that Socrates is a person, does not identify "Socrates" and "person" in such a way that they always coincide. One does not have to be Socrates to be a person.

The Aristotelian universal, then, does not mean that all the instances are united collectively in a whole. They are united with the universal object, here a "person," only one by one or severally. They are not united all together with one another to form a whole in such a way that wherever one instance is found, the other instances have to accompany it. But the same universal object is predicated in identity with each, though in turn. We see one individual chair in a room, then another chair, and then another. We see the one object "chair" in all three instances, and apply it to numerous other instances. That is the way Aristotle explains the universal in the rout simile at the end of the *Posterior Analytics* (2.19.100a3–b5), noting (a13–14) that the soul is of such a nature as to be affected in this manner. That, in a word, is our observation of the communal experience we undergo in understanding things. The sensible things are there and are known. We immediately and directly grasp the universal in them, and use it as our means of advancing to further and greater knowledge. Indirectly throughout all this process we are aware in concomitant fashion of our own cognitional activity, and are able to compare knowledge with things and make our judgments about its truth. That is what our observation shows us in regard to the way our universal knowledge is based upon what we see and know in particular things.

The same relations of the universals to the individual things and of our ever-widening knowledge through the development in the sciences may be seen sketched in the opening chapter of the *Metaphysics* (1.1.980a21–982a3). There we have the example of an observation that a certain remedy helped Callias and Socrates and many other individuals. That is a matter of experience. But when we investigate further and discover the cause of the cure, we have knowledge of a connection that goes with it in universal fashion for anyone with that disease. On universal knowledge of this type the vast array of the arts and sciences is brought about. Knowledge of the cause is accordingly required in order to know that the remedy in question is applicable to all instances one by one as the medical practitioner encounters them. But the notion of the universal itself, as an object present in more than one individual, is something that is spontaneously met with in our most primitive intellectual experience. There is nothing at all esoteric in the notion of the universal as Aristotle understands it in his observation of human cognition. The universal expresses the object that we are aware of as common in the different individuals, and when we come to know in one way or another the causal connection between this trait and the nature of the things in question, we know it in a way that can provide scientific knowledge. The way will differ in the various sciences, with absolute coverage in the metaphysical and mathematical reasoning, but only roughly and for the most part in the physical and practical and productive sciences.

However, the status of the universal in Aristotle's overall philosophy is not at all easy to grasp. The philosophical background upon which his gaze was directed lay in Platonic thinking. Plato had undertaken the task of explaining the presence of a one identical and abiding nature in a plurality of different and perishable individuals. He saw the explanation in a way in which each individual would share in the eternal and unchanging Idea of each of the respective natures. But this explanation required an existence for the Ideas that was separate from the world of individual things, with the result that truly scientific and philosophical knowledge had to be based upon supersensible Ideas rather than upon the sensible things that surround us.

In full conformity with the origin of human knowledge in sensible reality, Aristotle's attitude in the *Metaphysics* (7.7.1032a12–1034b19) was definite and firm. It was that the Ideas could serve no purpose in our understanding of things. The origin of sensible things was to be explained in terms of their own formal and material causes, together with the formal cause or causes in the agent that engendered or produced them. There was no need whatever for any separate Ideas upon which they would be modeled, and in the light of which they were to be explained. The origin of human knowledge in sensible things themselves was sufficient to account for the coming to be of those things, as also for human understanding of them in the universal required by scientific knowledge. Separate Ideas, accordingly, were from Aristotle's epistemological viewpoint superfluous, and therefore useless for our scientific inquiries (1033b26–1034a8).

Throughout his discussion of the Platonic Ideas, however, Aristotle never swerves from the requirement of the universal for human knowledge. Things are always "expressed and known by the universal definition" (10.1036a6–8). Cognition or the plane of universality is what distinguishes human intellection from sensible perception of those same things. The definition, from which reasoning commences, is "of the universal and the form" (11.1036a28–29). At first reading this might seem to equate the Aristotelian form with the universal. It would seem to look as though the Platonic forms were just taken over, and now located within the sensible things instead of being allotted separate status. But this is far from being the case. The Aristotelian form, rather, is to be understood in a way that distinguishes it sharply and radically from the Platonic conception of an Idea. For Aristotle the form of the thing is the thing's primary *ousia* or beingness (7.1032bl–2; 11.1037a5–29), while on the other hand no universal is an *ousia* (13.1039al4–15; 16.1041a3–5). In the context of book Zeta (3.1028b34–35), this was meant as Aristotle's definite answer to the stand that the universal could be regarded as the *ousia* of the individual thing. The universal, in its status as universal, is not the *ousia* of anything.

To appreciate the radical character of this Aristotelian distinction of form from universal, a glance at the function of form as *ousia* is perhaps the best introduction to the topic. In *Metaphysics* Alpha (3.983a27–28) the formal cause is labeled the *ousia* and the "essential being," and in book Delta (8.1017b21–26) one of the two ways in which *ousia* is understood is in the meaning of the "essential being" or physical form of each thing. Likewise in book Zeta (6.1031a18), the "essential being" continues to be regarded as the *ousia* of each thing. So understood, the form is what confers beingness on things, and in that way is their *ousia*. It is beingness in the Aristotelian sense that includes both the essence and the existence of the thing.[4] There is accordingly an internal gradation in the corporeal thing's being: form is prior to matter and has being in a higher degree; it will for the same reason be prior to the composite of both (3.1029a5–7). Internally, then, the form is the primary instance of being in the corporeal thing. It is the actuality that confers being on the matter, and by so doing gives rise to the composite substance. In this sense Aristotle repeatedly refers to the soul as the primary *ousia* of living things.[5] Upon this primacy of form to the composite follows the primacy of the substance itself to the accidents that are sustained by it (3.1029a10–16). Throughout all the composite structure, then, it is form in the category of substance that exercises the all-pervading priority in being. It is form that brings together all else in the structure of the thing. The basic form is what primarily makes the thing the being that it is.

When we turn from this function of form to the function of the universal, the contrast is glaring. The universal does not at all bring its manifold instances into a single being. The instances all remain separate from one another in reality. Each

4 Cf. *Metaphysics*, 7.1.1025b14–18.

5 *Metaphysics*, 7.11.1037a5; a28–29. Cf. *De Anima*, 2.1.412a8–9.

stays a closed instance in itself. The unity in the universal "person" does not bring Socrates and Plato and Callias into a unitary composite that would have its own being. Rather, it adds no being, either substantial or accidental, to any of the individual instances. The universal, consequently, does not make the instances be anything further than what they already are. It effects no beingness in them. For the knower, it is the way they are attained through cognition on the intellectual level. Nothing is in the individuals in themselves by reason of that knowledge. It is the individuals themselves that are being known, without any real addition in themselves through that activity. The knowing does not affect the reality, in speculative thinking, no matter how much the theoretical knowledge is used to advantage in conduct and production. From the standpoint of addition to real being, Aristotle's declaration that no universal can be *ousia* in the sense of beingness holds full sway. A universal does not confer any beingness that would knit its particulars into a whole in the way the physical form or essential being unites the constituents into the one being.

Also from the standpoint of predication Aristotle (13.1038b1–1039a23) argues polemically that the universal is always held to be something said of a subject, since it is something common to that subject and to similar instances. The *ousia* or beingness of a thing, on the contrary, is always proper to the subject to which it gives being, and is predicated of that subject only.[6] At the end of the passage (a19–23), however, Aristotle leaves this argument open for reconsideration from the angle that in one way the definition may still be of the universal even though in another way the *ousia* or beingness is proper to the particular thing.

Decidedly, then, there is no possibility of regarding the Aristotelian form simply as a universal. Rather, the distinction of the one from the other is profound. But at the same time the close connection of universal with form needs to be carefully assessed. A thing's definition, which expresses what the particular thing is, will be "of the universal and the form" (11.1036a28–29). In the context, the conjunction "and" in this sentence is quite clearly explicative in character. It reads as though the two terms, "form" and "universal," coincided in expressing the one notion. The reason is not hard to see. Matter is unknowable just by itself. All the intelligibility of the sensible things comes from their form. Always these individual things "are expressed and known through the universal definition" (10.1036a8). Even the requirement of matter and the possibility of plurality of individuals in the same species is known through the corporeal form. The corporeal form is of such a kind that it cannot come to be in reality unless it thereby is actuating matter. Otherwise it could allow only one instance of itself. The singular things in the species, in consequence, differ from each other by reason of their matter, but are the same through their specific form (8.1034a7–8). The unity of

6 The separate status and "thisness" of the form had been stressed earlier in Zeta (3.1029a27–30).

different individuals in the one species is accordingly based directly upon the form. It is in the specific form that all the singulars coincide while differing in their matter. That is the force of the term "universal." So much is this the case that in Aristotle's Greek the same word, *eidos*, is used interchangeably for both physical form and universal species.

But if the physical form is not a universal, and is the *ousia* or beingness of the individual composite, must it itself be individual? It actuates the physical matter. This would seem at first mention to require individual status for the form as such. The form definitely cannot be individual in the way the singular instance is an individual in the species. Is there any other way, then, in which it may be regarded as individual in contrast to the universal? Aristotle has shown how the thing's "essential being," which is its form, may in one way be regarded as identical with the individual thing and in another way as different from it.[7] Is there some further difference in individuality itself by which a form may be regarded as individual without thereby taking on the status of a singular instance of a universal species?

There is, in fact, a use of terminology in Aristotelian metaphysics that points in this direction. Throughout the present discussion of universality and the individual, a new phrase, "a this," keeps making its appearance. "A this" is not found as a philosophical term before Aristotle.[8] Grammatically, the indefinite pronoun *ti* should give the expression a distributive sense. The demonstrative *tode* points rather emphatically, but in general fashion, to anything in question. Its philosophical meaning has to be worked out from the Aristotelian text itself. In the text, the expression is generally used in the sense of a composite singular, regarded as an instance within a species. Yet in a number of passages "a this" stands for the form alone as contrasted with the matter.[9] In the *De Anima* (2.1.412a7–9), moreover, the matter is said to be "not 'a this' by reason of itself," though it is called "a this" by virtue of the form, with mention of the composite immediately after.[10] That way of speaking would indicate that the form is being regarded as the cause of "thisness" for the matter and the composite. It would imply that the form is the primary instance of "thisness," with the matter and the composite as secondary instances.

The full import of this primacy of form in regard to both universality and individuality can be left for the study of the form as cause of both being and unity,

7 *Metaphysics*, 7.6.1031a15–1032a11.

8 See Wladyslaw Tatarkiewicz, *Die Disposition der aristotelischen Principien* (Marburg: n.p., 1910), 24.

9 See Harold Cherniss, *Aristotle's Criticism of Plato and the Academy* (Baltimore: Johns Hopkins University Press, 1944), 351–352, n. 261, for a discussion of these texts.

10 *De Anima*, 2.1.412a7–9.

a study given in the concluding chapter of book Zeta. For the present, there is no problem in the case of a form that exists without matter, that is, with an Aristotelian separate substance. There, form subsists just in itself, so that in this case the form is an individual in the full sense of that term. Form and individual coincide. There is no material component that would allow a specifically identical form to exist in different individuals, as the form of dog or tree is present in a plurality of numerically different instances. No genuine universal, in the sense of a univocally identical object in all, is able to unify separate forms into one species, or bring them under a common genus. Aristotle can group them together only on the basis of their different relations to the various movements observable in the heavens. In the separate substances themselves, individual and form fully coincide in each instance.

On the other hand, where the form is a corporeal form, it can have being only as the actuation of matter. That requirement pertains to its very nature as a corporeal form. It can only be in matter. Of its nature it thereby allows a plurality of instances. It itself is not a further instance, but is the formal element that is present in all the instances, and that grounds the cognition of the things in universal fashion. These material instances are the original objects of our cognition. From them our concept of the individual takes its rise. Consequently when we ask if the real corporeal form itself is individual, we have to free our thought from the implication that the form considered just in itself is a material composite. A distinction between the individual as an undivided whole and the individual as a singular instance of a species has to be introduced. It can be maintained by using the term "singular" for individual instances of a species, while allowing "individual" to extend to objects that have in themselves a unity that separates them from other corresponding objects. In this perspective each separate Aristotelian substance is an individual form, though it is not a singular in a species. In that way every corporeal form may be regarded as individual in virtue of itself, even though as just in itself it does not stand in direct contrast to the universal.

What is the bearing of this consideration upon the question whether the form is a universal? Its bearing on the problem should be quite apparent. The Aristotelian form cannot be a universal because the form is an *ousia* or beingness, and no universal can be an *ousia*. At the same time, the form cannot be a singular in a species, because the singular is directly opposed to the universal. In English, the contradiction is glaring. In the Greek, the adverbial character of the expression *to katholou* mitigates the harshness in the opposition of the two. The Greek carries the notion of "that which is taken as a whole," suggesting something that has the character of universality rather than the universality just in itself. So regarded, the object under consideration is the intelligible content seen in the instances of trees or horses or persons, and present in reality there in the individuals. That is the content that is being considered universally. The suggestion is not that of a new object set in contrast to the singular instances. Rather, in accordance with the etymology of the Greek term for universal, the contrast is between the singular instances known separately in sensation, on the one hand, and, on the other hand, the aspect in each of them that allows them all to be brought together in a recognizable whole. The universal characteristic can then be predicated of them severally, that is, of one at a time, without making them one and the same real thing. No new instance alongside the other instances is brought into being by the universal. Only the manner in which the instances are known in intellectual cognition is brought into consideration.

The universal, then, cannot at all be regarded as and treated as a singular, as long as the term "singular" is understood against its Latin background in the distributive numerals. From this viewpoint Aristotle's stand that no universal can be *ousia* remains unshaken. Accordingly the form, which is the primary *ousia* in the corporeal thing, cannot be a universal. But need that stand prevent the form from being regarded as individual? Etymologically "individual" carries the notion of something undivided. Certainly the physical form that makes Socrates be Socrates and at the same time be a person, is not divided in any way when other individuals such as Plato and Callias are brought under the one universal notion of "person." From this viewpoint the physical form of Socrates may readily be accepted as individual, even though it is the element that furnishes the basis for regarding Socrates as an instance of the one universal species that includes Plato and Callias and every other human who has lived or ever will live. In that way the physical form of Socrates may be classed as "a this," even though it is not "a this" in exactly the same sense as the man Socrates and every other individual thing as perceived in sensation is "a this." "Individual" and "a this" will in consequence be looked upon as notions that have various meanings, quite in accord with the way Aristotle classes so many other important philosophical objects.

With this situation in mind, one need not be surprised to see Aristotle finding primary and secondary instances in the notion of "a this," parallel to the way primary and secondary instances occur in leading philosophical notions. Accordingly *Metaphysics* Zeta (2.1029a27–30) can regard separate status and "thisness" as belonging in the highest degree to *ousia*, with the result that the form and the composite would seem to have being in a higher degree than the matter. What does this assertion imply? It seems quite obviously to be looking at a gradated order of being in the corporeal thing. It is drawing the conclusion that the form and the composite of matter and form possess a higher grade of being than does the matter. From the standpoint of grades in "thisness," it is supposing that in the category of substance the form is the primary *ousia* and that the composite thing is an *ousia*.[11] With regard to separate status, one readily concludes that the corporeal things encountered in sensation have their being in themselves and accordingly cannot be looked upon as accidents of some underlying sub-

11 See *Metaphysics*, 7.3.1029a5–7.

stance. To that extent they have separate status. Likewise each of the corporeal things is "a this," since it is from them that we get our original notion of "thisness," for example in this stone or that stone. What we know as a being we know as something one. That norm is accepted without question in book Zeta (4.1030b10–12), with express mention of "a this" as synonymous with substance as the first in order in the gradation of substance and accidents. The full implications of this ranking, however, are left to the concluding chapter of book Zeta, in its discussion of form as the cause of being in regard to matter and to the composite thing.

The point at issue in the present question is whether in the Aristotelian context individuality necessarily makes something be a singular in a species. The answer is definitely that it does not. A separate form is individual without thereby being an instance alongside other instances of the same specific nature. Matter is not necessarily required for individuation, though it is a condition for singular status in a species. The form of Socrates is proper and individual to Socrates. It is not the form of Plato or the form of Callias. Its presence in an individual that is spatially and perhaps even temporally separate from Plato and Callias is enough to assure its difference from the physical forms of those two other individuals. This, however, is a problem that calls for study in the way the physical form functions as the cause of all other being in the corporeal composite. The problem is how the form, as the cause of being, is simultaneously the cause that makes the corporeal thing one as an individual in itself, and that places it nevertheless in the one species that it shares in universal fashion with a number of other singulars. It makes Socrates both the individual that he is by himself and the person that he is in common with every other human being who has lived or ever will live.

Returning then to the question whether the physical form just in itself is universal or individual, one may answer that of itself it is not universal. If its nature required it to be universal, it could never be individual. But in each singular instance it is "a this," and thereby can function as the primary *ousia* in the corporeal thing and the cause of being to all else in the thing. On the other hand, it is not a singular instance within a species. It is the cause of the "thisness" of the singular instance, but without becoming a singular thing just in itself. To be a singular thing just in itself, it would require matter in its composition. But here it is being considered in express contrast to the matter it informs. It accordingly is not something singular by reason of its own nature, but only in virtue of the matter it actuates.

The answer to the question about its universality or singularity, therefore, is that the physical form considered just by itself is neither. It is open to universality in the human mind's consideration of it, when it is seen in universal fashion in a number of different instances. From that viewpoint the corporeal things, which are singular, are being known universally, as is brought out by the etymology of the Greek term for "universal," namely "that which is taken as a whole." The instances are all singulars, but they are being viewed as each an instance of the one whole. But that viewpoint does not arise from the form itself just as form, but from the way it is known in the human intellect. In a word, because the physical form is the primary instance of *ousia* in the corporeal thing, it cannot be a universal just in itself, and because in itself it has no material constituent it cannot be just in itself a singular. For universal status it has to be known by the human mind, and for the status of a singular it has to inform matter. Alone in itself it is neither of those two alternatives.

One might ask, though, if the physical form could not be universal in the way separate substance in *Metaphysics* Epsilon is universal as though a "class" consisting of particular beings? As a particular being, a separate substance can be universal as a final cause to the beings that strive to emulate its perfection. Can there not be a like relation here in regard to particulars that tend to perpetuate their form by enabling it to continue in perpetuity in ever-new instances? The answer, however, has to be no. The kind of universal that Aristotle is excluding from the realm of *ousia* is explicitly the type in which the same notion is shared in common by a plurality of instances (13.1038b10–15), and which is always predicated of some substrate (b15–16). Both those conditions characterize the universality that is in question here. They distinguish it sharply from the *pros hen* universality present in the relations of the secondary instances of being to the primary instance, and distinguished in book Zeta (4.1030b3) as *kath' hen* in contrast to the *pros hen* type. The universal that Aristotle is here distinguishing from physical form is clearly the type in which the same notion is commonly shared by all the instances, and not the type in which secondary instances are related in various ways to the one primary instance. It is a universal notion that is shared in equal fashion by all the instances, and not something that is found as a nature in the primary instance only, and in lesser degrees in all other instances.

In Aristotle, consequently, the form has to be looked upon as absolutely basic. In Octave Hamelin's phrasing, it explains all the rest and is self-sufficient in accounting for itself.[12] It is more basic than either the singular corporeal composite that is first known to us in sensation, or the universal notion by which we grasp it in intellection. Nor may the Aristotelian form be regarded as a medieval "common nature" upon which universality and particularity are superadded, added as differentiae. It is in itself individual, without any need of being made individual by an added differentia.[13] Rather, it itself imparts individuality to the

12 See quote from Hamelin supra, ch. 6, n. 10.

13 On the origin of the theme "common nature" in the Aristotelian tradition, see A. C. Lloyd, *Form and Universal in Aristotle* (Liverpool: Francis Cairns, 1981), 50. The medieval thinkers distinguished the common nature sharply from the universal, though they differ radically from one another in their ways of making the distinction. Yet, as Lloyd (1) notes, "his common nature is, save for certain irrelevant cases, independent of anyone's thought or language." See Lloyd's article "Aristotle's Principle of

composite singular. Correspondingly it is the foundation of universality, since it imparts to each singular instance the formal characteristics that allow the corporeal things to be classed in species and genera. It does not require or permit anything else to account for what it itself is. Even its requirement of matter for its being in reality proceeds from its own nature. In this way it is absolutely fundamental in Aristotle's thinking. How it exercises this basic philosophical function, in serving as the cause of being for all else in the corporeal thing, is the study undertaken in the seventeenth and final chapter of *Metaphysics* Zeta.

From what has been explained in this way about universality for Aristotle, one should be able to see clearly that in ordinary universality the same nature is common in the same way to all the instances. From that viewpoint each new instance may be compared to a clone, and be referred to as a "token" that repeats the same monetary value. On the other hand, in universality through focal reference the nature involved is present just by itself in the primary instance only. In all secondary instances it is present only through relation to that primary instance, as cooked spinach is not healthy through its own physiological condition but through the health that it is supposed to cause in the human body. Within a species, then, the individual instances coincide in nature, but in being every one of them is distinct from the others. Even in biological clones the being is different, in spite of the thoroughgoing identity in nature. With Aristotle, however, this differentiation has to be investigated in terms of the real identity of what a thing is and that the thing is, in contrast to the medieval approach in terms of essence and existence. But in every case the ultimate explanation has to be given through form as the cause of being.

Individuation," *Mind* 79 (1970), 519–529, for "individuation by form" (528) without "turning the *in re* form into an *in re* universal" (523). A survey of the various modern views on Aristotle's notion of individuality may be found in Mary Louise Gill's paper "Individuals and Individuation in Aristotle," in *Unity Identity and Explanation in Aristotle's Metaphysics* eds. T. Scaltsas, D. Charles, and M. L. Gill (Oxford, Clarendon Press, 1194), 55–71.

Chapter 10

Form as Cause of Being

The concluding chapter of *Metaphysics* Zeta (17.1041a6–7) proposes a fresh start in regard to the problem of *ousia* or beingness. It expresses the hope that a discussion of sensible *ousia* from this angle will throw light upon the kind of *ousia* that is separated from the sensible instances of it. The new starting point will be the function of *ousia* as principle (in the sense of origin) and cause. The reason given for this way of proceeding is that an explanation is always sought by asking why something pertains to something else (a10–11). To ask why something is itself is not to ask for anything, since one already has the answer and is not looking for anything else besides what one already has. No extension of knowledge could thereby be expected. The only explanation that might be suggested is the fact that everything is inseparable from itself. But that is only an offhand comment applicable in common to all things and yielding no new knowledge (a18–20). That the thing is there, is already known, for instance the thunder or the person. But what causes the thunder, or why the person is endowed with sensible cognition, may be asked and investigated. Likewise why these bricks and stones are a house may be posed as a question. In every such case the cause, which is something not already known, is being sought. The cause may be efficient, final, material, or formal. But always it is in some way distinct from what is already known. With regard to knowledge in separate substances, the case is radically different. They have no matter that could receive a form and accordingly be explained by that form. They are their own explanation. But where there is matter as the subject of formal causality, the question why the matter is what it is can be asked. That question is to be answered, then, in terms of formal, final, and efficient causality. But basically it is a problem of form, namely what the form is and what efficient and final causes are necessary in order to explain how that matter came to be actuated by this particular form (a21–b11). Thereby the form is shown to be the first of the causes, in the sense that the explanation of all the other causes has to be carried back to the form, as had been asserted in the opening book of the *Metaphysics* (1.3.983a28–29). The other causes – including the matter – are required in accord with the exigencies of the form.

In this way, then, the form is shown to have the status not of a mere constituent of the corporeal thing, but rather that of the origin and first principle (*archē*) of everything else in that composite (1041b25–31). The form is the "cause of being" in the sense that it makes the materials be the thing they are, such as flesh or a syllable, instead of a heap thrown together indiscriminately. As the *ousia* or beingness of each particular thing, the form is in this way "the primary cause of being."[1]

Moreover, and by the same token, the form is the primary cause of unity in the thing. The very notion of unity consists in the inescapable presence of the thing to itself. That is the basic meaning of oneness. The "essential being" of a unit, insofar as it is a unit, is the indivisibility of a thing from itself – *touto d' ēn to heni einai.*[2] If you ask why these many different items of building material are a house, Aristotle's answer is that the essential "being" of a house is present in them – *hoti huparchei ho ēn oikia einai.*[3] Correspondingly for him the "essential being" of a unit as a unit lies in the obvious requirement of each thing, whether substance or accident, to be undivided from itself. This requirement is not proposed here as the "principle of identity" or the "principle of non-contradiction" for grounding thought and speech and philosophical reasoning.[4] It is meant merely as a norm consequent upon being, or in much later language as a transcendental property of being.[5] In order to be at all, a thing must have the unity appropriate to the being that is attributed to it.

Aristotle's point here is that the cause of a thing's being is thereby the cause of that thing's unity, in the perspective in which that thing is regarded as a being. Beingness and absence of division are indeed different notions, but the one inevitably implies the other in any particular instance. Traced back to causal origin, this will mean that the cause of a thing's being is the cause of its unity, from the viewpoint of metaphysical explanation. The form that actuates the matter under consideration, and is therefore the cause of its being, is likewise the cause that makes the composite thing a unit.

Accordingly, each stone or each house, or each living thing as well as each "heap," is perceived in sensation as something individual. In that way it is known as a unit, with a substantial or an accidental form as the cause of the individual being and the individual unity exhibited in it. The form is the cause of all that is

1 *Metaphysics*, 7.17.1041b28. Cf. 7.3.1029a5–7; 8.3.1043a29–b14.

2 *Metaphysics*, 7.17.1041a19. The force of the imperfect tense of the Greek verb "to be" for the expression of the notion of being that is not affected by time stands out in this phrasing. Cf. 8.6.1045a7–33.

3 *Metaphysics*, 7.17.1041b6. Jaeger text.

4 Cf. the various designations and corresponding interpretations of this first principle of demonstration, see supra, ch.1, n. 1.

5 On the designation "transcendental" see also supra ch.1, n. 1.

knowable in the individual thing, since the matter as such is not a source of intelligibility in the thing. It is unknowable just in itself. From the standpoint of the formal determination in question here, the matter cannot be the deciding factor.[6] The form, rather, is the determining cause of the corporeal thing's individuality. Substantial form is what makes the thing an individual, namely something undivided from itself. Individuality is not something that the composite thing could receive from its matter, even though the form requires the material causality of a substrate in order to bring about the repeated occurrence of itself in the singulars of a species. But the matter, just as matter, has no determination to offer. Determination is something formal, even though it may also be existential where existence is ranked as actuation that is higher than the formal. Yet with Aristotle there is no such further actuation. With him the form, then, is the cause of the individual determination. The matter is the proximate cause of spread and dispersion. The form, on the other hand, is the cause of the undivided status that is required for individuation. The form is accordingly the cause of the individuation of every corporeal thing, just as it is the cause of the thing's being.

Yet the form is the cause also of each of the specific and generic determinations in corporeal things. By the form the undetermined matter is made in one case a stone, in another case a tree, and in another case a person. The form, precisely as a form, is the cause of all these determinations. The form is likewise the cause of the gradated order present in them, for the form makes the thing the kind of being that the thing is. It is in terms of these specific and generic perfections that the human mind knows and understands what the things are. In this perspective the form is the cause of any unity the thing exhibits, whether the unity be individual, specific, generic, analogous or accidental.[7] All these determinations are brought together in the thing's ultimate differentia. They function within the real unity of the form. There is no different substrate for each that would allow distinct beingness within the thing itself.[8] There is just the one beingness or *ousia*, namely the form, and it gives rise to unity. The distinct grading comes from our own intellectual activity in understanding and explaining the things. What is known is indeed there in the thing, but the distinctions within the form itself are made by the human intellect on the basis of observed activities and properties.

6 On the approach to the questions of the role of matter and the role of form in Aristotle's understanding of individualization. see A.C. Lloyd, "Aristotle's Principle of Individuation," *Mind* 79 (1970), 519–523. Both roles have to be taken into consideration in assessing Aristotle's notion of the individual.

7 On these various kinds of unity, see Aristotle, *Metaphysics*, 5.6.1015b16–1017a3. Even in regard to accidents, the form in the category of substance is what renders qualities and activities human or bovine or canine, bringing them into a unity in these various respects.

8 The ultimate differentia contains all the subordinate differentiae. See *Metaphysics*, 7.12.1038al8–35 and 7.17.1041b2–9.

In this vein Aristotle can likewise speak of the "essential being" of a unit insofar as it is a unit.[9] Just as he can refer repeatedly to the form as the *ousia* of the thing in listing the thing's causes, so he can look upon the form as the cause of the thing's unity. The form is the cause of the unity in the thing by its very function of causing the thing's being. It could not make the thing be without thereby making it a unit. In the case of immaterial substance, the individual unity follows at once from the lack of any possibility for spread through parts or for multiplication in singular instances. In material substances, on the contrary, the presence of matter allows for spread of the form through the material parts in the same individual and for plurality on the respective levels of specific and generic unity. All these specific and generic rankings of the thing meld together in reality as the thing's ultimate differentia, which is the physical form. Each works through the real unity of the form. The form is in this way the cause of all the unity exhibited by the corporeal thing, regardless of the level. But how may one thereby explain Aristotle's designation of that unity as the "essential being" of the unit? Should not the form be left rather in the status of the cause of the unity? How can it be regarded as synonymous with the unity itself? How can the form be the oneness of the thing just as it is the beingness (*ousia*) of the thing?

Here the problem of Aristotle's understanding of the human mind's encounter with its object has to be explicitly faced. As is commonly recognized, Aristotle locates the starting points of human cognition in external sensible things. His philosophical procedure is from external things, perceived immediately and directly in themselves, to things that are beyond sense perception. There is concomitant awareness of the cognition itself and of the concepts it thereby produces. But these internal products depend upon the directly known sensible things for their specification. They are not new sources for knowing what the things themselves are. The human mind works from those things, without having first gone from sensations or concepts to the external objects. That is acknowledged to be Aristotle's procedure. It has been dubbed naïve realism. It is certainly not any of the realisms that have been developed in the wake of Cartesian thought, for it does not make any attempt to start from ideas or sensations and then work toward a status outside the mind for objects corresponding to them. Aristotle's procedure is not at all a realism in that accepted notion of the term. Further, it is not at all naïve, as a study of its exceptionally keen intricacies will show. A glance at what it means, however, is necessary for understanding how for Aristotle individual and specific and other determinations can all merge together in the one real factor, the physical form of the composite thing.

The immediate problem here is to understand how for Aristotle the physical form can be the cause of being and unity in the thing, and at the same time can

9 *Metaphysics*, 7.17.1041a19; 10.1.1052b16. The force of the possessive dative in the Greek phrase emerges clearly in these instances.

be regarded as identical with that beingness and unity. The formal cause, as has been seen, is called by Aristotle the thing's *ousia* or beingness, and oneness is called the "essential being" of the unit.[10] For the exercise of the functions of cause of being and cause of unity, however, a real status in the corporeal thing is required. The exercise of those functions cannot come from the matter, which in itself lacks actual being and unity. The real being and real unity in the thing are from the form as a real cause. From the angles of both being and unity the form provides the metaphysical understanding of the corporeal thing, and as an intrinsic cause may well be termed the beingness and unity of the corporeal thing, on account of its very status as intrinsic cause. By its actual presence in the corporeal composite the thing's being and unity are brought about. The form is the cause of the being and the unity and yet, as an intrinsic cause in the thing itself, coincides with each of them.

Perhaps the difficulty here for the modern reader lies in the way the terms "cause" and "principle" are usually understood in post-Cartesian philosophy. The term "cause" seems to suggest today a thing that is different from its effect in the way an efficient cause or a final cause is something other than what is brought about. A carpenter is a different being from the house he builds, and the comfortable life envisaged in it is something other than the house itself. The Aristotelian formal and material causes, on the other hand, are within the thing they cause. The real form, just by its presence in the thing, imparts being and unity to the matter. Merely by its presence in the composite it endows the matter and the thing itself with being and unity. This conception is indeed difficult to grasp in a setting in which cause and effect are usually regarded as two different things each separate from the other. The cause and the effect are each presumed to be a thing by itself, and the causality is studied as a relation that joins the one with the other. The problems become even more difficult against a Cartesian background in which the basic division of the objects of human thought is into things and eternal truths, truths that have no existence outside thought.[11] So much is this the case, in fact, that Aristotle's alternative term "principle" (*archē*) now suggests only some kind of mental axiom. We are conscious of difficulty in calling the physical components of material things, namely their matter and their form, "principles." Even the use of the term "causes" to designate them is not too comfortable.

As a result, it is hard for us to regard the marble as a "principle" of a statue, or the figure of Hermes as the statue's formal "cause." Yet with Aristotle either of these two "principles" or "causes" as well as both together, may stand for what

10 At *Metaphysics*, 1.3.983a27–28, the formal cause was introduced as the "beingness" (*ousia*) and the "essential being" of the thing.

11 Descartes, *Principi Philosophiae*, I, 48; A-T, VIII, 22–23. These truths are sharply distinguished from "existing things," and are said to reside in our mind.

the thing is.[12] The statue is marble, it is the figure of Hermes, it is a statue. Accordingly the basis of our malaise with the use of the terms "principle" and "cause" in this context does not lie only in an accident of linguistic reference. It springs from a radically different philosophical outlook.

The philosophical outlook is the immediate and direct bearing of human cognition on external things, sensible things that are existent in themselves. The principles and causes are studied directly in those outside existents. Principles and causes are not imposed on things in virtue of categories or axioms that spring from the human mind. They are not deduced from the necessities of internal thought. They are firmly located in the real world, and, where they are intrinsic causes of the things, they are investigated within those things themselves.

This conception of knowledge requires an intimate and thoroughgoing unity of knower and things known, a unity and identity brought about in the actuality of the cognition. That kind of unity is explicitly maintained by Aristotle in his treatise on the soul, *De Anima*.[13] It is perhaps the feature of Aristotle's thought that brings out the highest degree of sales resistance on the part of modern readers, and results in the persistent rejection of his philosophy as basically a naïve realism. The study of the cognitional union and identity, however, is not undertaken in book Zeta of the *Metaphysics*. But the understanding of this unity and identity is dominated by the overall conception of unity that is developed in that metaphysical treatise. Book Zeta shows how the physical form is the cause of being, and thereby is the cause of unity. The form is the cause that makes things one. If in the actuality of the cognition the percipient and the thing perceived, the knower and the thing known, are one and identical, the reason has to lie in the form.

That is indeed the way cognition is explained in *De Anima*. The fact that knower and thing known, percipient and thing perceived, are one and the same in the actuality of cognition, is stated too frequently and too clearly in *De Anima* to leave any doubt about Aristotle's own adherence to it. But it has been found a hard saying, and little serious attention has been given to it in modern writing. Even in *De Anima*, however, the required union is explained in terms of form. The form of the perceptible thing is impressed in an immaterial manner upon the percipient by the efficient causality of that thing, acting upon the percipient either immediately or through physical media. So received, the form makes the percipient be that thing in the actuality of the cognition. The received form is in this way cause of the being and unity here involved. But to understand the full effect of that conception of unity and identity, the inquiries of book Zeta of the *Metaphysics* are indispensable. In consequence those investigations have to be called upon for explanation of how thing perceived and percipient, thing known and knower, can

12 *Metaphysics*, 7.7.1033a2–23.

13 See *De Anima*, 3.2.425b25–426a26; 3.4.429b5–7 and 430a5; 3.5.430a14–21; 3.7.431al–2; 3.8.431b9–432a3.

all become and be one and the same in the actuality of cognition. Conversely, however, the teachings of *De Anima* are required in order to understand how the reasoning in *Metaphysics* is based directly upon things existent in themselves, and not upon the sensations or ideas by which the things are perceived and known.

Here the problem bears upon philosophical teachings that are interlocking. It is not a question of trying to deduce the doctrine of *Metaphysics* from that of *De Anima*, or that of *De Anima* from the findings in *Metaphysics*. The deduction of the one from the other might be mandatory in an idealism, which would aim to develop all its conclusions from the same basic intellectual principles. But a deduction of this kind is not present or even possible in Aristotle. What is basic with him is the common world in which we live and do our philosophizing. Of that world we are immediately aware, and from it we deduce our philosophical conclusions. About its existence even the Greek Skeptics did not doubt. Nor could Descartes, Locke, or Hume really doubt about it. Those modern philosophers questioned only the legitimacy of using real external things as the basis for philosophical reasoning. With Aristotle, on the other hand, the external things of the sensible world served in point of fact as the basic principles for philosophical reasoning. But he also demonstrates in *De Anima* the philosophical legitimacy of using them as the starting points for metaphysical thinking. Today the justification of that procedure has to be sought in the study of *De Anima*. Yet to appreciate the epistemological doctrine in *De Anima*, the study in *Metaphysics* Zeta of form as the cause of being and unity is indispensable. The doctrines demand each other. The one basis for both is the common world that not even the most extreme solipsist can in fact deny as he seeks an audience for his contentions. An examined look at that world distinguishes the real from the fanciful and the mental. The problem is to show philosophically how real external things can be the starting points for human thought. That is the problem encountered in *De Anima*, and given explanation in terms of the immaterial reception of sensible forms by the human cognitive agent. But to understand Aristotle's explanation in *De Anima*, the study in *Metaphysics* Zeta of form as the cause of being and unity is indispensable. The two studies are complementary. Epistemology is not made the entrance into metaphysics, nor is metaphysics left without justification of its Aristotelian starting points.

How, then, does form account for the thoroughgoing unity of knower and thing known in the actuality of the cognition? The cognitional reception of form is characterized in *De Anima* as reception "without the matter." This puzzling phrase is not given any detailed analysis in the Aristotelian text. Its meaning is explained in *De Anima* through contrast with the material reception of the forms of iron or gold or bronze. That material reception changes the matter into iron or gold or bronze. But the cognitional reception of those forms when the iron or gold or bronze is seen and felt, does not physically change the percipient into any one of the three commodities. The form of the thing perceived is indeed received by the percipient, but in a way different from the physical reception of form by matter.[14] In the cognitional reception it does not bring about a third thing, as product, but makes the percipient be the thing perceived. Correspondingly on the intellectual level the form received makes the knower be the thing known, but not by any physical change of the one into the other. The Greek commentators on Aristotle gradually developed this notion of cognitive reception as reception of form into form instead of into matter, and accordingly brought about the phrasing of it as immaterial reception, or reception in an immaterial manner.[15]

In this way the notion of the immaterial reception of form as the initial fac-

14 See *De Anima*, 2.12.424a17–b12. Aristotle's own phrasing is that the form of the thing perceived or known is received by the percipient or knower "without the matter." The force of this expression is adverbial. It refers to the way the form is received. The matter in question here is neither the matter of the thing perceived, nor the matter of the percipient. Rather, the manner of the reception is meant. Material reception would be the way a form is received into physical matter. Immaterial reception, on the contrary, means the reception of form into form, according to the explanation gradually developed by the Greek commentators. The texts showing this gradual development are assembled in my paper "Aristotelian Soul as Cognitive of Sensibles, Intelligibles and Self," *Aristotle, The Collected Papers of Joseph Owens*, ed. John R. Catan (Albany: SUNY Press, 1981), 200–202. Accordingly the Scholastic tradition came to express the notion adverbially, namely as *immaterialiter*. See *ibid*., 202–203. However, Aristotle himself does not express the notion by an adverb. But the adjective does occur at *De Generatione et Corruptione*, 1.5.322a28–31, in the clearly explained sense of form without matter. Harold H. Joachim, *Aristotle on Coming to Be and Passing Away* (Oxford: Clarendon Press, 1922), 21, makes a case for emending the traditional text here from *aulos* ("immaterial") to *aulos* ("reed"). That way of reading the text does not seem to go back any further than the Latin translation by F. Vatablus in the Prussian Academy edition *Aristotelis Opera* (Berlin: G. Reimer, 1831–1870), 111, 179, at *Generatione et Corruptione*1.5.322b28–31. The point here is merely that this need not be considered an objection against translating Aristotle's expression "without the matter" by the English adverb "immaterially." That adverb itself does not occur in his text, but it conveys the exact sense.

15 When received in cognition, the form brings the percipient into identity with the external thing as that thing existed at the moment it emitted its efficient causality into the intervening media. The identity is to be understood in a literal sense. The length of time elapsing in the passage to the percipient does not affect this cognitional identity. The intervening time may be several billionths of a second, as in the case of seeing the desk immediately in front of your eyes or it may be thousands of light-years, as in the case of the three present-day astronomers seeing the explosion of Supernova 1967A just outside our Milky Way, and even billions of light-years for scientists who watch the violent birth of distant galaxies. In these cases what is literally seen is the distant event in its real self. The last neurophysiological modification within the observer's brain is not something seen. It is something known only through subsequent and intricate scientific reasoning.

tor in the human cognitive processes passed over into the medieval Scholastic tradition. But from the Islamic philosophers on, the distinction between a thing and its existence enabled the medieval thinkers to explain cognition as a new existence in the knower for the thing known. For Aristotle, with whom what the thing is coincided with its existence, this existential type of explanation was not open. The union of knower and thing known had to be explained in terms of form. Form was the principle and cause of being and unity. The form of the thing perceived made the percipient be that thing in the actuality of the cognition. Received as form into form instead of into matter, it did not set up any new instance of what was perceived. Rather, it enriched the form of the percipient and knower with a new form, the form of the thing perceived and known.

Since this was not reception of form into matter, it allowed the received forms to merge into unity with the form of the percipient in a manner that may be compared to the way in which the ultimate differentia contains within itself all the other essential determinations of the thing, as set out in *Metaphysics* Zeta (12.1038a19–26). The specific and generic determinations are not received into matter that would be really distinct for each grade. Accordingly the one real form of the knower, so enriched, enables the cognitive agent to elicit the unitary cognitional act in which knower and thing known, percipient and thing perceived, as well as all the distinct determinations attained in their regard, are grasped in cognition. The real physical form of the human cognitive agent is in this way the unifying principle in the cognitive act. Through its dominance over both, the world about which we philosophize is the world in which we live.

On this resounding note of the physical form as the primary cause of being and unity throughout the corporeal thing, book Zeta of the *Metaphysics* culminates its philosophical achievement. The individual physical form in the category of substance is thereby shown to be par excellence the thing's *ousia* or beingness. In the microcosm recognizable in any corporeal composite, that basic form is the *archē* that governs all the rest. The Greek term *archē* did indeed carry the overtones of ruling and governing. The role of form was to maintain the overall aspect of order, an order that was dear to the Greeks and was pitted by them against barbarism and chaos. For Aristotle the one real form in the category of substance was accordingly the basic source of being and unity and order in each corporeal composite. Correspondingly each of the accidental forms was ruler in its respective accidental domain. The rule of one form instead of chaotic plurality held firm throughout all these microcosmic areas. Everywhere the gradations in being arose from form, with form as the source of being to the matter and to the composite.

On the other hand, universality was conferred by the human mind in knowing the thing. It did not inject any real being. It could not make the thing really different. Metaphysically, it could not function as *ousia*. Many centuries later, Bertrand Russell would turn his back on the idealism in which his early philosophical training had taken place. He came to the point where he "could no longer believe that knowing makes any difference to what is known."[16] For Aristotle the conclusion was that in *Metaphysics* no universal can be regarded as *ousia* or beingness. Universality is not a cause of being for the thing. The real form, on the other hand, is the overall cause of the thing's being and unity. It is what rules and governs, maintaining order in the microcosms. It, not Ideas, makes each thing what each is.

From these considerations one may readily see that for Aristotle the form is not a mental construct or pattern that is imposed upon external materials. It is a physical actuality, a real constituent of the corporeal thing, whether it is called form or "essential being," or whether it is identified with the ultimate differentia in that thing. From all these angles it is a real actuality, present in the corporeal things independently of the mind's consideration of them. In this respect it is not at all like a universal. It is individual, though the formal unities it grounds furnish the basis for universal knowledge. It functions as something real in endowing the corporeal thing with order, in its role of primary *ousia*.

Correspondingly in the macrocosm the primary instance of being is separate substance, which likewise is something real and individualistic in the way outlined in *Metaphysics* Epsilon. The notion of being that it grounds is not just a concept introduced by knowledge of it in the human mind. Rather, being qua being is the reality that is present in separate substance, and serves as the primary instance in relation to which the other instances are understood as beings. The findings of astronomy require that this primary instance be placed in a plurality of separate moving principles in order to account for the various eternal motions in the heavens. Yet the unity in all the multiplicity of these heavenly motions has to require one supreme cause that regulates them all. Likewise in the microcosm, just as in the macrocosm, there is room for applying Aristotle's own special interpretation of the Homeric adage that rule by many is not good. The obvious consequence to be drawn is that in both these areas, though in their respective ways, the governing principle finds its location in form as the cause of being. In form, ultimately, the gradations outlined in books Epsilon and Zeta of *Metaphysics* have their dominating source. Moreover, quite as the being that is predicated of each thing in the universe is the being that is caused by separate substance, so, correspondingly, the intelligible content of each individual composite is both caused by and identical with the thing's own form.

16 Bertrand Russell, "Logical Atomism," in *Contemporary British Philosophy*, ed. J. H. Muirhead (London: George Allen & Unwin, 1924), 360.

Epilogue

In today's philosophical world the notion of gradations in being will face a hostilely disposed public. The reason for the strong and widespread opposition to it has been voiced trenchantly by a defender of its presence in Aristotle: "Our contemporary metaphysical prejudices are so opposed to degrees of being that people find themselves unable to make any sense of such a doctrine."[1] In fact, the relevant difficulties spring from the very starting points of modern philosophizing. If one's philosophical starting points are located in concepts or in words, the inclination is understandably toward a precision that allows only one clear and distinct meaning to the concept "being" or to the word "being." Multiplicity of senses for the same word or for the same concept is thereby excluded in the name of philosophical rigor. The meaning each time has to be precise.

But if the starting points are the perceptible things of the external world, understood as things in themselves and as grasped immediately and directly by the human mind, the outlook changes radically. The prospect lies open for exploration of ways in which an aspect of things may have a meaning that remains basically the same in all its instances even though it presents itself differently in different cases. Basically, the same aspect is seen in all the instances. It is accordingly expressed in the one concept and named by the one word in all its occurrences. But the aspect is such that it allows a multiplicity of meanings in the totality of the instances in which it makes itself manifest. These differences are internal to its own nature. They are not brought in from the outside. This is readily seen in the case of being. There is nothing outside being to bring about differentiation in being. The differentia would first have to be, in order to exercise this differentiating effect. Obviously, then, being is not something generic. Its range is too wide for that.

1 Donald Morrison, "The Evidence for Degrees of Being in Aristotle," *Classical Quarterly*, 37 (second series) (1987), 382. In this connection Morrison notes the Platonic background that was discussed by Gregory Vlastos in "Degrees of Reality in Plato" in Vlastos's collection *Platonic Studies* (Princeton, N.J.: Princeton University Press, 1973), 58–75. Vlastos (65) remarks, "As we commonly use the word 'existence,' degrees of it (as distinct from degrees of perfection of things in existence) make no sense whatever; the idea of one individual thing existing more, or less, than another, would be a rank absurdity." Vlastos (74) suggested that "more real" and "less real" are themselves rather misleading expressions in this context.

In this perspective, being is an aspect that manifests itself in substances and in accidents, in real things and in things that exist only in our cognition. But it manifests itself in graded fashion. For Aristotle the absolutely primary instance of being is form without matter, namely separate substance. Within a sensible thing, the thing's form is the primary instance of being, with the composite and the matter as secondary instances. Likewise the sensible thing exists primarily in the real world, and only secondarily in human cognitions according to Aristotle's explanation.

From the Aristotelian viewpoint of external sensible things in themselves as the first object of human cognition, there should accordingly be no special difficulty in acknowledging gradations in being. In those things the aspect of being appears in both primary and secondary fashions. It is the same aspect, but in fact is present in various ways in the different instances. The difficulty arises when one starts out with a concept or a word, and insists on a precise meaning for it that will remain exactly the same throughout all the instances. Existence, beings, essence, whatness, etc., are each given a different meaning and have to be regarded as keeping precisely that meaning wherever the word or the concept is used. Against that background the Aristotelian gradations in being will certainly appear "uncongenial."[2] But if the starting points of one's philosophizing are located

2 "To me, grades of existence are uncongenial. There are no half-way stages about belonging to a universe of discourse, and being admitted as a value of a variable of quantification and quantification is the way of schematizing the existence concept that seems clearest to me." W. V. Quine, "Thoughts on Reading Father Owens," *Proceedings of the Seventh Inter-American Congress of Philosophy* (Québec: Les Presses de l'Université Laval, 1967), 62. Here what is expressly claimed to be at issue is "the existence concept." In the Aristotelian context one and the same concept could of course cover being, existence, thing and unit, since for Aristotle (*Metaphysics*, 4.2.1003b26–34) these four coincide. Accordingly, with that one comprehensive Aristotelian concept as starting point for the discussion, each difference in being would indeed give rise to a distinct unit. But that unit need not be a quantitative unit. It can be a difference in quality or grade. Accordingly, degrees may be seen in being, in the way the categories differ from one another in kind and not just numerically. A different grade is a different kind of being, but not a new quantity in an already given grade of being.

In that Aristotelian context, then, the pertinent difference will be regarded as an entitative unit, but not necessarily as a quantitative unit. In the modern analytic framework, on the other hand, the basic model for the unit is decidedly quantitative in character. With this current approach, the existence of a new relation or of a new time or of a new grade may come to be schematized as the addition of something further to the totality of things, quite as though it were a new quantitative unit. Very differently for Aristotle in the passage, just quoted (1003b26–34), the unit is conceptualized expressly in terms of the supergeneric being that both antecedes and permeates all categories of being. For Aristotle everything is a unit expressly insofar as it is a thing

firmly in the sensible things themselves, no incongruity will make itself felt. The radical difference in viewpoint here follows inevitably from the difference in philosophical starting points.

In this setting, when books Epsilon and Zeta are read in conjunction with each other from the standpoint of their respective gradations of being, a striking parallelism emerges. In both those books the primary instance of being is forms, though in different ways. For book Epsilon immaterial or separate form is the primary being in the macrocosmic universe. For book Zeta, on the other hand, the physical form of the perceptible thing is the primary *ousia* or beingness. In book Epsilon, separate form is being qua being, and as such is the final cause of all else in the world. In book Zeta, quite differently, the physical form is exercising the type of causality that is properly formal. It is thereby endowing the thing's mat-

or a nature. That is the context in which he may be said today to have schematized "the existence concept."

What does this mean? In a perceptible object it should not be too difficult to visualize. The difference between an ordinary grade of red and a deeper red is something real. That difference has accordingly its own real existence and unity. The light rays that underlie colors do differ in measurements. But as a grade in quality the deeper red does not mean a larger red patch but rather a different grade in the category of quality for the same-sized red patch. As a reality and an existent, then, the difference between the two grades of red has its own proper unity, and that unity is to be conceptualized not as a quantitative unit but as a unit of the type that everywhere follows upon being and corresponds exactly to the respective type of being that is enjoyed by the thing at issue. That is what is meant by an entitative unit, in contrast to a quantitative unit. In this way any new kind or grade of existence in the object may be classified as a further addition, and in this supergeneric sense a further unit.

When so understood, any grade of existence absolutely involves the exclusion of the opposed kind of non-existence. Being always contradicts not-being, as asserted in the traditional "principle of non-contradiction." Consequently there can be no "halfway stages" of existence. Every stage, no matter how slight, absolutely renders impossible the corresponding non-existence. In any given context the thing either exists or does not exist, regardless of the grade of existence at issue.

Quantification, then, is hardly an acceptable way of "schematizing the existence concept" with Aristotle. As understood in today's context, quantification takes its notion of the unit from a particular category of being, the category of quantity. In that univocal sense, it would explain existence everywhere. In Aristotle, on the contrary, existence is expressly schematized in terms of thing and nature, and the unit thereby involved is the entitative unit that is required in the very notions of thing and existent. For him one might say that in opposite fashion quantity is schematized as a category of being, rather than existence as an expression of quantification. In any case, the text (1003b22–34) under consideration maintains clearly that while thing or nature, and being, and unit, may each be conceptualized separately, it is more advantageous in metaphysical treatment to keep them conceptualized as always united.

ter, and the whole composite, with being. Consequently in both cases form is the cause of being, though in the two different ways. In each of those ways the permanence that characterizes being is imparted. In this regard their parallelism is quite apparent.

Further, in both those ways the aspect of universality is attained. Separate substance is being qua being. Thereby it is universal to all beings by way of focal reference. Correspondingly the physical form, by way of its intrinsic presence in the perceptible thing, grounds universal extension of the thing's formal meaning to all the other singulars of the species. The formal nature of a tree, for instance, is universally present in all individual trees. In both Epsilon and Zeta, then, form is the ground of universality, though in two radically different ways.

In both ways of universalization, moreover, the form is identical with what is predicated universally. In Epsilon, being qua being coincides with separate form, and in Zeta all the intelligibility in a perceptible thing is identical with the content of its form. Matter and composite, accordingly, are intelligible objects only through their form. This parallels the way in which all material things are beings through the primary instance of being, which is separate substance.

In books Epsilon and Zeta of *Metaphysics*, these different gradations of being explain in parallel fashion the unity required by both the macrocosm of the visible universe and the microcosm of the perceptible thing. Aristotle's philosophical reasoning in these two books of *Metaphysics* is intricate and profound. But if it is to be understood at all it has to be kept firmly based upon its own distinctive starting points. These starting points are the external things in the perceptible world. They are known directly as things in themselves. Yet Aristotle is not in any way naïve in maintaining as his own philosophical stand, the ordinarily accepted view that the things perceived are things in themselves outside human cognition. He explains carefully in *De Anima* how by acting through the appropriate physical media the external things impress upon the percipient the form that is the cause of their being. So received, that form makes the percipient be those things in the actuality of the cognition. Further, in *Metaphysics* (12.9.1074b35–36), he maintains that human cognition is always of an object that is other than the particular cognitive act by which it is attained. Concomitantly and *in obliquo* there is awareness of the percipient's own self and cognitive activity, within the cognitional identity brought about by the actuality of the perception. Is not this explanation radically different from any naïve acceptance of a common sense conviction?

With his philosophical thinking firmly grounded in the things of the sensible world, things that are multiple in character and at all times subject to ongoing change, Aristotle is amply able to impart a deep appreciation of the human need for multiplicity and widespread qualitative differentiation throughout one's life and activities, along with the requirement of a highly variegated environment. But nowhere does he allow this need to dominate and give rise to confusion. Everywhere for him order is achieved by the dominance of form, since form is the cause of all being and of a thoroughgoing unity throughout the universe. The order requires gradations in being, with primary instances regulating the secondary ones. Confusion is thereby avoided. The respective gradations in being that are discussed with penetrating acumen in books Epsilon and Zeta of *Metaphysics* assure and explain the ever-present unity. They allow genuine being to the secondary as well as to the primary instances, though in graded fashion. They build the way to the towering conclusion at the end of book Lambda, as expressed in the proclamation that beings do not want themselves to be governed badly. In that panorama Aristotle interprets and applies the ancient Homeric adage that rule by many is not good, and that everywhere one definite ruling principle is required if the appropriate order is to be maintained. The order is sharply hierarchical with dependence on primary instances the basic and all-pervading characteristic of the universe.

From that Aristotelian viewpoint, the equality that reigns will consist in the required adherence of every part in the whole to the respective function of each. For the primary instances, this adherence is thoroughgoing identity by nature. For secondary instances it is dutiful acceptance of the relation that each of the instances bears to the primary instance. Through this proportional equality in obligation the overall welfare both of the whole and of each of its parts is harmoniously achieved. But the inevitable result is that when the individual instances of the notion or word are viewed apart from one another in the focal reference schematization, there will be intrinsic inequality among them. The primary instance of the aspect will be supreme in its own order. Through relation to the primary instance in one way or another, the other instances will share its meaning and its perfection in varying degrees. From this viewpoint the individual instances do not exhibit democratic equality. Rather, they have a hierarchical grading. Regarded intrinsically they do not all have equal status. Only as sharing in a perfection common in this focal way will each of the instantiations denote the fullness of the perfection at issue. But for that type of sharing in its meaning, intrinsic inequality in the secondary instances cannot be avoided.

One may well regard this intrinsic inequality as the law of the universe. Whether in sports or in commerce or in war, excellence is what everywhere dominates. Throughout all those areas does not excellence regularly receive the preference? Opportunity is indeed present for all the participants, but in an intrinsically graded manner. Not every player is chosen as quarterback on the football team. Not every toiler rises to directorship in the business world. Not every general is qualified, as Foch was, to function as generalissimo for allied armies. But all the participants will share in the final triumph, each in her or his own way. The final triumph belongs to them all without exception, and its thrill vibrates in every secondary instance by way of the focal reference. Each individual team member is a winner, each office employee receives a paycheck for entrance into the good life; each soldier on the winning side is a victor as the annual remembrances are celebrated. An English poet, moreover, could speak of "our tainted nature's solitary boast,"[3] without implying lack of divine grace in all other children of Adam. In this regard a single primary instance could be seen in the poetic verse as encompassing all the other instances and as containing within its own self all their relevant perfection. The example here is theological, and in it the implications have to be established by theological study.

In these cases, then, the one perfection is found present in all the instances, but in graded fashion. Everywhere there is the requirement of order in a manner that locates the one perfection in all the participants, though in varying degrees. Each participant shares it in the way appropriate for each. Intrinsically each secondary instance of the aspect remains different from the other secondary instances as well as from the primary instance. Definitely, intrinsic difference with accompanying inequality is required in the schematization. Intrinsically the instances are not equal to each other or equal to the primary instance. Yet the same focally shared meaning is spread throughout all the various occurrences of that one and the same aspect.

The secondary instances in the focal schematization, accordingly, are not tokens struck in exact conformity with each other. In commercial coinage, indeed, the individual tokens of a given denomination have each the same monetary value. Each U.S. dime is worth exactly ten cents, no matter how often the coins are struck. In this type the universality is of the kind exhibited in the classification of singulars into species and genera in the Porphyrian tree. But above the divisions into species and genera in that tree there is the overall predicate of being. This highest predicate is not shared in the univocal fashion seen in the specific and generic characteristics. Rather, it is shared by way of reference to a primary instance. Against that background the Aristotelian doctrine of focal meaning can provide the framework in which both the intrinsic inequalities among the instances and the common aspect pervading them all can be philosophically probed and understood and appreciated. Dependence of secondary instances in various ways upon a primary instance is characteristic of the ordered universe in which we live. Aristotle's metaphysical outlook thereby enables us to come to grips intellectually with the real universe around us. Explicitly as beings the things of this universe repel chaos and yearn for ordered governance, both in the assemblage as a whole and in the particular groupings in which each instance finds itself.[4] Status for the individuals is not egalitarian. Rather, it is profoundly hierarchical.

3 Wordsworth, "The Virgin," line 4, in *Ecclesiastical Sonnets*, ed. Abbie Findly Potts (New Haven, Conn.: Yale University Press, 1922), 151. On the status of Mary as first from a common Christian viewpoint, see Nicholas Ayo, *The Hail Mary* (Notre Dame, Ind.: University of Notre Dame Press, 1994).

4 A recent tendency has aimed at giving chaos a basic role in the universe. On the topic, see Leon Glass and Michael C. Mackey, *From Clocks to Chaos* (Princeton, N.J.: Princeton University Press, 1988).

This respective order places the variability first of all in the things themselves. Variability of the aspect in the things antecedes both the conceptualizing and the naming of it in human understanding and communication. In this way the primary instance of the aspect is supreme in its own order. Through relation to it in one way or another each secondary instance will carry the meaning expressed by the focal notion. All the secondary instances will be presented as sharing, each in its own way, that focally common aspect. Nevertheless its full perfection, as such, is located in the primary instance only. Intrinsically each secondary instance of the aspect remains different in itself from the other secondary instances as well as from the primary instance. In that way intrinsic difference with accompanying inequality pervades the schematization. Accordingly, practitioner, discussion, book, prescription, tonic, regimen, and so on, all differ from one another as instances of "medical," with the primary instance of the notion located in the art of medicine. Intrinsically those secondary instances are not at all equal to each other or to the primary instance. But the same definite perfection that is present by its own nature in the primary instance is imparted in one way or another to each of the secondary instances. All share in that same perfection, each in its own appropriate way. The characteristic "medical" belongs to all, but in graded fashion. The secondary instances are not at all made equal to the primary instance in the ways they share the perfection. The perfection itself remains the same. It is indeed an aspect that is shared by all its instances, but only in a focal manner. In its own intrinsic fullness it is found in the primary instance only. But in that way each has the best.

The focally shared aspect, then, is seen in all the instances. From that angle it allows no exception. But solely in the primary instance does it reside in the fullness of its proper meaning. In the case of being, this fullness is located by Aristotle in separate form. Separate form is accordingly for him the absolutely primary instance of being, and is thereby the cause of being for all other instances of it. In that way it is the cause that regulates them all and firmly establishes the thoroughgoing order present throughout the whole universe of beings in which we live.

Always, however, if one is to appreciate the depth and coherence of Aristotle's thinking, one must realize that its starting points are the things of the external world. These things themselves, and not our concepts or verbal designations of them, are what is immediately and directly known. But that should not be too hard to acknowledge when one reflects for a moment on what we actually see or hear. Internal modifications of the cortex are not the object of our immediate awareness. Rather, knowledge of those modifications is reached only through long and intricate scientific study. What we immediately and directly see or hear are the colored and resounding things in the external world. From those external things we reason to our own modifications in perceiving them. Surely everyone whose mind is unhampered by Cartesian influence should be willing to acknowledge this actual working of our own cognition and to grant to Aristotle the full right to proceed as he does in his *Metaphysics*. This effort today is hard to make. But it has to be made, if Aristotle is to be understood.

General Index

Index Locorum